THE
QUEST

EXPLORING A SENSE OF SOUL

Growth and nourishment
for your spiritual journey

Joycelin Dawes, Janice Dolley, Ike Isaksen

BOOKS

Winchester, UK
Washington, USA

THE QUEST co-authors

Joycelin Dawes, Editor and Project Leader, and member of writing team. Joycelin has experience as a political and economic researcher at the UK House of Commons, in education as a teacher, school governor and parent, and in voluntary community work. She is a Quaker interested in the meeting point of traditional faith and contemporary spirituality.

Janice Dolley, Education and Network Liaison and member of writing team. Janice worked as a lecturer and Senior Training Officer at the Open University, UK from 1971 until she retired in 2000. Co-author of *Christian Evolution: Moving Towards a Global Spirituality*. Trustee of the Findhorn Foundation, Executive Director of the Wrekin Trust and University for Spirit Forum.

Ike Isaksen, Business Development and member of writing team. Ike is a freelance writer, and education consultant. He worked for the Findhorn Foundation, Scotland 1973-1999 where he was director of the Arts Centre for 8 years and then co-focaliser of the Education Area at the Foundation 1997-1999. Ike is currently living and working in Colombia.

Information about **The Quest** is available from www.thequest.org.uk

Copyright © 2005 O Books
O Books is an imprint of John Hunt Publishing Ltd.,
Deershot Lodge, Park Lane, Ropley, Hants, SO24 0BE, UK
office@johnhunt-publishing.com
www.o-books.net

Distribution in;
UK
Orca Book Services
orders@orcabookservices.co.uk
Tel: 01202 665432 Fax: 01202 666219 Int. code (44)

USA and Canada
NBN
custserv@nbnbooks.com
Tel: 1 800 462 6420 Fax: 1 800 338 4550

Australia
Brumby Books
sales@brumbybooks.com
Tel: 61 3 9761 5535 Fax: 61 3 9761 7095

New Zealand
Peaceful Living
books@peaceful-living.co.nz
Tel: 64 7 57 18105 Fax: 64 7 57 18513

Singapore
STP
davidbuckland@tlp.com.sg
Tel: 65 6276 Fax: 65 6276 7119

South Africa
Alternative Books
altbook@global.co.za
Tel: 27 011 792 7730 Fax: 27 011 972 7787
Text: © 2005 The Quest

Design: Nautilus Design(UK) Ltd
Cover design: Krave Ltd., London

ISBN 1 903816 93 9

The intent of the authors is only to offer information of a general nature to help you in your
quest for personal and spiritual well-being. In the event that you use any of the information in
this book for yourself, which it is your constitutional right, the authors and the publisher assume
no responsibility for your actions.

The rights of Joycelin Dawes, Janice Dolley and Ike Isaksen as authors have been asserted in
accordance with the Copyright, Designs and Patents Act 1988.
A CIP catalogue record for this book is available from the British Library.

Printed in the USA by Maple-Vail Manufacturing Group

CONTENTS

Being Loving
Living Lovingly
Living Lovingly With Others: Shifts And Conflicts
Living Lovingly On The Earth

DIAGRAMS AND TABLES

GETTING STARTED

"Surely there is more to life than this?" you might exclaim as you grapple with the ups and downs of life or when your hopes for an enduring sense of fulfillment are dashed again.

Sometimes people find that a gap opens up when long-sought material dreams do not bring contentment. Others find they are no longer satisfied with the spiritual beliefs and traditions with which they grew up and they search for a wider, more universal spirituality that draws on the wisdom of many faiths. Still others want to engage with the forms of spirituality that have sprung up in recent years but are bewildered by the variety. These are quests – examples of people feeling drawn to what *The Quest* calls "exploring your sense of soul."

As the turn of the century approached, the three co-creators of *The Quest* met and explored some of these questions ourselves. We had each been pursuing our spiritual life and inquiry for many years and had varied experience: community and political activity, teaching, professional experience in writing open learning courses, theatre and arts, and living in a spiritual community.

We gathered together a group of friends and colleagues for a weekend of sharing our stories and searching for a sense of soul. Next, we formed a small team of people who complemented our ideas, skills, and experience and shared our commitment to writing material that might help others wrestle with similar questions. During team meetings and with others, we explored our spiritual life and the spiritual, cultural, and economic transitions that seem to be affecting people widely across the planet. We tried to identify what helped us find our way amid all this change. We listened also to our inner sense of what spirituality meant to us, and wondered how we might more effectively live in the world together.

The Quest is the result of this work and we hope it will provide a guide for your search. It is a framework of questions, activities, resources, and ideas that help you establish, or deepen, an inner life that is real and meaningful. It is neutral in that the activities and examples in *The Quest* point you toward your own answers rather than a particular set of beliefs or practices that might be advocated. Throughout *The Quest* exploring your sense of soul embraces your beliefs, valuing your experience of spirituality, and those things that bring purpose and vitality to your life. It helps you become clearer in knowing who you are and more in touch with your innermost fullness. You will also develop a practice of spiritual reflection to anchor and deepen your sense of soul.

The "thought-bubbles" on the next page summarize the different things that people have said they were looking for in starting *The Quest*. Some of the bubbles are blank so you can add your own hopes and aspirations. *The Quest,* however, is meant to be flexible so you have choice about how to use it:

○ **As a book to read and work through**, on your own, with a partner, or by bringing together a group of friends
○ **As daily meditation or reading** that prompts questioning and reflection
○ **As an intuitive journey** that directs you
○ **As a "toolbox"** for exploring ideas and experiences as your interest or need guides you
○ **As a course for professional development** where spirituality is a current or emerging interest
○ **As a friend and companion** you can turn to when needed.

However you choose to use *The Quest*, we recommend you make time to do the activities as this is how you find and clarify your answers to the questions that *The Quest* asks. We suggest you keep a record of your thoughts, feelings, ideas, insights, and responses to the activities in *The Quest*. There is no set way to do this; some people like to write, others draw, keep mementoes and reminders, talk on tape, write a poem, write music, choreograph a dance ... choose any method that helps you and perhaps try to use different ones from time to time. When you return to your record, it helps you see what's changed, how you've developed, and in what way.

SETTING OFF

Exploring your sense of soul begins with you and your experience, so the first activity builds a picture of yourself as you get started with *The Quest*.

Activity: Picturing The Present

Read through the activity to see what it involves. Then gather together anything you might want to have handy, such as paper and pens, music, favorite objects.

Imagine that you are going to meet an old friend and bring them up to date on your life.

●*Where are you as you begin* The Quest? *Look around and recognize what*

Fig 1: Why Follow **The Quest?**

is important or meaningful now so you can remember it.
- *What is your life like today?*

As you imagine bringing your old friend up to date, take time to dwell, however briefly, in the current experience of your life. It may be helpful to stop using words and just be aware of this, without having to think about it or describe it. Then focus on the main elements, what matters most, and what is uppermost in your attention at this point.

Then make a record of this activity in a way that suits you – write, draw, paint, speak onto tape, bring together some important mementoes. It does not need to be detailed; the important thing is that in the future you can recall what was happening and how you are feeling now.

David Spangler (1998) says in *The Call*: ".... some of the most powerful calls that we may receive in our lives, the calls that come from the deepest places in ourselves, are not summonings at all, but are more like awakenings. They call us to attention."

In *The Quest* you pay attention to the significance and potential of such calls. They are thresholds, which hold the possibility of opening into something new or an opportunity for seeing with fresh eyes, openings to potential and transformation. Beginning *The Quest* is such a threshold and the next activity looks at this more closely.

Activity: As You Begin *The Quest*

Take a little time to feel centered, reflective, and quiet. Read through the questions, quickly noting any immediate responses. Then go through them again and reflect more deeply, noting whatever comes to mind, what you feel or what you notice in yourself.

- *What do you hope to get out of exploring your sense of soul?*
- *What might be difficult for you?*
- *What aspects of your personal and spiritual life feel settled at this point?*
- *What aspects of your personal and spiritual life are seeking your attention?*
- *Are there any questions, whispers, promptings, hunches, or intuitive ways of knowing that you notice at the moment?*
- *What are they telling you?*
- *What help or support might you need, e.g. someone to talk to and share it with, time to yourself, etc? How or where can you find it?*
- *What will encourage you to keep going and face some things that might be challenging?*
- *Do you want to follow* The Quest *on your own or look for a friend/find or form a group to follow it with others?*

ACTIVITIES AND IMAGERY IN *THE QUEST*

The Quest is built around activities that focus on your experience, like those you have just done. Each activity begins with some guidelines; these will work in most cases, but sometimes the method we suggest will not suit you. If this happens, we suggest you read the activity to understand its purpose, then adapt it so you arrive at a similar outcome in your own way.

Sometimes activities stir up things you may find hard to look at. When this happens, it's best to take stock of how you feel: are you ready to be challenged and how far do you want to cope with feeling uncomfortable? Remember, too, that your discomfort may help you become more aware of things you avoid, spotting when your "dislike" of an activity conceals a habit or pattern that you prefer not to notice. In *The Quest* you also revisit past events that may re-stimulate any difficult feelings associated with them. If you can work on these feelings, even a little, you can help yourself move on. There may be other occasions when you feel the time is not right for you to work on these feelings; if so, put the activity aside and come back to it when you feel ready.

The image of a labyrinth is used in *The Quest*.

Fig 2: **The Quest** *Labyrinth*

It is an ancient symbol, indicating that life is never straightforward but twists and turns. Nevertheless, a labyrinth has a single path wherever it seems to wander. At times we seem to be on an inner route toward the center and other times on an outer one of return to the wider world. The arrowheads on *The Quest* labyrinth indicate direction; you may find your sense of direction from your values, or from feeling aligned – between "heaven" and "earth" – or they may suggest a direction toward personal transformation or global change. Exploring your sense of soul is a journey of movement and change, like the twists and turns of the labyrinth, sometimes toward the center and sometimes toward the outer world. Ultimately, it leads to the heart of the labyrinth, denoted by the shaded circle, where you encounter and experience the sense of soul that is central to the spiritual quest.

THE LANGUAGE OF SPIRITUALITY

When writing *The Quest*, we were challenged to find the right words – our language of spirituality. Words and phrases for spirituality have many shades of meaning and we each use them in slightly different ways. When we use a word or phrase in *The Quest*, therefore, we try to be clear what we mean; this does not mean it is the only legitimate meaning, but that we use it in a reasonably consistent way. At various points in *The Quest* you will find activities that help you look at the language about spirituality that is meaningful for you. In this section, though, we set out the meaning we intend in the way we use words and phrases.

The most important phrase we use is *a sense of soul*. So it's worth giving that a little more attention first of all:

Activity: **What Does *A Sense Of Soul* Mean To You?**

- *What does* a sense of soul *mean to you at this point?*
- *Is there any way you can describe this?*
- *What does it feel like?*

When we talk about a **sense of soul** in *The Quest* we mean a sense of your essence, an inner core that holds your potential and wholeness and is a vital, living source; for some, it is also infused with connection to a Presence or Ultimate Reality, the ground or fabric of existence that feels "radically alive" (Moss, 1987). You can be aware of a sense of soul even though it is difficult to observe the soul directly, to identify and know what it is. Your sense of soul is experienced through insight, intimations, hints, and windows that open, witnessed through your values, attitudes, beliefs, and actions, and deepened through practices for spiritual reflection. The journey of *The Quest* is to explore more fully what this means to you. It is a journey about *spirituality*, concerned with your experience of Spirit rather than focusing on dogma or theology and you begin to engage with this in the chapters **Heart of The Quest** and **Developing Your Skills**.

In *The Quest*, the **personal** and **spiritual** experiences in your life are seen as complementary. The **personal** relates to the content of your personality;

working on this helps you move toward independence, individuality, and autonomy, more open and available to your sense of soul. The *spiritual* aspect offers a route to meaning and purpose, the possibility of integrating and transcending your day-to-day identity through a sense of being part of something greater than yourself. We each have different expressions and encounters with *spiritual experience* but its nature is often associated with a longing for such qualities as love, beauty, goodness, and truth. In the chapters *Telling Your Story* and *A Growing Sense of Soul* you look in depth at personal and spiritual experiences in your life. In *Passion and Change* you address your passions and purpose through the perspective of change, while *Dark Nights* continues the same theme through the difficult and arid periods in life so that a clearer sense of your soul emerges.

Throughout *The Quest,* you explore ideas of inner and outer aspects of yourself. We use *inner* to include your emotions, attitudes, thoughts, and values, which remain private unless you talk or act in a way that outwardly expresses them. Your inner constantly interacts with your *outer*, meaning the actions, behavior, and speech that can be observed and provide your means of interaction with others and your environment. You consider the relationship between inner and outer and between yourself, others, and your environment in the chapter *Wholeness and Connection*. Later you focus on your ideas and experience of the *sacred* – those things that evoke awe, wonder, and respect; ultimately, we believe that all things can be held to be sacred, a part of Spirit. To become real, however, a sense of the sacred needs to be embodied – put into practice. In *The Quest* this is explored further in *Living in a Sacred Way*.

Spirit describes a powerful dimension, encompassing more than your sense of soul. It is not just passive or "feel-good" but is widely perceived as an energy or force that can change individual lives, society and the planet; for example, we described your sense of soul as perhaps accompanied by connection to a Presence or Ultimate Reality understood as the ground or fabric of existence. Over time, different peoples and religious traditions have built up treasuries of experience and techniques to access this dimension. Many people find their connection with *Spirit* through the riches of a specific religion, such as Christianity, Judaism, Islam, Hinduism, or Buddhism. Others do not subscribe to a particular religious path and access this dimension in other ways.

The material in *The Quest* is rooted in an age-old conviction found in all traditions, cultures, backgrounds, and faiths that there is *"something more"* than that which we can see, hear, touch, taste, or feel in the material world. Sometimes "something more" is referred to as *Spirit*. In the varied religious traditions *Spirit* is known by many names, such as: God, Allah, Brahman, Tao, Presence, Great Spirit, the Void, Shekhinah, the Sacred, Divine, Holy Spirit, the Goddess, the Big Holy, Mystery, the Unknown, the Beloved, the Source. We use some of these words interchangeably in different places in *The Quest*. In *Changing Faces of Faith* you review the building blocks of your "faith" in the light of changing expressions of Spirit in today's world.

Throughout *The Quest* we refer you to the major religious traditions. But *The Quest* is not based on any single dogma or creed. It draws widely on ideas and universal truths, common to all spiritual teachings, and contemporary explorations of spirituality that can act as guiding principles on the spiritual quest and support you, whatever your views and beliefs. In *Encountering Direct Experience* you go more deeply into your encounter with Spirit and maps and practices that help anchor and deepen your spiritual life.

Activity: What Works For Me?

Throughout The Quest *it's important that you don't take what we have written for granted. Use it as a guide that helps you find your own way.*

•*How far do the meanings explained above accord with your own ideas?*

THE NEXT STEP

Many people worldwide are on a quest to discover a sense of soul that is authentic for them yet still honors and learns from diverse wisdom, traditions, and religions. It is a "zeitgeist" or spirit of our time and *The Quest* signposts a way to explore this contemporary expression of spirituality. Thomas Berry (1988) wrote, "It's all a question of story. We are in trouble now because we do not have a good story. We are in between stories. The old story, the account of how we fit into it, is no longer effective. Yet we have not learned the new story."

Berry draws attention to this period of transition between old and new stories; such major changes are paradigm shifts. Paradigms are conceptual umbrellas that help you make sense of your experience; they frame the questions you ask and the kinds of answers that are acceptable. In writing *The Quest* we tried to identify what might help you find your way amid profound change and listen to your sense of what spirituality means today.

The purpose of *The Quest* is to help us each participate in creating a new story for humanity. To play your part, you need to be willing to explore yourself in many different ways. Time and time again, you will find *The Quest* asking you "What do you experience and know directly for yourself?" and "What do you make of this?" The emphasis is on the kind of knowing that builds on experience rather than abstract knowledge. So your research material is your life, relationships, interests, qualities, beliefs, passions, and difficulties.

Many people find their quest is enriched by sharing it with others. Religious communities have long recognized the need for community, a "sangha" of like-minded persons with whom to share fellowship, experience, and understanding. You might consider bringing a few friends together to follow

The Quest, or advertise in your local library or community center to start a group; *The Quest* website has some ideas and suggestions on how to do so (www.thequest.org.uk). The idea of spiritual friendship and mentoring is gaining currency; you may find ways to develop it for yourself or you can consult *The Quest* website for links, ideas, and information.

There is no set time for working through *The Quest*. People who have already followed *The Quest* used the materials over a minimum of four to eight months. Many people spend much longer. You may also find that you return to it at different times and at different levels. But however long you spend and whatever your starting point, remember that now is the only moment to be open to all that is around and within you, and prepare to take your next step.

HEART OF THE QUEST

You encounter many questions on the spiritual journey. Such questions include:

○ What does "spiritual" mean?
○ What has felt real or authentic to you?
○ What times, places, activities, people help you to be more in touch with your most meaningful experiences?
○ What kind of spiritual reflection helps you?

Finding your own answers to such questions, and developing a way to stay in touch with your sense of soul, are key elements in *The Quest*. So **Heart of The Quest** outlines a framework for exploring your sense of soul and trying out skills drawn from spiritual traditions around the world; cultivating awareness is a central aspect of all such skills.

A SENSE OF THE PRESENT

You might notice how sometimes you are completely absorbed in, and feeling part of, what is happening. These moments may focus on ordinary and mundane things, like doing the daily chores, but you are fully engaged in them. You are not carrying on another conversation in your head at the same time or creating stories to yourself about a different past or future. Time seems to stand still or cease to matter. The moment might seem magical, precious, or have some other special quality. You might feel more than usually aware in the moment and of it as it passes on.

We don't allow ourselves to experience this kind of absorption in the moment very often because we are too busy: rushing, feeling anxious, doing too many different things, and so on. So the purpose of the next activity is for you to find a time when you can just enjoy something you choose to do, without being distracted by other things.

One writer, Tony Parsons (1995), describes such an experience:

"One day I was walking across a park in a suburb of London. I noticed as I walked that my mind was totally occupied with expectations about future events that might or might not happen. I apparently made the choice to let go of these projections and simply be with my walking. I noticed that each footstep was totally unique in feel and pressure, and that it was there one moment and gone the next, never to be repeated in the same way ever again."

Tony Parsons then went on to describe another and more profound shift that happened as he was just "having an experience":

"As all of this was happening, there was a transition from me watching my walking to simply the presence of walking. What happened then is simply beyond description. I can only inadequately say in words that total stillness and presence seemed to descend over everything."

It will not necessarily be like this when you do the next activity, but the important thing is to focus on "having an experience" – whatever that turns out to be like. As you are doing the activity, there are four actions we ask you to do. But don't let "doing them" take over from "having an experience" by getting caught up or too concerned about what we ask you to do. Read the activity first and imagine yourself carrying out these four actions. Then put the instructions aside and just do it.

Activity: Having An Experience

Choose an activity that you enjoy and can get absorbed in. It needs to be reasonably easy to do and should not be mentally intricate. Allow enough time so you are not worried about other things you should be doing. You might choose to go for a walk, garden, sit quietly, cook, paint, play music, mess around in a workshed, sew, read, watch the night sky – whatever you choose!

As you do the activity, practice the following:

●*Give your full attention to this activity – yourself, here, now, just fully experiencing what you notice and feel, accepting the moment as it is. If other thoughts intrude, or your attention is drawn to other things, just bring your attention back to being focused on having this experience*
●*At some point while you are engaged with your activity, watch or observe yourself in the act of doing it, as if you are watching a child doing the same thing*
●*Be open to what touches, moves, delights, or is of value to you, including any awareness of connection or presence*
●*Reflect briefly on how you might bring such qualities more fully into your day.*

You may well find this activity an enjoyable experience. However, if you find that your experience while doing it is not enjoyable, the same principles still apply; you may need to give more attention to accepting things as they are first, in order to open yourself to your experience.

As an example of the activity, one of *The Quest* writers, Ike, chose to do something he does often. There are many ducks living around a pond between his flat and the supermarket. He likes to buy an old loaf of bread in the supermarket and then feed the ducks. This time, however, he set off to feed the ducks and immerse himself in the world of ducks more consciously.

He put aside other thoughts and just noticed the little fights and squabbles of the ducks, how they protect their young, the fondnesses and flirtations and the whole sense of extended family. Then he let his attention move a little outward, to other wildlife such as frogs, toads, newts, and fish that might be in the pond or in the rushes and reeds around it. He took in the pond itself, the trees, bushes, and grassy areas of the park, the weather clouds overhead and the quality of light. He noticed the warmth of the sun on his face and felt his feet on the ground as he listened to the noises close by and further away in the distance. He became aware of the people around him and what they were doing – the closer interactions and the wider spaces in between them. What struck Ike was how the world was just being there at that moment, how much it was part of him and he was part of it.

Since then, Ike notices that he values moments when he feels as if time and the world stand still. When he slows down enough to give his full attention to what is in the moment, then the beauty, joy and life-force of everything flood in. He thinks he can feel the same connection when he is rushing or when life is difficult if he gives his attention fully to the moment rather than giving part of it to something else at the same time. He also sees that he needs to build further on this single example.

Activity: Anchoring Your Experience

It's useful to anchor your experience in some way before moving on.

●*Imagine observing yourself having this experience; how would you describe it?*
●*How did it feel to try to "just have an experience"?*
●*What did you observe as you watched yourself?*
●*What was in the experience that you valued or was meaningful?*
●*How might you bring the same quality into your life on another occasion?*
●*What would remind you of the experience?*
●*Lastly, try to notice whether or not your experience has any impact on you over the next few days.*

UNPACKING *HAVING AN EXPERIENCE*

The Quest is a process of exploring your sense of soul and finding how to stay in touch with it by nurturing a habit of spiritual reflection. You practiced the basic skills of spiritual reflection in the four actions that were part of *Having An Experience*; in later chapters these basic skills are developed further and incorporate spiritual practices found in spiritual traditions around the world. The table below shows how these actions relate to spiritual practice.

Four actions used in *Having An Experience:*	Skills of Spiritual Reflection based on spiritual practices of:
1. Giving your full attention to this activity – yourself, here, now, just fully experience this, what you notice and feel, accepting the moment as it is.	Stillness and Being Centred
2. Watching and observing yourself as if you were watching a child.	Observing and Reflecting
3. Being open to what touches, moves, delights or is of value to you, including any awareness of connection or presence.	Opening
4. Asking yourself how you might bring such qualities more fully into each day.	Integrating

Fig 3: Four actions from Having an Experience

The purpose of developing a habit of spiritual reflection is "an effort to be aware of and to reflect on the movement of the Spirit in the course of the day" (Loring, 1997). The activities in *The Quest* use the skills of spiritual reflection in varied ways so you will practice and develop your skills as you do them. As the skills become more familiar, you will be able to adapt them to your needs and integrate them with any existing practice you may have. Gradually, you establish awareness in your daily life through spiritual reflection.

Through **stillness and being centered** you give your full attention to what is; through **observing and reflecting** you direct attention toward your inward self and become more sensitive to the connections between external things and internal ripples; through **opening** you become more aware of what is meaningful, and foster connection; **integrating** embodies action with awareness more fully every day. The four actions introduced in *Having An Experience* are now named as *Stillness and Being Centered, Observing and Reflecting, Opening,* and *Integrating* as in Figure 4 below.

These skills promote awareness, being present, and connection. This creates a space in which you can be more conscious of your sense of soul, the central element of a spiritual life. So *The Quest* places your sense of soul, indicated by the symbol of a shaded circle taken from our labyrinth, at the center of *The Quest* framework. This sense of soul is nurtured by spiritual reflection, building an "inner holding" that then feeds back into your daily life. This whole process is what *The Quest* calls *exploring a sense of soul.*

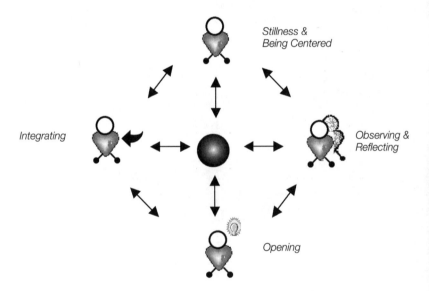

Fig 4: **The Quest** *Framework For Exploring Your Sense Of Soul*

However, exploring *your* sense of soul is not neat and uniform; the arrows going in many directions suggest a less structured process. But, if you look at the diagram again you will see that the elements of spiritual reflection are connected to each other and to your sense of soul; this rhythm fosters a conscious spiritual life. Yet exploring your sense of soul is fluid and flexible and will be different for everyone.

Activity: What Is A "Conscious Spiritual Life"?

Read the quotation below. Jot down ideas, pictures, words or phrases that depict the kind of spiritual life you would like to develop. This may be a clear or a very fragmentary picture at this point.

"Spiritual life is a life of commitment to being present to what is, and open to the potentiality of the Spirit within it." (Patricia Loring, 1997)

- *What are key features of a meaningful spiritual life for you?*
- *What habits and practices will help you attune to your sense of soul?*
- *What will keep your creative energy flowing?*
- *What will help you maintain this connection when life is challenging or busy?*

Heart of The Quest has set out a framework for developing awareness, introducing basic skills of spiritual reflection that help you explore and embody your sense of soul. In the next chapter you develop and practice them.

DEVELOPING YOUR SKILLS

In *Developing Your Skills* you practice a key example of each of the skills of spiritual reflection introduced in *Heart of The Quest*. The four skills are based on the same four actions from *Having An Experience* but now you encounter them more deeply and in forms that are more akin to spiritual practices from across the religious traditions.

Each activity, a *Skill Of Spiritual Reflection*, focuses on one key example. Try it as it is, reflect on the experience, and then experiment with the suggested variations so you can adapt the skill in ways that suit you.

THE PRACTICE OF STILLNESS AND BEING CENTERED

Stillness involves self-discipline but needn't be complicated, nor are you required to sit in a particular position or place. The aim is to become fully present in each moment, and be aware of that moment. By being centered in the moment, you allow yourself to still the body, emotions, and mind. By accepting the moment, letting go of any negativity or desire to change it, you become more receptive.

Most religious traditions point to the experience of being still and centered as a doorway to deeper strengths and wisdom. In Buddhism, for example, there is a strong tradition of mindfulness and meditation, while in Christianity it is embraced in prayer and contemplation. You may find you can be distracted by external stimuli, and a practice of stillness helps you remain centered in the present moment; that what is happening now is the only moment there is. The past has gone and the future is still ahead and unknown. The activity focuses on basic steps in finding inner stillness that can be used as preparation for quiet time, meditation or just in a brief moment in daily life.

Activity: **Skills of Spiritual Reflection:**
Practicing Stillness And Being Centered

FINDING INNER STILLNESS

WHAT DOES IT MEAN?

Finding inner stillness is gently quietening the mind, minimizing the clamor of thought and bodily needs, withdrawing from everyday activities so that it is possible to get in touch with a center within; this is frequently experienced in terms of peace and stillness. This skill also provides an opportunity to review and take stock of your thoughts, feelings, and activities from a more centered, and less busy or charged, perspective. Some people describe inner stillness as finding an inner point where they feel more balanced and clear. Finding inner stillness, or finding one's center, can be practiced without adherence to any religion or philosophy, and there are countless ways of practicing.

STARTING OUT

Start with practicing inner stillness for five minutes, and build up to 10-20 minutes or so. Many people practice on a daily basis in the morning but you will find a rhythm that suits you.

1. Sit in a comfortable but alert position with a straight spine and close your eyes. There is no need to sit in any special position. Be aware of noises and sensations around you without letting them disturb you. Keep bringing your attention back to this moment and this place, and allow your body to relax.

2. Move your attention inward, and focus on your breathing. Do not change the rhythm in any way. Simply give your attention to its movement. Feel yourself becoming steadier and more still.

3. Rest in the rhythm and let go of any distracting thoughts and sensations. If they surface, acknowledge them and return to your breathing, aiming to establish a sense of being centered and balanced.

4. Allow yourself to experience just "being" for some while. Your mind is stilled, and you are just at rest in your center.

5. Come back to everyday awareness slowly and gently. Appreciate the quiet time you have had.

REFLECTION: WHAT HAVE YOU LEARNED FROM THIS PRACTICE?

After you have experimented with Finding Inner Stillness, *review your experience:*

- *How was it for you?*
- *What happened as you focused on relaxing, taking your attention inward and paying attention to the quality of the experience?*
- *To what extent were you able to let go of distracting thoughts and sensations and bring your attention back to the moment?*
- *What changes, if any, did you notice in the level of inner activity of your emotions, thoughts, and memories?*

Make a note of your experience with this practice.

PRACTICING

Finding inner stillness is a first step towards the kind of meditative practices found at the heart of many spiritual traditions. People report a variety of experiences from visions, voices and sounds, colors and images, to warmth, pleasant sensations, feelings of peace and tranquility, and connectedness with creation. Don't worry if you find it difficult at first to still the mind. Stay relaxed and keep bringing your focus back.

Use the suggestions below as ways to vary your practice.

1. Focus on flowers, a candle, a symbol or object that is meaningful to you. You can also focus on an image in the mind or an abstract quality that is important to you such as love, joy, friendship.

2. On each out breath, let go of all negative thoughts and emotions. As you breathe in, bring in peace, joy, or calmness or flood your body with white light. Notice how these images affect you and vary them to find one that is helpful for you.

3. Notice where your body feels tense and relax it. Notice where your emotions and feelings are reactive or distressed and let them settle. Notice when your thoughts are teeming and stay focused on inner stillness.

4. As your body, emotions, and mind are stilled, receive in a non-judgmental way anything that enters your mind. The mind is not ruling you in the way it usually does; it is simply bringing your inner wisdom into consciousness. You can always review afterwards, with discrimination, what you received in this inner stillness.

5. When you reach a place of stillness, sit resting your hands on your legs, palms upward in a gesture of holding. Imagine unconditionally holding yourself, then your surroundings, gradually extending this holding to whomever and whatever you wish.

This activity may be difficult whether this sort of skill is new to you or not; most people, even those with many years' experience in similar spiritual practices, find it difficult to keep their focus. Initially you may become even more aware of the amount of inner chatter that goes on. And while sometimes it is easier to quieten your "monkey mind", it always pops up again. Like any skill, regular use helps train the "muscle"; the knack is just to persist as best you can.

The sensation of inner stillness that may come in the midst of what you are doing is not easy to describe. It may feel empty, in a clear light, noticing distractions falling away or quietening. It is recognizable often as much by how you feel as what happens. The most important thing is simply that you practice. And you may find that gradually stillness and being centered integrates into your moment-to-moment awareness.

THE PRACTICE OF OBSERVING AND REFLECTING

Observing what's happening to you, whether that is a single event, a period in your life, feelings, or relationships, helps you notice what you are experiencing. Reflecting – where you question, listen, or wait for insight to arise, and interpret your experiences – can clarify the present and provide you with signposts for the future. Finally, recording it in some way helps you "ground" the experience and make it alive. You may come back and review this reflection, identify what has changed, or check if you would now respond in a different way.

Activity: Skills of Spiritual Reflection:
Practicing Observing and Reflecting

BEING YOUR OWN OBSERVER

WHAT DOES IT MEAN?

This practice links closely to Finding Inner Stillness *described in the previous activity, with a subtle shift, which helps it to become a skill for effective reflection. In* Being Your Own Observer *you try to develop a capacity to observe, or witness, yourself from an independent position, without judgment or opinion. You cultivate a clear sense of standing outside your normal awareness, almost like someone standing at your shoulder. You may notice things that would otherwise escape you, with an attitude of "Oh, that's interesting". The observer, or witness, is not caught up in judging. Most spiritual systems teach that we have an inner place, which is the point of connection between the individual and the whole or divine consciousness.*

With this practice, you are also able to bring compassion to the way you watch and notice yourself, and you realize that you are just a "player". It's as if you usually wear a mask, taking it for granted that what you are, what you do, what you say is the truth. But everything you say or do is subjective, and being your own observer is a step towards unmasking that subjectivity.

STARTING OUT

1. Begin with a small period of time, say 15 minutes. During that period, imagine that you are your own best and compassionate friend observing what is going on, standing at your own shoulder, silent and listening. You are not intervening in any way, but just noticing what is happening.

2. Notice that the main difference between being an observer of yourself and of someone else is that you can focus on the inner landscape, as well as what is happening on the outside. You can notice the emotions, thoughts, body sensations, assumptions, and so on.

3. Describe out loud what is happening, both the inner and the outer experiences.

4. As you speak, be aware of when your noticing starts to introduce judgments or opinions. Try to remain neutral, and simply to describe what is.

REFLECTION: WHAT HAVE YOU LEARNED FROM THIS PRACTICE?

After you have experimented with Being Your Own Observer, *review your experience:*

●*What, if anything, do you notice in yourself when you observe and reflect on your experience?*
●*Are there any patterns, thoughts, feelings, or responses that recur?*
●*What moments of insight or difficulties did you encounter?*
●*How could you experiment with different ways of recording what you notice in yourself?*

PRACTICING

1. Imagine that you are watching yourself as if you are in a film or play. The actors, of whom you are one, are playing roles in that film. You may be the hero, the love interest, the villain. In another film, you may play a different role, perhaps mother, wise friend, temptress. Notice the role you play in this film, and observe yourself with detachment. Notice at another time a different role you play. Which role(s) feel most true to yourself?

2. Another way of looking at the same phenomenon is to imagine that you are made up of players in an orchestra. You are all striving for the same harmony, but you may play different tunes at different times. Observe how sometimes different players can seem out of tune with each other, but at other times they harmonize well. Watch how you play here, and notice when your different roles seem to conflict.

3. *Piero Ferrucci (1982) suggests that you have an inner core, from which you can observe what you are thinking or feeling, without identifying with it. The figure below shows an adaptation of this theory. When the self is in one of the open circles, you say, for example: "I am angry. I am going to ... " When you become the observer, represented by the black dot, you observe: "I feel anger but I am not my anger." Then you just notice your anger, but are not dominated by it.*

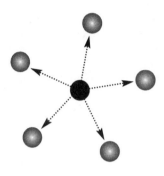

Fig 5: Being Your Own Observer

Learning to become an observer requires you to see clearly what is, and not what you judge or desire it to be, and to resist identification with what you observe, believe, or feel. Instead, you can be both fully engaged in the present and yet remain centered and non-attached.

Later in *The Quest* there is an activity that introduces *Journaling* as a skill associated with observing and reflecting (page 116); many people use journaling as a way to record and process the experience of being their own observer.

THE PRACTICE OF OPENING

Being open consciously can become a regular habit. *The Quest* calls it *opening*, as you are opening up to new input and awareness of what has meaning and value to you. You may do this in many different ways, by opening to nature, other people, books, music, dance, movement, sport, ecstasy, body-work, or inspiration from spiritual resources. You can be curious about things, ask questions, and keep an open mind. It doesn't matter, as long as you recognize inspiration and new possibilities, and are mindful of them. Essentially, the practice alerts you to what delights, touches, moves, and inspires you, to what is of value and has meaning and what helps you feel connected and whole.

Moments of personal inspiration, when a light bulb flashes on, can happen at any time. "Most of us can remember the strangely moving power of passages in certain poems read when we were young," wrote William James (1961), a pioneer of modern psychology, "irrational doorways as they were through which the mysteries of fact, the wildness and the pang of life, stole into our hearts and thrilled them … we are alive or dead to the eternal inner message of the arts according as we have kept or lost this mystical susceptibility."

Inspiration doesn't necessarily change your whole life in an instant, although it may do; but it does keep you in touch with those moments that "stole into our hearts and thrilled them." You often don't have to do anything, except be open to your inspiration, know and be able to recognize your triggers. These "triggers" are experiences which help you to discover and remember those things that make life precious and meaningful in some way; they refresh and renew your sense of purpose, restoring your feelings of trust and courage, encouraging you to try again and reminding you of a wider or deeper spiritual connection. Triggers could be readings, music, nature, art … the list is endless.

Activity: Skills of Spiritual Reflection:
Practicing Opening

OPENING TO CREATIVE INSPIRATION

WHAT DOES IT MEAN?

We commonly imagine that creativity is reserved for outstanding people, such as great artists, sculptors, writers, poets, composers, philosophers. But we all have a creative spark, and the capacity to live and express ourselves spontaneously, with authenticity. Being open to this creativity takes courage and conviction, seeing things freshly, harnessing imagination to take a leap into the unknown.

Creativity can help you to explore spirituality without any requirement to adhere to a specific religious path. The act of reaching beyond your normal awareness and tapping into the imagination opens up deeper wellsprings that make a connection with the underlying creative impulse of the cosmos of which you are part.

The seat of creativity is inspiration, a life force that flows through each of us. The act of creativity involves your whole being – body, mind, feelings, and soul. Carl Rogers (1977) linked creativity to the drive to "express and activate all the capacities of the organism or the self," while Natalie Rogers (1993) suggests: "Using our creativity for awareness, release, insight and action leads us to the path of spirituality."

STARTING OUT

Often, we don't believe in our own creativity sufficiently to allow its life force to come to the surface. However, a source of inspiration can help to create conditions within that allow the creative spark to live and flower. That source may come from many different triggers. What the triggers do is help open up new ways of being, thinking and doing.

Creativity takes many forms, and so it is difficult to give you steps that say "Do this'", and then "Do that" and you will be successful. Try out, however, the following tips.

1. Be reassured that you have always, throughout your life so far, been creative. Look at what you have already created around you, in your everyday life. This might be in the form of a home, a garden, a family, friends, colleagues, a working environment, a community life, and so on. They may not be what you would normally define as "creative" but someone created them. You may feel that you had nothing to do with it, but think about it for a while. Many of the things around you are directly influenced by you and your own actions.

2. Become aware of what it is that gives you inspiration. Look for those things in your everyday life that make you feel good, that make you stop and stare, or that excite you.

3. What happens to you when you do find these triggers? Do you want to be able to paint a landscape you see? Do you want to write something or make music or teach? Try to think through what kind of creative act would be most meaningful for you. Remember that creativity doesn't have to be "artistic". It can also be destructive of old ways, or it can clarify, simplify or enlighten actions and events. Try to experiment with different creative forms that you are less practised in.

4. Don't be too critical of yourself, or feel you need the approval of other people for your creative acts; this may only stifle the creative spark within you. Be prepared sometimes to struggle with frustration and despair, even about ever unlocking your creative potential. Be open to possibility, take risks, get things wrong sometimes, but try expressing yourself with spontaneity and the courage of your convictions.

REFLECTION: WHAT HAVE YOU LEARNED FROM THIS PRACTICE?

After you have experimented with Opening to Creative Inspiration, review your experience:

●What are the triggers that inspire you? You might think in terms of experiences that transform you, refresh and renew you. It could be something that illuminates, or gives you insight. It might be something that gives you joy, a sense of peace and goodwill.
●What have you created this day? Where have you made choices? How far were

you able to make choices in the light of the values and potential that inspire you? What, when and how has this been difficult?

PRACTICING

1. Remind yourself that being creative is part of human nature. Evans and Russell (1992) say:

> *"As you read these words you are exercising creativity; you are bringing images and ideas into existence in your mind. You are expressing creativity in every decision you make; whether it be in resolving a conflict, organising a presentation, or preparing a meal. Whatever we do, we are causing the world to change, we are bringing new forms into existence. Every thought and every action we ever make is an expression of creativity. To be alive is to be creative."*

2. Try to look at familiar situations from a different point of view. Sometimes a physical act can shift your point of view and help you to see through new eyes. In a discussion with others, move out of your chair to stand behind or next to someone else with a different viewpoint. Try to imagine yourself 'in their shoes'.

3. Imagine a triangle, where one base point is you and the other base point is the situation calling for your creativity. Both the points are connected to a single point above that represents the highest possible outcome. Your creative potential is activated by asking what is the highest possibility that you could imagine at work here.

4. Practise using techniques of thinking that take you outside your usual patterns. If these techniques are new to you, try brainstorming or using pictures and diagrams instead of words. Trust your intuition more.

5. Consider attending workshops on creativity or working through courses on creativity in books that provide an experiential and recommended approach.

Later activities in *The Quest* encourage you to consider a variety of triggers for inspiration. For now, the lyric of this song by Mike Scott sums up what it means to be open.

OPEN

Open to the world
open to spirit
open to the changing wind
open to touch
open to nature

DEVELOPING YOUR SKILLS ◈

open to the world within
open to change
open to adventure
open to the new
open to love
open to miracles
open Beloved to You

Open to learn
open to laughter
open to being blessed
open to joy
open to service
open to saying "Yes!"
open to risk
open to passion
to peace and silence too
open to love
open to beauty
open Beloved to You

(Mike Scott, 1992, from CD album *Still Burning*.
Words and Music by Mike Scott © 1996 Sony Music Publishing Limited.
All Rights Reserved.)

THE PRACTICE OF INTEGRATING

How do you bring what you're learning back into your life? How does it affect your relationships, with self, with others, community, and environment? What you learn might change your behavior in a significant way, but it's equally likely to be small gradual changes. However, they all have the same beginning – acting with awareness.

Activity: Skills of Spiritual Reflection:
Practicing Integrating

ACTING WITH AWARENESS

WHAT DOES IT MEAN?

Acting with awareness means using your senses and keeping your attention on the present moment, so that you consciously notice the experiences you are having in the very moment they are happening. If you can approach each instant as a new and rich experience, unique and unrepeatable, then you are more able to appreciate the gifts that it might bring. Even with everyday actions – brushing

33

your teeth, traveling from one place to another – try consciously to bring every part of you fully present. Start to notice small, subtle details that may otherwise be overlooked, things like the way your muscles work, or how droplets of water on a flower petal form patterns. Be attentive to your inner world of thoughts and feelings as well as your outer world of perceptions and actions.

Through acting with awareness, you can increase your enjoyment of living and your capacity to focus or concentrate on what you wish. You may well find that by acting with awareness, you remain calmer even when the present moment is noisy, challenging, exciting, painful or distressing. You will find yourself less likely to be taken over by your current emotion, while at the same time being very aware of what that is, and able to make conscious choices.

STARTING OUT

In the Zen Buddhist tradition, a teacher may give the student just one instruction: "Attention. Attention. Attention."

1. Just notice. Be aware of where you are, who is with you and the surroundings. This moment is immeasurably precious. If the moment is difficult or you notice yourself having negative feelings, try to accept the moment as it is. Try to set aside your resistance; whatever your feelings, at this moment the fact is that things are as they are, so let them be.

2. Try to do one thing at a time, being aware of what you're doing. Give the action your full attention. Notice your body, your feelings, your thoughts, without getting caught up in them. Focus fully on just the present moment and bring your attention to what you are doing in that moment.

3. Pay attention to the quality of the experience. Look for and appreciate the things for which you can give thanks. Every experience, even an uncomfortable one, will have some aspect that you can appreciate. Make conscious choices about your actions and behavior, inner and outer.

4. If you find that your attention strays away, consciously bring it back. But do not give yourself a hard time over the number of times it strays.

REFLECTION: WHAT HAVE YOU LEARNED FROM THIS PRACTICE?

After you have experimented with acting with awareness, review your experience:

- *Was anything different for you when you acted with awareness?*
- *What was valuable for you in the way you did it?*
- *What did it mean to you in the context of the moment?*

Next recall a contrasting situation where you felt that you were on automatic pilot or where your action seemed very routine and mechanical.

● Can you identify how the situations were different for you?
● How did you feel?
● What difference, if any, does acting with awareness make?

PRACTICING

1. **Conscious Choice.** William Blake (1804) said: "Do good by minute particulars." As often as possible, and especially when you make significant decisions, ask yourself what values you want to express, what potential can you help open, what impact your choice and action will have. If you feel the situation is negative, consider how you can minimize harm and keep options open.

2. **Active Listening.** When you have a conversation with someone, give them your wholehearted attention, being open and keeping eye contact. Let them know you have heard what they say – by your body language and by asking questions, seeking clarification and reassurance. Do not prepare your next remarks until after they finish speaking. Do not give advice unless it is asked for.

3. **Symbolic Action.** Identify a small but meaningful action that you can take that harmonizes with your values. It could be something like recycling your waste or valuing yourself and doing something that takes care of yourself. Take this action and do so carefully, thinking of it as making a statement about something you believe to be important in your life.

4. **Concerned Citizenship.** Think of something that concerns you. It might be your local supermarket stocking a healthy or organic product, or a political decision. Decide on some action you could take, such as a letter asking for the decision to be re-considered or putting your reasons for a change to be made – and do it.

5. **A Practice Of Mindfulness.** Set the alarm of a watch or clock to sound every hour. As it does so, pause momentarily in what you are doing. Bring your attention fully to how you are feeling, and what is happening around you. Alternatively, when the telephone rings, allow it to ring a couple of times before you answer. When you answer, give the call your full attention, being completely aware of what is around you, what is happening, and what you feel.

The point of acting with awareness is to accept and be present with what is, aware of what is meaningful and choosing to bring this to the center of your attention.

BUILDING A HABIT OF SPIRITUAL REFLECTION

Exploring your sense of soul is a continuous flow of experience, insight and understanding supported by spiritual reflection; *The Quest* framework for exploring your sense of soul summarizes the core elements and this multi-directional flow.

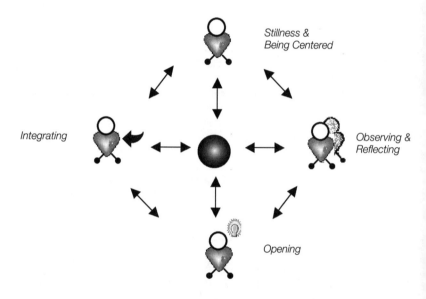

Stillness &
Being Centered

Integrating

Observing &
Reflecting

Opening

Fig 6: A Framework For Exploring Your Sense Of Soul

You won't need to say to yourself: "Ah, now I'm reflecting on an experience, and next I'll check for inspiration." But, over a week or so, pay attention to using all four types of skills. Then, gradually, awareness and consciousness illuminate and anchor what you learn. You may find that your values and purpose change and you feel a greater connection with something deeper.

By the time you have worked with *The Quest* for some while, you may find that *Having An Experience* becomes embedded in you and the skills support and nurture your growing sense of soul. It can come as a surprise to find out that even a limited amount of practice changes your perceptions and raises your level of awareness. To see where you've got to so far, try the following activity.

Activity: **Using Spiritual Reflection**

Is there anything that you've learned so far in The Quest *that has meaning for you or has struck a chord? Is there anything new that you want to bring into your life?*

- *What has been your experience so far in working with the skills in the activities?*
- *What, if anything, has changed for you so far?*
- *How easy or difficult was it to make the change?*
- *What effect has this had on your sense of soul?*
- *How might you adapt the skills of spiritual reflection so they suit you and your needs?*

*Now you have used the four types of skills, reflect on your experience of **Stillness and Being Centered**, **Observing and Reflecting**, **Opening to Creative Inspiration**, and **Integrating** and consider how you can bring what you learn into daily life.*

Take your time over this activity, and return to it now and then to remind yourself of where you were at this time.

In *Heart of The Quest* and *Developing Your Skills* you have experienced the spiritual reflection that underpins *The Quest* and practiced key examples of the skills. You continue to use these skills in activities throughout *The Quest* although we don't necessarily label them as such. Where there are activities that focus on developing new skills they are identified by the title *Skills Of Spiritual Reflection*; wherever you develop a new skill, you might find it useful to refresh the basic skills in this chapter and, in particular, make use of the questions under *Reflection: What Have You Learned From This Practice?* from each one. There is an index at the end of the book that lists all the skills and provides follow-up references.

Spiritual reflection is one key component of *The Quest*. In the activity *Picturing The Present* in **Getting Started** you met the other key component of *The Quest* – you and your experience. In the next chapter, *Telling Your Story*, you use the kind of skills you have been learning to start looking at what has brought you to where you are today.

TELLING YOUR STORY

"We are closer to God when we are asking questions"
than when we think we have the answers.

Rabbi Abraham Heschel (1997)

In *Telling Your Story* you begin by telling the story of your life as it has unfolded to date. As you explore your journey, you move further into reflecting on themes, patterns, and blocks in your life and recognize what has positive meaning for you. This is essential work in exploring your sense of soul. You will be uncovering the obstacles and hindrances that stand in your way, and identifying values and core principles through which you express your unique embodiment of Spirit. Questions you will ask include:

○ What has been important in your life?
○ What matters most to you?
○ What has challenged or stretched you?
○ What will help you let go of fear and experience more love?

YOUR STORY

Experience, *your experience*, is the starting-point of self-awareness and inner knowledge. As you reflect on events and experience, you become alert to inner perceptions and the way they affect you. Levine (1997) suggests: "The first element is the exploration of what has gone before as a way of clearing the path for what is to come ... the life review goes beneath the surface of past actions to the states of mind from which these acts originated."

The first step in establishing an idea of who you think you are is telling your story. Initially, it may seem daunting to look back over your life and identify which events stand out for you and why. Some people seem to have lives that contain nothing but memorable or significant events. For others, life seems a blur and they find it hard to remember any specific events.

Generally, there are some experiences and events that you recollect most readily and, as you begin to think about your life, more will surface. Looking through old photo albums, diaries, letters, and other mementoes or a "do you remember … ?" session with family or old friends can jog your memory. Or you may feel that you have reviewed your life story so often there's nothing new to say, that the same things come up again; however, setting out to find a different way to express your memories can stimulate new recollections and new ways of seeing events and experiences.

Activity: Telling Your Story

This activity gives you two different ways to begin telling your story; the first one may suit you if you are not already familiar with this kind of exercise and the second one may be useful if you have done it before.

Sit quietly for a short time, relax, breathe evenly and let your mind slow down.

(a) Let memories, images, sounds, smells, colors, words, incidents in your life arise. You might remember significant events or periods in your life by asking yourself about:

- *People*
- *Places*
- *Times of year*
- *Emotions*
- *Sensations such as smell, touch, taste, sounds*
- *Favorite pieces of music, books, works of art*
- *Times when things seemed straightforward and times when you seemed to be wandering down side-alleys*
- *Highs and lows*

(b) If you have recounted your story many times before, you can try a different way of doing so now by using the labyrinth (see Fig 8, page 41). Let your finger walk through the labyrinth, beginning where the white path starts in the lower left-hand side. Use the questions below to prompt your recollections.

- *As you stand at the threshold of the labyrinth, how do you feel as you recall your story?*
- *Was there a time in your life when you knew, or felt as if, you were on a path?*
- *What significant moments or milestones represent turning points?*
- *When did you feel as if you knew where you were going? When did your life feel more like an unlit passage full of challenges, obstacles, and concerns?*
- *Have there been any "arrows" helping to guide your direction, particularly when you were lost or the way was dark? If so, what names would you put to the arrows?*
- *When has your life been concerned with an inner track — a path in to the center*

– and when has it been more focused on outer events and demands?

● Has there been anything in your life that might relate to the center of the labyrinth?

● When you choose to let your finger walk out of the labyrinth, do the arrows suggest any directions that are important to you now?

You could use words, maps, charts, or pictures or make a collection of photos or objects. Some people make a chronological list of events, or draw it to look like a winding path or a temperature chart. Others draw or paint or create a dance or write a poem. You might prefer to do this activity orally by telling someone else your ideas or recording what you say on tape before replaying it and making notes. It doesn't matter, so long as you understand what your record stands for and that your record has meaning for you.

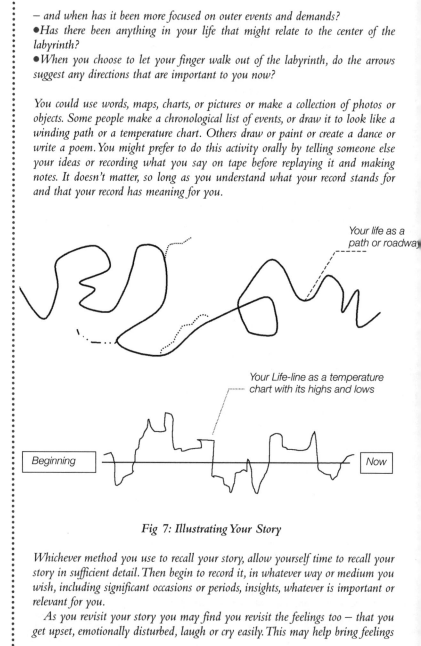

Your life as a path or roadway

Your Life-line as a temperature chart with its highs and lows

Beginning

Now

Fig 7: Illustrating Your Story

Whichever method you use to recall your story, allow yourself time to recall your story in sufficient detail. Then begin to record it, in whatever way or medium you wish, including significant occasions or periods, insights, whatever is important or relevant for you.

As you revisit your story you may find you revisit the feelings too – that you get upset, emotionally disturbed, laugh or cry easily. This may help bring feelings

Fig 8: Telling Your Story Through The Labyrinth

into the open and discover what lies behind them. Revisiting such times and feelings may create movement in your memories and help you let go of energy that has been wrapped up in them for a long time.

When you have finished, look back at your story and add any further record you need.

- Notice what stands out for you
- Is there something that looks new or different to how it seemed before?
- Are there things you have included that surprise you?
- Do you have any new insights or realization about events and feelings or the relative importance you have given them?

This is a core activity and you will be returning to it several times in different ways and at different levels. You may also find that over the next few days or week, you have more recollections, thoughts, or insights which can be added to your record.

41

PATTERNS AND THEMES

As you were doing the previous activity, you may have noticed recurring themes or patterns in your story. Sometimes your approach to situations or reaction to events is dictated by something that happened early in life that goes on to influence the way you deal with future situations, each one having a further impact on the next. You learn lessons from when you are a small child about your place in the world, what you should do, or how you ought to behave, and build up habitual responses that you continue to use later in life.

Activity: Exploring Patterns And Themes From The Outside

Review your notes, drawings, and record from the activities in Telling Your Story, *looking for themes and patterns in your:*

- *Education*
- *Career or profession*
- *Personal relationships*
- *Places*
- *Politics*
- *Influences*

Can you see any patterns or themes emerging, whether they are the kind you see as "positive" or those you see as "negative"? People who know you well, friends or family, may be able to tell you if they notice repeating kinds of episodes or ongoing threads in your story.

However, themes and patterns are not restricted to life events and circumstances. When you look back at the significant events highlighted in your life story, you may find connections between your feelings and what was happening; for instance, similar events may be associated with excitement, anger, happiness, or frustration.

Activity: Exploring Patterns And Themes From The Inside

Now look at your most significant events in terms of how you felt or what was going on inside you at the time.

- *How did you feel during the "negative" events?*
- *Were the feelings different from the "positive" and, if so, in what way?*

It might trigger your awareness if you try to remember times when you felt most:

- *Calm or at peace*
- *Joyful*
- *Alive*
- *Angry*
- *Hurt or betrayed*
- *Confused or doubtful*
- *Depressed or despairing.*

Some events prompt you to think or act differently. Look back and see if during these times you developed new qualities or strengths. Did any learning and change take place?

WHO AM I?

Up to this point you've been considering yourself by looking at patterns and themes, things that have shaped the way you are, and which still have an effect on you today. Noticing such themes and patterns brings you in touch with your quest for authenticity. Barber and Bates (2000) explain authenticity as: "best felt at times when you just share your natural being, rather than when you are struggling to be something you feel 'ought to be' or what others say you 'should be'. It is akin to the soul coming home."

In reaching toward your own authenticity, you need to expand your picture of yourself, to include your ideas about the kind of person you know yourself to be from the inside. What makes you unique? What do you most value in who you are and what you do? Where do your particular skills and talents lie?

Activity: Who Am I?

Read through the whole activity. You might find it easier, or more effective, to complete the sentences out loud and record them or, if you feel comfortable with a listener, you could ask someone else to jot them down for you.

Close your eyes and relax briefly. Then try completing the following phrases by writing the first five things that come into your head for each phrase without allowing your "critic inside" or "inner judge" to censor them before you get them onto paper.

- *What I like about myself is …*
- *The things I am good at are…*
- *My best personal qualities are …*
- *What other people like about me is …*
- *The qualities I most admire in other people are …*

●The image of myself as I most like myself to be is ...
Read back the statements you have written about yourself.

●Do they reveal any unexpected sides of you?
●What, if any, new insights do they give you?
●Pick out those that are an essential part of who you are and what is unique and important about you.

Finally, ask a friend or your family what they like, respect, and value about you; their response may give you another perspective on who you are.

Recognizing your qualities within, knowing what people appreciate in you, can be very reassuring; knowing yourself as accepted and loved is hugely important.

BLOCKS AND BARRIERS

However, sometimes your experience of yourself may be dominated by feeling as if you are a mess inside. But what is the "mess inside" that you may be aware of? You may try to appear on the outside as if you are OK, while the inside is very different. Inside, you might feel confused, muddled, unsure, insecure, upside-down, less good-natured than you appear, less calm, and many other things. However, if you can recognize yourself in this to any extent, feel reassured that you are not alone! Most of us try to hide the mess inside, hoping that it will not be overwhelming or that at least no one else will notice. However, this is actually quite a normal aspect of life, an inevitable piece of luggage that we carry. We all have weaknesses, fears, and vulnerabilities, defenses that help us cope with difficult situations. So, it's useful to try to figure out, firstly, what they are, and, secondly, why they're there.

Activity: Checking Out Blockages

In this activity, you will be reviewing things from your past which still seem to hinder you. It is not an easy activity to do. If you are still hanging on to events from your past, this indicates that they are important to you.

Read through the activity and notice any memories, thoughts, physical feelings, or emotions that arise as you read. Try to note them down. You may find that once you have noticed they are there, it becomes easier to reflect on them.

●Have particular periods or events in your past life given you seemingly negative messages?
●Do you notice that you seem to land up back in a place or situation where you've been before?

- *Do you feel as if you are stuck with an issue or upset in your past?*
- *Are there some issues and upsets that seem to keep re-surfacing, as if you cannot let go of them?*
- *Are there events from which you haven't been able to move on?*

Look again at your life events, and try answering the following:

- *What kinds of events in your past still have the power to upset, disturb, or anger you?*
- *What have you held on to that you can't get over?*
- *Do you still feel as if you are stuck with anything in the past?*

You might need to come back to this activity a number of times before you get anywhere; it might work better to think about these questions when you find yourself upset or angry again over something. You might also find it helpful to talk it over with someone you can trust.

Acknowledging that there are particular kinds of situations that still have a hold over you can, in itself, be liberating. The first step is to know that these blocks are there, and then to become aware of why they exist. They have often served a useful function, acting as protection and defense mechanisms when you were most vulnerable and enabling you to contain your fear or distress. On the other hand, if you begin to see that they constrain and limit your actions and feelings, it's worth identifying them and bringing them out into the open. This may well help you to dissolve them when you feel ready, bringing healing, forgiveness, and possibly reconciliation.

Although everyone's experience is unique, it can also be helpful to recognize that there are common childhood and/or cultural blocks or barriers. They may include:

Childhood conditioning, following models given by parents, elder family members, teachers, e.g. mother's assertion that men can't be trusted, adults' statements that children should be seen not heard.

Being labeled by others, e.g. you'll never amount to much.

Self-judgments based on unhappy, bad experiences, e.g. I don't deserve to be happy, I am not good enough, I'm stupid.

Messages concerned with community, ethnicity, religion, gender, age, e.g. elderly people are less useful members of society, men should have authority, being rich means you are a better person, the color of your skin determines your value or intelligence.

Feelings of not fitting in, e.g. I am stupid, not rich enough, from the wrong part of town, I'm too young, they'll never take someone my age, I've never felt part of this, I'm strange or different.

Do any of these, or similar statements, strike a chord with you? It's useful to be aware you may have made such messages part of yourself although they are only other people's opinions or the attitudes and prejudices of the society in which you grew up.

The themes, patterns, and blocks you have been exploring are obstacles and hindrances that inhibit deeper spiritual development. They represent accumulations of fear and distress that build around the personality and constrain the expression of love. In his book, *A Path with Heart*, Jack Kornfield (1994) explains that:

> "...each ... hindrance is an emotional or spiritual contraction, and ... each is generated out of fear. It is this contraction and grasping that the Buddha described as the source of all human suffering ... Our fear creates a contracted and false sense of self. This false or small sense of self grasps our limited body, feelings and thoughts and tries to hold and protect them. From this limited sense of self arise deficiency and need, defensive anger, and the barriers we build for protection. We are afraid to open, to change, to live fully, to feel the whole of life ... out of this fear, all our greed, hatred and delusion arise. Yet underneath it we will find an openness and wholeness that can be called our true nature."

While the hindrances and obstacles are founded in fear, your true nature is the expression of love, in all its many forms. Thus, a parallel aspect of exploring your sense of soul is clarifying the events and experiences that have been life-affirming and helped you build up a sense of who you are. This can be a lifelong process. It is often difficult both to appreciate yourself and be realistic about your frailties. This next activity helps begin this appreciation.

Activity: Qualities You Respect In Others

Bring to mind someone whom you respect or love. This person could be someone you know well, or someone you admire from afar. Try to work out what makes you respect, admire, or love them.

- *What are the qualities that you respect in this person?*
- *What is it about their behavior that you admire?*
- *What does this person do, or has done, that you would like to do or have done yourself?*

Reflect also for a while on the possibility that you have these qualities in you, at least in potential.

- *Now think of someone who does not command your respect or love.*
- *Why, and what is it that does not appeal to you?*

Reflect for a while on the possibility that you have some of the same qualities in you too.
   Now, return to those qualities that you notice and respect in others. Imagine what you would be like if you were expressing these qualities more fully.
   Record your responses to this activity in any way that is meaningful to you.

In the last activity, knowingly or unknowingly, you will have encountered *projection*: when you see, or notice, in others qualities that you have in yourself but do not recognize. Sometimes this is because you find it difficult to accept your own "star qualities"; you see such qualities as generosity, wisdom, kindness in others rather than recognize the quality in yourself. Equally, for all of us there are parts of ourselves that are too painful or challenging to recognize and so we notice them and complain about them in others – *their* negativity, coldness, and so on. You were specifically asked to reflect on the possibility that you may have the qualities you identified in others. You may find that you need to work on this for a while to spot your own projections.

VALUES

The Quest uses the term values in the sense of active principles that you can notice, in yourself and others, and consciously cultivate. As active principles they underpin choices you make about how you behave; such as being loving, bringing joy and creativity into life, appreciating beauty.
   Linda Marks (1989) defines values as: "those things that we hold dear in our hearts and which matter most to us." They are central to your attitudes and behavior, and in the way you view other people and events. Halberstam (1993) calls this "*integrity*":

> "Integrity means wholeness. People who have integrity have values that belong with one another. They make sure to discard those values that are alien to their true selves. Their politics, their family life, their friendships, their career judgements are all of one piece and reflect the same moral code. Those without that cohesive core disintegrate."

The next activity helps you to identify your personal values and sense of integrity in life.

Activity: Skills of Spiritual Reflection:
Your Personal Values

This activity introduces a new skill of spiritual reflection associated with Observing and Reflecting

WORKING WITH VALUES

WHAT DOES IT MEAN?

Personal values reflect individual identity, whilst shared values reflect those of your culture, environment, and any faith tradition. However, be aware that personal values can also be distortions and contribute to antisocial behavior. In The Quest, *values are used:*

1. *To evoke the highest form of a quality, such as love or beauty.*
2. *To focus attitudes and intentions on the deeper qualities of life.*

STARTING OUT

This exercise works best if you can either record the questions on tape and play them back or ask a friend to read them to you, pausing for a few minutes between each one for you to reflect and record. If this is not practical for you, then read them to yourself one-by-one, with a gap between each; during this gap you can jot down anything that you wish to remember.

1. *Before you begin, relax and center yourself, allowing other thoughts and concerns to quieten.*

- *What matters deeply to you? For example, it may be a place, quality, activity, or relationship.*
- *What inspires, excites or enthuses you?*
- *What angers or upsets you?*
- *What do you see as your main guiding principle or responsibility in life?*
- *What is important to you in a close relationship?*
- *What do you like to give to other people?*
- *What do you need for yourself?*

2. *Spend a while reflecting on your responses to these questions. Then list those values that matter most to you, plus others that are important to people close to you.*

3. *Gandhi said: "My life is my message." Imagine that your values are a unique expression of God or Spirit working through you. What message is being expressed? Try to find a word or short phrase that sums up your 'message'. It might be something like honesty, integrity, wholeness, love, and so on.*

PRACTICING

1. Make a set of cards with a different value written on each card; the list on page 242 may help. (You can also buy "Angel" cards; see bibliography and notes)Choose a card, daily or weekly; think about it and how you might bring it into your daily life.

2. During the day ask yourself how to bring more of a chosen value into the situation you are in. For example, how could you bring more joy into your life at work, or how could you bring more peace into your home life?

3. When it seems that your values conflict with those held by other people, use a value to consider how you can act for the greatest good of all.

Most of us prefer to believe that the values we hold dear are good, leading toward behavior that is positive or, at least, neutral in its impact on others and the environment. But it is not always like this. You may also hold values based on fear and insecurity, or reflect a part of your identity that is antagonistic or self-seeking. However, *The Quest* holds the principle that everyone can identify core values in themselves that embody their constructive and positive potential and this is what you amplify.

Although there are clearly differences in values across cultures, religions, and nationalities, it is also widely accepted that some values are universal. Despite the horrors of violence, strife, and injustice, there are some things that people around the world frequently identify as being core to their lives.

Activity: Universal Values

What do you see as values shared by virtually all people? Note them down and add others that you notice over the next few days as you listen to the radio or television and talk with others.

You may have responded with values such as love, family loyalty, justice, fairness, and peace. So just how important are such core values? You may also have noticed that what is happening in the world frequently leaves you feeling upset, if not frustrated, angry, and alienated. Discomfort results when you feel that your values are offended or compromised. You may encounter similar discomfort around you, in your family, at work, in your neighborhood. As you reflect on integrity and wholeness, it becomes increasingly challenging to stay in such situations without compromising your values.

Activity: Upholding Your Values

Remember a time when you were uncomfortable in an event or situation because you were uneasy at the way it worked out, or how someone else managed it.

•Can you pick out what it was that made you uncomfortable?
•How did you react at the time?
•In an ideal world, how might you respond so that you feel you are upholding your own values, both in what you say or do and how you do it?

Sometimes the only answer is to leave; however, many people find meaning in staying where they are, continuing a daily practice of putting positive values gently and quietly into action. Making a difference can be an important motivation on your quest and often allows you to put up with things that cause discomfort.

The Quest sees values connecting you to your sense of soul and the way in which Spirit expresses itself through you; it is this that makes you unique. A conscious and intentional focus on your values and the way you practice them is soul-based work. The next activity is a practical way of engaging with this.

Activity: Taking Action On Qualities

For this activity, choose a quality from the earlier activity Your Personal Values *(page 48), the list below, or the fuller list on page 242. Choose a quality that you would like to develop or enhance in yourself. For at least one day, concentrate on that quality and on how you can bring it into your life more.*

Try to understand what it means to you in practice, when you consciously let it have an effect on every action that you take. You might ask yourself how you could bring more of your chosen quality into your attitude or behavior or you might wonder what difference more of that quality would bring. You could visualize that quality flowing into the situation you are experiencing.

Love	*Compassion*	*Joy*
Honesty	*Humour*	*Purpose*
Harmony	*Contentment*	*Tolerance*

When you have tried this, record what happened, how you felt, how easy or difficult it was, and how you think it might have affected other people.

Next, reflect on what might have stopped you from living that quality even more fully. Did you encounter obstacles as you tried to live the quality? What might need to happen or change if you wanted live it even more fully?

Finding a way of living that fits with your values and beliefs, and which uses your qualities to the utmost, offers you a way of expressing your sense of soul through what you do, taking it out into the world.

PUTTING IT ALL IN CONTEXT

Stories are about making sense of everything around you. In the same way, telling your story is your way of understanding and plotting where you have traveled so far. However, out of all the memories and events of your life what you record is only a selection; this is necessary to bring order and meaning to the limitless streams of data that come into your awareness.

This process of selection and interpretation gives one picture of your life, but a fuller picture may remain hidden. Some of these other truths concern memories and understanding that don't fit in with the accepted truth about yourself in your culture, your family, and in relation to how you see the world.

If you look at the particular way you depict your life in the previous activities, it tells you something about yourself that is true. But, at the same time, the way you represent your story, its selection and description, contains assumptions made, quite unconsciously, about your life and about yourself. As a narrative about your life, it is true, but it is not the truth, it is just one story you have shaped from the possible narratives.

As Halberstam (1993) wrote:

> "The challenge to make your life whole applies not only to your values but also to the events of your life. You don't have control over everything that happens to you. Your life is dotted with experiences and you choose how to connect the dots.
>
> All stories, including your life story, string together separate events. In telling your story to yourself and others, you emphasise some events as crucial links in the narrative while neglecting others as being irrelevant. It is in the telling and remembering that events gain their significance. You can amplify or reduce the significance of anything that happens to you by altering your attitude to it. You've marched down many a blind alley and put your heart into projects that now seem useless to you but you don't have to see it that way. Your life isn't a straight line; no one's is.
>
> The twists and turns got you to where you are now, and there will be many more zigs and zags to come. A thriving life is a complex story with subplots, digressions and surprises. View your life as an expedition rather than a series of aimless meanderings."

The next activity will help you to uncover some of the ways in which you "connected the dots" of your story and reflect on other ways of seeing them.

Activity: A Second Look At Your Story

You will need to have with you your record from Telling Your Story *and your diagrams and notes from the activities that followed.*

- *What do you notice about the symbols and style that you used to tell your story?*
- *Imagine how someone else might tell your story, with fresh eyes: what overall impression would they get, what would the style, color, images convey?*
- *Do you notice anything about what you chose to put in compared to what you left out?*
- *Do you have any ideas or hunches about what lies behind your selection?*
- *Can you see any way that you might have represented your life and experience differently?*

Here is a further challenge: find a trusted friend or partner and tell your life story again. BUT now, try to tell your story differently. You might try to put in all the things you left out first time around.

Often the first time you tell your story, you tell it quite factually, and the second time you focus more on such aspects as feelings or things that are painful or about which you feel ashamed or guilty. It helps you to access deeper parts, which may have been too sensitive at first.

YOUR *EDGE*

Telling Your Story is also a preparation for your next steps. The activities so far build up a picture of how you have arrived at your present position. The next activity explores your intention as you follow *The Quest*, whether you wish to examine everything in your life or concentrate on one particular area. Whatever this focus – broad or narrow – we call it your *edge*.

Your *edge* is the edge of your comfort zone – the limit of what you feel capable of. We call it an edge because you feel you need to go beyond what you have been used to. It may feel like going over an edge or being called to what lies just over the horizon. Perhaps you came to *The Quest* recognizing a desire to take a fresh look at yourself, your life, and spirituality as a whole. You may not know what your edge might be, but you have a feeling of looking for something.

Activity: Your *Edge*

Before beginning this activity, you will need to have drawing paper, pens, and colored pencils ready.

   Focus first on something that is an issue or challenge for you. Choose something that pushes at the limit of your comfort zone or capabilities at the moment.

Now broaden this: what does – or might – really stretch you?

Take a sheet of paper and draw a shape, any shape that represents your comfort zone. As you draw make sure that you leave enough room on the paper for the area that lies outside your comfort zone. How much space do you feel you should leave for that?

Next draw, write, or in some way mark in those things in your life that fall within your comfort zone; examples might include having coffee with a neighbor, walking the dog, going to a football match. Then put in some of those things that lie outside your comfort zone; examples might include making a public speech or sitting with someone who is dying. They may be things that you avoid or are reluctant to do. Use the blank paper to help you show how near or far each thing is from your comfort zone. Pay particular attention to which things you put on the borderline – your edge – and notice which ones are current in your life.

At this point in your journey with The Quest, you might choose to keep it just as a record of what challenges you right now.

You may also use an edge – a challenge to do something that lies outside your comfort zone – as a focus for your work through The Quest and keep returning to it. There will be numerous activities where you can choose to work further with your edge.

In this activity, you identified more clearly some of the things that challenge you. However you choose to use what you learnt from this, we suggest that over the next few weeks you watch for those times when you feel as if you are on an edge; you can intentionally use something you are finding out about yourself as an opportunity to push out the boundary of your comfort zone – just a little!

NOBODY'S PERFECT

But while being realistic and clear-eyed about yourself, your weaknesses and vulnerabilities, this needs to be tempered with being compassionate and tender toward yourself. Baron von Hugel (1995) wrote: "The deeper we get into reality, the more numerous will be the questions we cannot answer." Having worked through the activities in *Telling Your Story* so far, you will see a lot that remains unresolved and aspects of your development in which you haven't moved as far as you'd like to have done. If that's the case, take some time out to sit down, relax, and read the following poem. It is a poignant reminder that part of life's journey is to embrace all the elements that make us who we are and that we can't expect an immediate quick-fix solution to the parts we're still working on.

"I want to beg you as much as I can to be patient
Towards all that's unsolved in your heart,
And to learn to love the questions themselves,
Like locked rooms,
Or like books that are written in a foreign tongue.
Do not seek the answers that cannot be given to you,
Because you would not be able to live them,
And the point is to live everything.
Live the questions now,
Perhaps you will then, gradually,
Without noticing it,
Live along some distant day
Into the answer."

Rainer Maria Rilke (orig.1903)

Activity: Different Ways To Express Yourself!

Have you ever tried writing poetry like this? It can be a very effective way of expressing yourself. You don't have to write in stanzas or use rhyme, and the beauty of poetry is that you don't have to form proper grammatical sentences either, just say exactly what you want, just as it comes.

Try to express how you are feeling right now as a poem. Write it now – just as it comes. Don't judge it to be good or bad poetry, just let it be.

The work you have done through this chapter helps your heart open. "Opening the heart is a matter of working through the layers of defense we have used to protect it. The coverings are the result of various hurts ... To dissolve these layers of protection, we need to feel whatever it was that caused us to retract in the first place" (Jasmin Lee Cori, 2000). You are "tendered" by this process, more ready and open to your sense of soul; in touch with others, nature, and a Presence or Ultimate Reality, the ground of existence that is your spiritual experience.

A GROWING SENSE
OF SOUL

"As we reflect on our experience, intimations may emerge about the nature of God. In this we are helped by the experiences of others which enlighten our path."

Britain Yearly Meeting (1995)

Exploring your sense of soul is primarily a search for your connection with your essence, with others, nature, and a Presence or Ultimate Reality. *The Quest* uses *spiritual experience* as an umbrella term for encounters with this sense of soul that stimulates such questions as:

○ What brings me alive?
○ What deadens me?
○ How do I describe my sense of soul to others?
○ What is living life with a greater level of meaning?
○ Have I ever had a sense of closeness or connectedness
   to a greater whole?

JOINING UP THE DOTS

In *Telling Your Story* you began by telling your story and went on to explore it in several ways, concentrating primarily on the personal aspects. *The Quest* regards *personal* and *spiritual* as two complementary facets of your whole self. *A Growing Sense Of Soul* starts, therefore, by considering if, and how, these two are intertwined in your life; it's looking at your life story again but connecting up the dots in a different way that highlights your spiritual experience.

Activity: Mapping The Spiritual Onto The Personal

Go back through your life again (with or without the help of your earlier story). Start with your earliest memories and scroll forward. Make a note or recall any occasions that have spiritual significance, such as:

- *Hearing or feeling a call to do something or go somewhere*
- *A peak moment*
- *Times of joy or times of pain*
- *Religion or beliefs playing a part in your life*
- *Significant inspirations – travel, books, nature, music, etc.*
- *Feeling that you may have lived another life, in a different place or time perhaps.*

Now bring both these notes and those from Telling Your Story *in front of you. As you sit with them alongside each other, begin to look for connections, overlaps, and other ways in which the two maps link together.*

You may notice that sometimes events in your story sparked spiritual peak moments or that the spiritual highs led to changes in the rest of your life. You may see values, insights, etc. that helped bring about changes you subsequently made. It may appear that the spiritual experience has popped up periodically, reminding you that you're part of something larger than just yourself, like a doorbell that rings occasionally until you choose to open the door. It may be that it has always been present and important to you.

WHAT IS SPIRITUAL EXPERIENCE?

People understand the variety of their experiences differently and different faiths and philosophies offer different interpretations of them. In order to give attention to your experience, understand and integrate it more fully, we begin with two examples of how other writers have expressed their understanding of spiritual experience. You can find many other examples by talking, sharing with others, and listening to the ideas of different faiths and views, and reading.

Roberto Assagioli (1991), founder of psychosynthesis, wrote:

"More than anything else spirituality is concerned with considering life's problems from a higher, enlightened, synthetic[1], point of view, testing everything on the basis of true values, endeavoring to reach the essence of every fact, neither allowing oneself to stop at external appearances nor to be taken in by traditionally accepted views, by the way the world at large looks at things, or by our own inclinations, emotions and preconceived ideas."

[1]**synthetic** – to synthesise or bring together

Alison Leonard (1995), the author of *Telling Our Stories*, wrote:

"For me, the spiritual journey is a search for meaning: for a deeper, broader awareness of my existence than the material or even the emotional or the psychological can give. It is a search for truth: the truth for myself, of myself, and the truth for others, and then the search for links between those differing glimpses."

RECOGNIZING YOUR SPIRITUAL EXPERIENCES

In the later nineteenth century, William James, one of the pioneers of modern psychology, became deeply interested in religious experience as a window into the soul. Later he wrote (1902, in 2002 edition), "It is that our normal waking consciousness, rational consciousness as we call it, is but one special type of consciousness, while all about it, parted from it by the filmiest of screens, there lie potential forms of consciousness entirely different."

Diana Whitmore (1990), a psychosynthesis psychotherapist highly experienced in working with people's spiritual journeys, identifies some universally characteristic forms of experience beyond everyday awareness:

- An insight
- The sudden solution of a difficult problem
- Seeing one's life in perspective and having a clear sense of purpose
- A transfigured vision of some external reality
- The understanding of some truth concerning the nature of the universe
- A sense of unity with all beings and of sharing everyone's destiny
- Illumination
- An extraordinary inner silence
- Waves of luminous joy
- Liberation
- Cosmic humor
- A deep sense of gratefulness
- An exhilarating sense of dance
- Resonating with the essence of beings and things that we come in contact with
- Loving all persons in one person
- Feeling oneself to be a channel for a wider, stronger force to flow through
- Ecstasy
- An intimation of profound mystery and wonder
- The delight of beauty
- Creative inspiration
- A sense of boundless compassion
- Transcendence of time and space as we know them.

Surveys in the United Kingdom and the USA generally show that a significant proportion of people recall similar incidents in their life. The Kendal Project in the UK reports recent data based on a research project begun in 2000. The researchers surveyed Kendal, a market town on the southern edge of the Lake District in north-west England, with a population of around 28,000.

The researchers, Heelas, Woodhead and Szerszynski from Lancaster University (2004), say:

> "Our main aim was simply to find out what is happening, and to see how things are changing. Our second aim was to use our findings to test the most influential claims about what is happening to contemporary religion and spirituality, including our own hunch that some sort of "spiritual revolution" may be currently underway."

They investigated two domains, the visible "congregational domain" of people associated with the activities of a church or chapel and the less visible domain that they termed the "holistic milieu". They go on to say, "We called these the 'heartlands' of the sacred in Kendal because these are the key settings in which people come together, on a voluntary basis, to engage with what they believe to be sacred, and to do so by way of face-to-face activities with like-minded people."

From among the fascinating data the research is producing, the results of people's reported experiences are most useful here. The researchers extensively mapped activities taking place in Kendal which involved "a subjective-life spirituality" in the holistic milieu. They identified 600 people who facilitated or participated in these activities, 237 of whom responded to a survey questionnaire. One question in the survey offered respondents a range of experiences and they were asked to say which they had experienced. Their responses are shown in the chart on the next page (Fig 9).

You may be able readily to recall occasions in your life that you interpret as spiritual. On the other hand, they may be less clear as it can be hard to pinpoint such moments. Be triggered by the descriptions of Whitmore and the findings from the Kendal Project.

Activity: What Has Been Your Experience?

Relax, and let your mind fall quiet, letting go of whatever you have been doing. Focus on breathing steadily in and out. Try to respond to the following:

- *Describe an occasion in your life that you see as a spiritual experience*
- *What marked it as special or different from other experiences?*

You may find that images or words/phrases represent your spiritual experience

Q: Some people describe special personal experiences. Have any of the following ever happened to you?

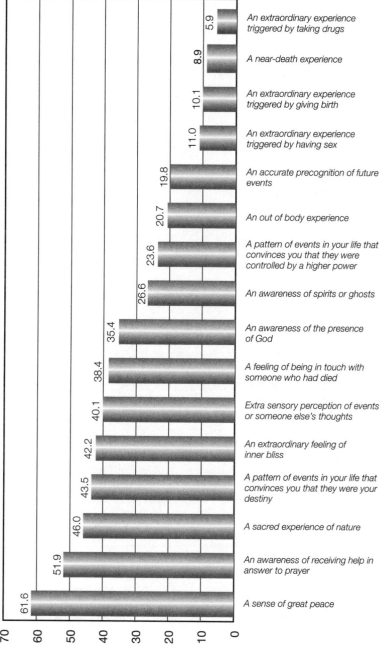

- An extraordinary experience triggered by taking drugs — 5.9
- A near-death experience — 8.9
- An extraordinary experience triggered by giving birth — 10.1
- An extraordinary experience triggered by having sex — 11.0
- An accurate precognition of future events — 19.8
- An out of body experience — 20.7
- A pattern of events in your life that convinces you that they were controlled by a higher power — 23.6
- An awareness of spirits or ghosts — 26.6
- An awareness of the presence of God — 35.4
- A feeling of being in touch with someone who had died — 38.4
- Extra sensory perception of events or someone else's thoughts — 40.1
- An extraordinary feeling of inner bliss — 42.2
- A pattern of events in your life that convinces you that they were your destiny — 43.5
- A sacred experience of nature — 46.0
- An awareness of receiving help in answer to prayer — 51.9
- A sense of great peace — 61.6

Fig 9: The Kendal Project

and you can draw or note them. Record your responses as best you can, remembering that it is in the nature of spiritual experience that it is often ineffable – cannot be put into words.

It's often difficult to express what a spiritual experience felt like. Part of the depth and strength of that feeling is its inexpressibility in words; it's hard to find adequate language and to use words that don't limit or make assumptions about your experience.

Robin Skynner and John Cleese (1996) wrote a book called *Life and How to Survive It*. In the book they observe that the characteristics of these kinds of moments are:

> "... they are overwhelmingly persuasive: whoever experiences them 'knows' they are true... they bring a sense of meaning and hence of security ... for a person who is religiously inclined, they bring a sense of direct contact with the spiritual force in the cosmos, which must, of course, be the highest possible value for him or her ... they give a deep sense of connectedness through an infinite network of cause and effect ..."

THE LANGUAGE OF SPIRITUAL EXPERIENCE

In attempting to define a spiritual experience, language itself – the words you have to express your experience and yourself – shapes and limits what you can say. In English there are few words to express direct experience of Spirit; the single word that means just that is *mysticism*, a word often associated with unconventional or odd things that are not part of everyday conversation. The ancient Greeks, however, had 12 words that described the spiritual dimension, e.g. *pneuma*, meaning wind, breath, or spirit, and Hindus have about 35 such words, e.g. *satcidananda* meaning eternal wisdom and bliss.

Pause for a moment and give a thought to what these observations about language mean; the (un-)ease of describing spiritual experience, its place in conversation, the recognition (or lack of it) of spiritual experience as real and normal within your culture. If English is not your only language, does it make any difference in which language you express your connection with your spiritual life?

In the following quotations, for instance, two people describe spiritual experience in quite different terms.

Eckhart Tolle (2001), a contemporary mystic: "I am the awareness, a part of a whole, in which thoughts, emotions and actions happen in a context of 'life situations' – the timeless inner space in which the content of my life unfolds."

Robin Skynner (in Skynner and Cleese, 1996), a psychotherapist: "everything is like it is, only more so ... but the 'only more so' bit transforms everything."

Activity: Finding Your Own Language

•*Do either of the quotations above tally with your understanding of your spiritual experiences?*
•*Have you come across any quotations that feel closer to your experience?*
•*Try to express it in your own words and share it with someone else.*

Having established more comfortable language for you to describe spiritual experience, the next activities develop understanding of your spiritual experience so you become more able to work consciously with it rather than experiencing brief, peak moments as random, peripheral events; the activity *Having An Experience* in **Heart of The Quest** is a practical example of the kind of awareness that helps embed spiritual experience.

In the following activity you recall and re-enter these experiences then look at how you can re-create a setting in which you can intentionally access this dimension and anchor it in daily life.

Activity: Exploring Your Spiritual Experience

Before beginning this activity, have to hand any materials you need to record your responses in whatever form is meaningful to you. Prepare yourself for this activity by finding a quiet place where you will not be interrupted.

Close your eyes, let your breathing settle, and place your attention on your inner world.

Recall a time when you had what you regard as a spiritual experience. Go back into that experience and feel it as if it is happening again for the first time.

•*Where are you? What is happening? How do you feel?*
•*Are there any colors, sounds, smells, and physical sensations?*
•*What is special or significant about it?*
•*How would you express this particular moment in words, colors, shapes, sounds, movement?*
•*Is there anything else that is a key part of your experience? (e.g. a meditation exercise, a special place, a time of day, a piece of music, an object etc.)*

Now record your experience in whatever way will serve to help you re-enter it and to remind you that it was real.

You can use such instances of spiritual experience to give added weight and meaning to a regular practice of spiritual reflection. Regular practice can help to 'ground' or anchor a spiritual experience and significant spiritual experience may bring a clearer sense of purpose to your spiritual reflection.

DEEPENING YOUR SENSE OF SOUL

It's all very well to have had these spiritual experiences, but they can still seem no more than fleeting moments – what Virginia Woolf (1927) called "matches struck unexpectedly in the dark." As you deepen your sense of soul you face two major questions. Can you bring these moments of supreme spiritual awareness into a central principle in your life in a way that you can work with and develop? How is your spiritual experience related to everyday life?

You may already be clear in your response to these questions. But, you may be unsure or you may think it's time to take another look. So in the next two activities you will be asking yourself whether spiritual experience is just about events or circumstances in your life or whether it is connected in some more fundamental way with who you are.

Researchers, like Carl Jung and Roberto Assagioli, came to the conclusion that we have an organizing and integrating center within ourselves. It's experienced as if it is part of who you are. But it is not physical like an arm or a leg. A wheel is sometimes used as an image of this dimension; the center of a wheel is the focus of balance and power, connecting and integrating the rest of the wheel. But, whatever words you use – back to the difficulty of language – it is important that you sense for yourself how to be in touch with this center and able to draw on it. As you give it your attention, you can deepen "a sense of 'self' which underlies our ever-changing sensations, emotions, and thoughts." (Molly Young Brown, 1997)

Activity: Connecting With Your Sense Of Center

You may need to have paper, pencils, and colors ready. It may be helpful to record the visualization below onto a tape, ask a friend to read the activity to you, or do one part at a time. Prepare yourself by relaxing and focusing on your inner world, leaving the demands of the day on one side.

1. Become aware of your body, just noticing all the physical sensations that you can. Feel yourself as you sit, your contact with the ground, your clothes on your skin. Move inside your skin and pass from your feet up your body, noticing what you feel, where there is tension or relaxation in your muscles, ease or discomfort. Be aware of your breathing. When you have scanned your body, release it from your attention.

2. Become aware of your emotions, just noticing those present in you now. Recall, as best you can, the emotions that were present in you yesterday. You might notice which emotions are most common in your life. Be aware of those you might consider positive, such as love, happiness, and those you might consider negative, such as fear, jealousy, and despair. Allow them all to be recalled and noticed.

When you are ready, let them fade, and let go of your attention on your feelings.

3. Become aware of your desires, just noticing the things that motivate you most and most often. You might notice a desire for comfort and warmth, a desire for money, safety, order, sun, sexual experience. You might recognize a desire for things, alcohol, cigarettes, fashion. Just notice these things without making any judgment about them; if they are accompanied by feelings such as shame or guilt or excitement or concern, just note this too. When you feel ready, allow your desires to fade and let them go.

4. Become aware of your thoughts, just noticing how one thought is followed by another in your mind. If you think that you are not having a thought, realize that this too is a thought. Watch them come in and out, thoughts, memories, ideas, opinions, images, a constant flow. When you have watched it flow for a while, then again put it aside and let your thoughts go like clouds moving across the sky.

5. There is a part of you that has been noticing and giving attention to these aspects of yourself. Turn your attention in this direction. Reflect on this part of you, the "I", who is watching and noticing your body, feelings, desires and thoughts. Who is "I"? Let the question settle and then note what images, feelings, body sensations, ideas, and experiences emerge.

When you have completed this activity, take time to record your experience of it in a way that will help you to recall these sensations another time. It is important that you can re-enter and remind yourself of each aspect. Pay close attention to how you feel you can best record your sense of "I" watching yourself.

[This activity draws on exercises by Piero Ferrucci, What We May Be, *Diana Whitmore,* The Joy of Learning *and Molly Young Brown,* Growing Whole*]*

Roberto Assagioli, the original creator of this exercise, called this process "dis-identification", When you identify yourself <u>with</u> something – whether it is an emotion, role or object of desire – it controls or defines who you are. The purpose of dis-identification is that you progressively let go of your identification with the different aspects of yourself until you reach a focus on an enduring and unchanging part, your sense of center. You become freer to exercise choice to switch between different emotions, roles, and so on according to what is appropriate in that moment.

As such activities strengthen your sense of center, you may also experience a wider awareness; in *Getting Started* we said that for some, a sense of soul is also infused with connection to a Presence or Ultimate Reality, the ground or basic fabric of existence that feels 'radically alive' (Moss, 1987). For example, in Hindu philosophy, the soul has two parts called the Jiva and the Atman. The

Jiva corresponds to the individual soul making successive journeys toward union with God whereas Atman is pure Spirit and of the same essence as God.

There are many ways in which people, over the ages, have tried to articulate what this means to them. In *The High Flyer*, a novel by Susan Howatch (1999), one of her characters calls it "tuning in to the great integrating principle in your unconscious mind and thus lining yourself up with the power which sustains all life everywhere."

In 1762 John Woolman wrote: "There is a principle which is pure, placed in the human mind, which in different places and ages hath different names; it is, however, pure and proceeds from God. It is deep and inward, confined to no forms of religion nor excluded from any where the heart stands in perfect sincerity."

Albert Schweitzer (1993) wrote: "What does the word 'soul' mean? ... No one can give a definition of the soul. But we know what it feels like. The soul is the sense of something higher than ourselves, something that stirs in us thoughts, hopes and aspirations which go out to the world of goodness, truth and beauty. The soul is a burning desire to breathe in this world of light and never to lose it – to remain children of light."

And John O'Donohue (2004) described it as:

"My understanding of 'soul' would be that it is the unseen, hidden dimension of the self, and that it is the place beneath or beside or above the mind and consciousness. To put it in imagistic terms and spatial terms, I think it's the kind of field of presence or color or light that suffuses the body and that holds the body, so that the body is actually in the soul."

In this next activity, you will be taking time to review your current sense of soul and how you may be able to express it.

Activity: What Is A Sense Of Soul For You?

Find a time when you can be quiet. You might like to do this activity whilst out walking, or in the garden. You need to feel still and be able to listen to your inner thoughts and emotions.

Allow yourself to look back over all the work you have been doing in The Quest *so far. Pay special attention to the activities on spiritual experience and your sense of an enduring aspect of yourself.*

●*Consider the perceptions of soul above: "the power which sustains all life everywhere"; "a principle which is pure"; "a sense of something higher than ourselves"; a "field of presence or color or light that suffuses the body and that* holds the body, so that the body is actually in the soul". What do they mean to you?

●Does your sense of soul have a name, or is there an image or symbol?

●What is its place in your life?

"SPIRITUAL INTELLIGENCE"?

However you experience or describe it, a sense of soul encapsulates something precious about the way you are and how you act in the world. Some writers now suggest you even have a kind of intelligence that relates to such spiritual experience.

Intelligence used to mean simply mental capacities and intellectual skills. Then Howard Gardner's research (1993) suggested that we are all blessed with multiple intelligences which have since been correlated with seven different ways of learning: verbal, logical, visual, musical, physical, extrovert, and introvert: you may have noticed that you prefer to learn more in one way than another.

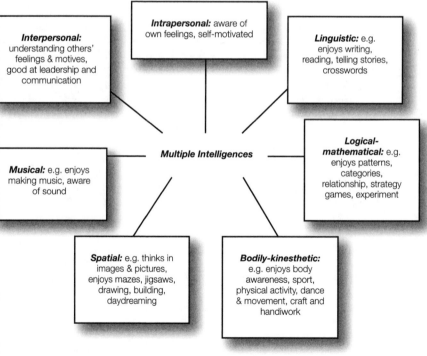

Fig 10: Gardner's Multiple Intelligences

Since Gardner's groundbreaking work, identification of other intelligences, such as Goleman's naming of *Emotional Intelligence* (1996), has widened the field further. Through the work of those such as Danah Zohar and Ian Marshall (2000) and Michal Levin (2000), it has widened again to include *spiritual intelligence* – SQ.

CHARACTERISTICS OF SQ

Zohar and Marshall (*op cit*) list the following as hallmarks of spiritual intelligence:

- Flexibility – a capacity not to be stuck in basics, rules, and regulations but to be open to the new
- A high degree of self-awareness
- A capacity to face, transcend and use pain and suffering, including your mistakes
- The quality of being inspired by vision and values
- A tendency to ask "Why?" and "What if?" about fundamental issues
- An ability to be holistic, to see the connections between different things
- Being what psychologists call "field independent" i.e. a capacity for working against convention and standing out against the crowd
- An openness to diversity and the possibility of optional paths from A to B
- A sense of conscience as an inner compass and an inner directedness
- A quality of deep spontaneity, which can be responsive to others and to deeper realities.

Activity: Developing Your SQ

Zohar and Marshall suggest that SQ helps you reach toward the true potential that lies deep within you and to live life at a greater level of meaning. They identify five guidelines that help to enrich and deepen SQ. These are:

- *Being aware of where you are now*
- *Feeling strongly that you want to change*
- *Reflecting on what your center is and on what are your deepest motivations*
- *Looking for connections between things, becoming more reflective, being more self-aware and honest with yourself*
- *Committing yourself to a path while remaining aware that there are many paths.*

Take each of Zohar and Marshall's five guidelines in turn as your focus for a day. Begin the day by reminding yourself of the guideline, reflect on what it means to you, and imagine how it might be to put it into practice. Throughout the day, recall the guideline as often as feels comfortable. Notice what happens. Before you go to bed review the day and the impact the guideline had on you, your interactions with others, and reactions to what was around you.

You may find that your awareness of the guidelines is strengthened if you return to this activity over a period of time.

Your growing sense of soul requires regular nourishment. Paul Lacey (1999) wrote: "If I can speak with authority it is of what nourishes my life and what drains it of spiritual vitality." Richard Thompson (2000), a teacher in a secondary school in Bradford, engaged his students in looking at how to care for themselves holistically. The students identified 5 aspects of Me: body, self-confidence, thoughts, feelings, and soul. The next activity uses the exercises they wrote with Richard Thompson to nourish their inner strength.

Activity: Caring for Your Sense of Soul

- *Give thanks – find 100 things a day*
- *Be still for some time every day*
- *Keep your capacity for awe and wonder*
- *Share with each other the hidden depth in ordinary things*
- *Invest a daily action with a special significance*
- *Pay attention to the details of an ordinary experience such as being alive.*

(*Extract from* The Friend, *Richard Thompson, 2000.*)

You might add some ideas of your own to develop your own inner strength.

> "The heart is a sanctuary at the center of which there is a little space wherein the Great Spirit dwells, and this is the Eye. This is the Eye of the Great Spirit by which He sees all things, and through which we see Him. If the heart is not pure, the Great Spirit cannot be seen."
>
> **Black Elk**

PULLING IT ALL TOGETHER

In *Telling Your Story* and *A Growing Sense of Soul* your focus has been primarily on reviewing your story and looking at it in different ways. Before moving on, we want you to bring together the ideas and activities from both *Telling Your Story* and *A Growing Sense of Soul* to collect any changes, insights, or deepening that have emerged so far.

Activity: **What's New or Seen in a Different Light?**

You will need to have your notes and drawings, etc. from the activities in **Telling Your Story** *and* **A Growing Sense of Soul** *available. You may want to refer to them.*

Recall the quotation from Alison Leonard (page 57):

"For me, the spiritual journey is a search for meaning: for a deeper, broader awareness of my existence than the material or even the emotional or the psychological can give. It is a search for truth: the truth for myself, of myself, and the truth for others, and then the search for links between those differing glimpses."

From the work you have done so far, what are your current awareness, thoughts, and feelings about:

• *"A search for meaning"*
• *"A deeper, broader awareness of my existence than the material or even the emotional or the psychological can give"*
• *"A search for truth"*
• *"The truth for myself, of myself, and the truth for others"*
• *"The search for links between those differing glimpses."*

If you were having a conversation with a friend, perhaps someone else following The Quest, how would you complete these sentences?

• *The way my sense of soul looks at this point is …*
• *What I have learnt that is new / interesting / exciting is …*
• *What I have learnt that is challenging is …*
• *I shall need to explore further into …*
• *I am still unclear about …*
• *My current challenge is …*

CHANGING FACES
OF FAITH

"Faith is the bird that feels the light
when the dawn is still dark."

Rabindranath Tagore(Indian sage)

Changing Faces of Faith uses *faith* to indicate a broad conviction that the universe is underpinned by a Source or held together in a way that is not always apparent at the day-to-day level. The religions and wisdom traditions of the world offer diverse expressions of such *faith* and we are all heirs to the insight that created these channels and held them together over centuries.

Your personal faith, however, flows out of more than this wisdom, or indeed out of just the individual experiences you have looked at so far. It is also shaped by the influences, learning, the culture and traditions you have known since your childhood. However, familiar traditions, and the values and explanations they offer, are increasingly subject to scrutiny and question. The faces of faith are changing, radically affected by new understanding in fields such as science, psychology, and ecology. Things that used to be true, expressed through a wide variety of media including word, myth, symbol, ritual, art, and music, are being challenged.

As you unpack what you believe, why and where it comes from, you encounter the changing nature of the times in which you live, bringing you face to face with questions such as:

○ What do you believe?
○ What are the roots of your belief?
○ What has influenced you?
○ What have you encountered that has led you to modify your faith?

In the past, the faith you held was likely to depend on culture, upbringing, history, and the language of the society in which you grew up. Today, mass media, communications, and travel have made knowledge and experience of different cultures more accessible; there are opportunities to discover and explore wisdom and faith traditions beyond that of your own society. In the past, faith was handed down and emphasized knowing about God (or the name used in a particular tradition); today, as the bonds of hierarchical authority loosen, many people seek a less structured, more direct and personal experience of faith.

FOUNDATIONS OF YOUR FAITH

Each of us holds a *world-view*; our story of how things are that underpin social structures such as family, friends, work, politics, and values. World-views begin to form in childhood, when patterns of family behavior may become so ingrained they are scarcely noticeable. Nevertheless they provide patterns that guide aspirations, choices, and behavior. This also applies to the influence of religious upbringing, so that experience of a particular religion – or absence of it – forms part of your value system and wider philosophy of life.

The next few activities help you examine how your faith and wider philosophy of life formed. For each activity, read it through, jotting down any immediate responses. Then put it aside for a while, so you can mull it over before recording your detailed responses. This is a major sequence of activities and you may find yourself adding to your recollections as time goes by. You may wish to keep your responses to all the activities together in one place; the chart at the end of the series (page 72) offers one way to do so, or a mind-map (like the one on page 82) might help you organize your recollections so you can expand them to include new information.

Activity: You, Yourself, Childhood, And Adolescence

Look back at your life map (from Telling Your Story, *page 39). With various incidents to jog your memory, think about all the influences in your life that, since your earliest years, have contributed to the formation of your present faith. Your faith might include your religious beliefs, or none, your spiritual world-view, your values, attitudes, qualities, and attributes.*

- *What do you remember believing?*
- *What were the prevailing beliefs of the culture in which you grew up?*
- *What, if any, were your experiences of religion in childhood such as ritual, ceremony, place of worship such as going to church/ mosque/ temple?*
- *Who were key influences in your early years, e.g. mother, father, grandparents, other relations, and what were their beliefs?*
- *How did your peer group affect you and at what age?*

- *Which other people were significant for you — living people, such as teachers, spiritual leaders, public figures, the local shopkeeper, or historical figures, such as religious teachers, political figures, artists, social revolutionaries?*
- *Can you recall any innate sense or experience of spiritual knowledge during childhood and adolescence and how it was confirmed or denied by other people?*
- *What have been other central forming experiences or beliefs?*
- *Were there times when you questioned, challenged, or even broke away from the influences of your childhood and adolescence?*

As you grew older, education and the formal institutions of the society in which you lived would have played an increasing role in your life, influencing your views and having an impact on your faith.

Activity: **Education And Formal Institutions**

Begin by noting down the schools, colleges, universities, etc., you attended and what, if any, were the beliefs, values, attitudes, qualities they expected or instilled in you. Then work through the prompts below.

- *In what ways have your educational experiences played a formative role? It may have come through teachers, subjects studied, attitudes and qualities, and so on. Some of these experiences may have been positive and some may have been negative.*
- *While you were a student — from primary school through to completion of your education — what contact did you have with a church, other religious institution, philosophical or faith traditions? How did these influence you?*
- *Have any other institutions or experiences, such as health, leisure activities, law and policing, systems of social security, etc, had a significant impact on you?*
- *Have you been influenced by political and economic systems, views of political leaders, parties, or political or economic thinkers or social reformers?*

Throughout your life a wide range of inputs will have influenced you, whether you were aware of this or not. For instance, the media have a very important place in the formation of world-view and faith. We are exposed to television, radio, and cinema from an early age. As we learn to read we are exposed to books and magazines. In recent years the availability of computers, offering information, games, and access to the Internet, have provided an even broader range of influences on your world-view and your faith.

Activity: **The Impact Of The Media On Your Faith**

Look back over your life and note the different kinds of media that have been important to you, and at what age. Note any particularly strong memories or impressions that you have.

Continued on page 73

	Describe who or what influenced you and when	How did this affect you at the time – what you gained or lost? Does it affect you now, and, if so, how? What were any points of change, affirmation or insight?
You, yourself, your childhood and adolescence		
Education and formal institutions		
The media		
Culture and change		
Are there other important factors or influences not yet mentioned which you want to record?		
Do you notice any overall trends, patterns, stimuli, setbacks or growth points?		

Fig 11: Foundations Of Your Faith

- *What books have you read, in childhood and since, that have been significant to you?*
- *Have any holy books, sacred or spiritual texts been important for you and what was their impact?*
- *What other media, including film, television, theatre, arts, music, information technology, access to the Internet, have been important for you?*
- *In what ways have these had an impact on your faith?*

The final activity in this sequence turns to the culture of your early life and the impact of any different cultures you have experienced since then.

Activity: Culture And Change

- *Look back at the culture/s in which you spent the formative years of your life. Which beliefs, rituals, values, assumptions, and so on, have contributed to your world-view?*
- *Have you experienced shifts of perception through travel or other kinds of exposure to different lifestyles and practices?*
- *In what other ways have you experienced events or situations or encountered something that either reinforced or challenged your faith and belief?*

STIRRING THE FOUNDATIONS

In the past, change took place but, generally, at a speed that allowed it to be assimilated. Religious life was ordered and large numbers of people attended a place of worship regularly. The predominant religious framework influenced most people's lives and underpinned the majority of institutions regardless of whether or not any individual participated in worship.

In reflecting so far on what has formed your faith and shaped your world-view, you have focused on influences in your immediate environment. Beneath such individual frameworks of faith and world-views, however, is the prevailing paradigm of the culture in which you live. In **Getting Started** we described a *paradigm* as a conceptual umbrella. Now we probe paradigms and the impact of paradigm shifts further.

NEW SCIENCE

In the Middle Ages in Europe, most people believed the world was flat and the sun moved round the Earth. Those who first put forward elements of a new paradigm, such as Copernicus and Galileo, initially were scorned and rejected; the Vatican put Copernicus' work on the papal index of forbidden books and Galileo was forced to retract his seemingly heretical ideas. But periodic breakthroughs have occurred. After a period of ridicule and opposition, new paradigms become accepted as self-evident until, in turn, they are challenged.

Such ideas are so different from what has gone before that they feel totally new. In the thought world of the West, such a paradigm shift gathered momentum throughout the twentieth century as scientific and technological development radically stirred up the taken-for-granted way of seeing material reality. More recently, pictures sent back from space by astronauts, telescopes, and space probes give a new sense of Earth as a whole, as a place of beauty, and pose tantalizing questions about life on other planets.

Changes and discoveries in science have shifted the prevailing paradigm in two connected but distinct ways, both equally significant.

1) Before the sixteenth and seventeenth centuries, people's beliefs about the nature of the universe were derived from divine or traditional authority, expressed through biblical and church teaching and handed down from an elite in one generation to the next. However, natural philosophers, such as Kepler and Galileo, began to observe and measure what they saw around them and develop hypotheses that could be tested against their measurements. Theories built upon this method of observation and measurement undermined unquestioning belief and challenged religious authority; they were remarkable in contrast to earlier authority as they were empirically based, publicly verifiable, and open. The scientific method was also superior in explaining how the world functions and led to advances that have transformed our lives.

2) From early in the twentieth century, scientific discovery rapidly moved through different theories about the fundamental nature of the known world:

a) That *matter is primary*; energy is secondary (conventional physics).
b) That *matter and energy are equivalent* (relativity physics).
c) That *energy is primary*; matter is organized energy (quantum physics).

From the seventeenth to the twentieth century, the basis of the Western world-view, stemming from the work of thinkers such as Newton, Bacon, and Descartes, was that we lived in a clockwork universe. Matter – the material world – was the prime reality and was governed by linear relationships of cause and effect. This fitted in with a view of human development, also found in many religious traditions, of a hierarchical progression through material, emotional, and mental development culminating in the higher cognitive faculties demonstrated by human beings. Wilber (1998) wrote: "Virtually all the world's great wisdom traditions subscribe to a belief in the Great Chain of Being."

Einstein's groundbreaking work in relativity, early in the twentieth century, established an equivalence between matter and energy: $e=mc^2$. Although the frontiers of science are moving rapidly, it seems clear that new science is re-casting this view yet again. Solid matter is neither solid nor fixed; it is fields of energy and patterns of relationship in which everything is interconnected. Quantum theory suggests we live in a participatory universe where there is no such thing as a neutral observer; the act of observing changes what is being observed, therefore the observer participates in creating that which they observe. Reality is a vast sea of potential out of which the material world takes form; from this potential each of us forms specific patterns or configurations.

The earlier Western world-view was mechanical and as science developed the world-view was also shaped by other new discoveries and understanding in the physical sciences and engineering. Geology reveals the universe to be far older than imagined. Astronomy tells us that the universe is vast and expanding and our planet is one infinitesimal part. The exploration of Mars, and possible discovery of life on another planet, will revolutionize perceptions of ourselves again.

The contemporary scientific model combines these advances with fresh knowledge in the biological and human sciences. Biology contributed ideas and evidence of evolution. Ecology offers contemporary understanding of the vast and intricate webs of connection between all living things and all matter. Psychology has found that this external world parallels a complex internal world where light and dark forces vie for our attention. Questions about the nature of consciousness are at the leading edge of scientific endeavor.

Two relatively new concepts are at the heart of this new perspective. One is the realization that consciousness is not a property that has emerged as matter has evolved but is fundamental to the nature of matter itself – it underpins and precedes matter rather than arising from it. The second is a revolutionary definition of life that has gained credence in biology in the last few decades – *autopoesis* – which means that a living entity is one that continually creates itself, while holding its form and releasing what it no longer needs. This radically changes our notion of what we perceive as alive. Elisabet Sahtouris (2003), an evolution biologist, writes:

> "So when I looked at that definition of autopoesis I said "What's the simplest entity I can think of that continually creates itself?" What I came to was a whirlpool in water. It holds a form through a constant intake of new water and lets out what it no longer needs. Very like a human body: we eat food, drink water and breathe in air. We continually renew all our molecules, cells and organs and we hold a recognizable form through that process, letting go of what we no longer need."

The sum of all these discoveries also overturns earlier ideas derived from religious beliefs. Creation was not given once in a fixed form for all time. The universe does not comprise discrete objects connected in cause-and-effect relationships. Diarmuid O'Murchu (1997), a Jesuit priest, describes the new paradigm as a world where everything is interconnected so that things cannot be understood in isolation and alone. Schwartz and Russek (1999) describe everything as an integral part of a "living energy universe".

A CRISIS IN SPIRITUAL PERCEPTION?

Mystics have maintained that behind the material world is a reality that represents itself to them as pure consciousness:

> "That was the true Light, which lighteth every man that cometh into the world." (John 1:9)
> "The Lord of Love is above name and form. He is present in all and transcends all." (Mundaka Upanishad, trans. Easwaran, 1987)
> "God is the light of Heaven and of the Earth." (Qurăn, trans. Arberry, 1998)

With the emergence of quantum physics, some scientists are beginning to say something similar: that everything we know manifests from consciousness and that light is more fundamental than space, time, or matter. Peter Russell (2003) suggests that consciousness is the meeting point of science and religion: "When science sees consciousness to be a fundamental quality of reality, and religion takes God to be the light of consciousness shining within us all, the two world-views start to converge." People who explore transcendent aspects of reality through contemplation and deeper levels of meditation describe consciousness being like the light in a film projector, which shines through different images that are projected onto the screen. We live among these images in what we call the "real world" but contemplatives tell us that these are merely changing illusions and that the real world is a faculty of consciousness that lies deep within.

This has implications for spirituality: it implies that evolution is continuing, that revelation of Spirit can be ongoing and that we each participate intimately in a process of unfolding and, possibly, co-creation. Swimme and Berry (1994) capture the excitement of a "new awareness of how the ultimate mysteries of existence are being manifest in the universe about us." No matter how exciting these new understandings, however, they can precipitate a crisis in our spiritual perception. Suddenly it may seem as if the world has been tipped upside down and put back together a different way.

Activity: The Impact Of New Science

Doug Gwyn (1997) created the word "bi-spirituality" to explain the need to move flexibly between very different realities. These realities might include the reality of the religiously described world of your childhood, the reality of nature and creation as a pulsating web, and the reality of everyday perceptions and needs.

Prepare for this activity by setting aside a period of time when you can think without being interrupted. Have to hand any materials to write, draw, or capture your response in any way that is meaningful for you.

● *Recall and note what you have read of new fields of science and new exploration. What is your current understanding of the nature of the world in which you live? How has this changed since you were a child?*
● *How does this compare with or contradict what you learnt in childhood?*
● *Does this affect the way you perceive the world around you on a day-to-day basis? Or when you are in the natural world?*

Use your local library, television, radio, magazines, newspapers, and the Internet to search out new understandings of the broad changes that new discoveries and exploration bring.

SOCIAL, HUMAN, AND TECHNOLOGICAL CHANGE

The questioning and re-shaping of understanding that flows from science and philosophy has a counterpart in other profound shifts.

○ Psychology, epitomized by Freud, has made vast strides in mapping the human psyche. Growing knowledge of our inner worlds challenged the ideal of rational, objective thought and questioned the nature of religious experience. Some depth psychology made religious experience a pathology and stigmatized it as mental breakdown. By contrast, humanistic and transpersonal psychology, through thinkers such as Jung, Assagioli, and Rogers, give room for the growth of potential and hope.
○ Rapid social and technological developments mean that information and knowledge is dispersed rather than concentrated in the hands of a restricted group, e.g. instead of consulting a local wise person many people can use libraries and look for information through the Internet.
○ Advances in information technology have brought an information web that flows around the world with billions of messages shuttling back and forth at the speed of light. Russell (1998) depicts this as if we, the minds behind this "global brain, are being linked by the 'fibers' of our telecommunications systems in much the same way as the billions of cells in each of our brains."
○ Biologists have mapped the human genome and are coming closer to designing new forms of life. This heralds new possibilities while challenging our basic ideas about the beginnings of life and the

relationship between nature and nurture.
○ New political, economic, and ecological forces press the urgent need to address war, violence, poverty, hunger, and injustice. The domination and power of the Western world-view is challenged by the dispossession and lack of dignity that is the share of much of humanity.
○ The environmental and ecological crisis requires us to use existing and new technologies in different ways and with different priorities and objectives. Climate change is now a generally accepted phenomenon, though its likely causes and course are hotly debated.
○ The very forces that provide the impetus for change generate reaction too. There is increasing polarization in global opinion between conservative and radical forces in each of the fields above.

Some commentators take the view that the contemporary crisis results from the rapacious and greedy nature of human society as it developed and grew, from a too-ready human (often Judeo-Christian) assumption that the Earth was ours to plunder. Other commentators, while acknowledging the challenges, take a more benign view. Bloom (2004) writes, "We need to acknowledge that our modern challenges are not due to any inherent selfishness or stupidity. They derive from the sheer size and speed of the changes" and seeks to mitigate the vulnerability and fragility of the situation by enquiring "what moral and great ideas are going to inspire and guide us."

THE HOLISTIC REVOLUTION

Many of these changes press us toward a world-view that is congruent with new science yet encompasses a much wider field. This has been termed the holistic revolution. William Bloom, in his introduction to his anthology *The Holistic Revolution* (2000), describes the growth of the holistic revolution:

> "Originally perceived by many people as a passing fashion, the holistic and New Age movement can no longer be ignored by anyone. It threatens established religions. Its activists and thinkers have increasing credibility. It represents the cutting edge of much science, medicine and psychology. It is a daily feature of contemporary media. And no matter how the establishment intelligentsia may judge it, millions of people are turning to it."

For Bloom the holistic revolution encompasses fields that include new science, psychology, ecology and right livelihood, health and healing, feminism and the Goddess, tribal and shamanic traditions, mystic and esoteric religions, prophecy and channeling. He identifies the characteristics of this holistic revolution:

○"Its various aspects were genuinely relevant to certain human needs … it was unlike mainstream religion and medicine."

○"It actually encouraged personal involvement and enquiry."

○"Not only was it accessible, but it also offered new and practical strategies for addressing everyday challenges."

○"The holistic movement grew and still is growing because it offers useful ways of engaging and coping with the modern world."

○"It is absolutely logical, then, that religion and religious enquiry will also begin to reflect these new circumstances. It will tend to be international, universalist, process-oriented, pluralistic, diverse, democratic, networked and decentralised."

○"It celebrates the liberation from narrow paths that have too often been over-controlling if not completely corrupt. It sees no problem in people exploring and 'tasting' many different approaches."

○"People need to start from a point of informed choice and then make their own decisions. Just because in the past people have been constrained to single religious paths is no sign that it was either good or useful. People should be free to explore meaning and reality in as many ways as are available."

○"I call the holistic movement 'religious' because it explores the major metaphysical questions of wonder, meaning and identity."

Activity: Thinking About The Holistic Revolution

Note any experiences of your own that seem to have the same/similar characteristics as those that Bloom identifies.

Bloom's central proposition is that "the holistic revolution presents a creative and deeply hopeful answer." How far does this correspond to your experience?

HOLISTIC SUPERMARKET OR BROADER INQUIRY?

The holistic revolution covers a wide field. You can choose whether to pick-and-mix or delve deeply into one pathway; alternatively you may do both. You may have come across some practices and experiences of the holistic revolution without identifying them as such. The aim of the activity that follows is for you to gauge the extent and depth of your experience of the holistic revolution, building a picture of your experience of newness.

Activity: Experiences Of Newness

Turn to the "Newness brainstorm" on page 81. It classifies some of the many new practices and experiences on the holistic supermarket shelves today. You may not have heard of some of them and you may think of others that we have not mentioned.

Take a look at the list. Tick those you have heard of but not experienced; circle those you have experienced and add an asterisk if you have gone further than just a tasting.

THE CHALLENGE OF NEWNESS

Of course *new* does not necessarily mean good; you might see the pursuit of material things in the 1990s as a substitute for faith that accelerated ecological, sociological, and economic problems. Others interpret the changes as a shift away from authoritarianism enabling individuals to develop a new kind of "self-spirituality" (Heelas, 1996). To be credible "self-spirituality" must take account of emerging strands of spiritual exploration, especially those that critique the prevailing culture:

- ○ *Eco-spirituality:* re-evaluating indigenous wisdom, recovering a sense of wonder at the beauty of creation, re-connecting with the energies in the natural world and taking action to encourage ecological awareness
- ○ *Liberation theology:* responding to social, political, and economic inequalities in the world and the urgent need for peace and justice
- ○ *Feminist spirituality:* re-discovering a Goddess or feminine aspect of God, and highlighting the contribution of female visionaries in the past, the role of empathic relationship with creation, and the role of women in ecclesiastical and political life
- ○ *Process theology:* revelation was not given once for all time but there is an ongoing and fresh revelation each time a person encounters God
- ○ *Esoteric traditions:* re-surfacing and re-presenting ancient wisdom that was underground for centuries, such as that of the Egyptians or the Essenes. Early twentieth-century modes such as theosophy, anthroposophy (based on the work of Rudolf Steiner), or the mystery school teachings of Alice Bailey and others are in evidence
- ○ *Eastern practices:* Buddhism, Zen, Taoism, and Hinduism are examples of Eastern religious traditions that have become known in the West whilst Tai Chi or Feng Shui emphasize greater harmony with the subtle and dynamic forces of the universe
- ○ *New academic areas:* including human ecology, mysticism, transpersonal psychology, noetics, consciousness studies, critical-historical biblical studies
- ○ *Fundamentalism* is a growing phenomenon in both East and West, partly as a reaction to rapid changes in society, a perceived breakdown in faith and morals, and contemporary, more fluid, expressions of spirituality.

Religious Traditions:
e.g. Bahai, Buddhism, Christianity, Judaism, Hinduism, Islam, Paganism, Shamanism, Sufism, Taoism, Zen, Zoroastrianism...
Other ...

Newer Traditions & Teachings:
e.g. Anthroposophy, A Course in Miracles, Conversations with God, Gurdjieff, Swedenborg, Theosophy, Tolle ...
Other .....

Practices:
e.g. Angels, Astrology, Bodywork, Community, Communing with Nature, Contemplation, Daily review, Devotion, Dream diary, Fasting, Guru, Inner guidance, Knowledge, Koans, Mantras, Meditation, Movement, Parenting, Pilgrimage, Prayer, Purification, Retreat, Ritual, Sacred plants, Sacred space / place, Satsang / sacred discussion, Service, Study, Sweat lodge, Tai chi chuan, Vision quest, Visualisation, Work as 'love made visible', Yoga
Other ...

Miscellaneous:
e.g. Clairaudience / sentience / voyance, Cults, Hallucinogenic drugs, Near death experience, Tarot,
Other ...

Therapies:
e.g. Acupuncture, Acupressure, Chinese herbs, Flower Essences, Herbalism, Homeopathy, Massage, Psychotherapy, Psychosynthesis, Reiki, Shen, Shiatsu, Spiritual healing, Vibrational medicine...
Other ....

Fig 12: A "Newness" Brainstorm

Activity: Summarizing Your Own Experience Of Newness

Figure 13 on page 82 gives one person's example of the different strands of newness that are weaving themselves into her current world-view and faith expression.

Look at this example and let it trigger your awareness of how and where in your life you have encountered, and perhaps incorporated, strands of newness. You might identify them as "aha!" or points of breakthrough. Then try to draw your own mind-map of your experience of newness.

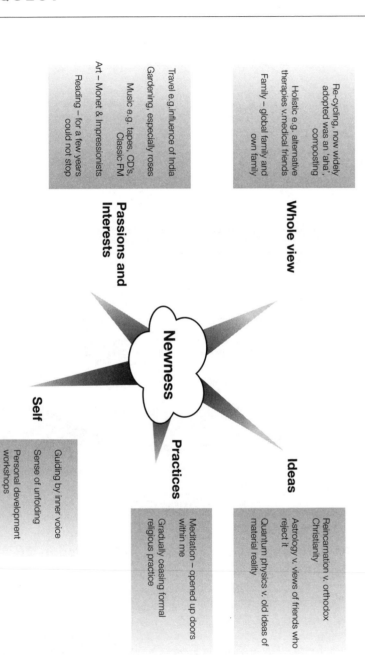

Re-cycling, now widely
adopted was an 'aha',
composting

Holistic e.g. alternative
therapies v.medical friends

Family – global family and
own family

Whole view

Travel e.g.influence of India

Gardening, especially roses

Music e.g. tapes, CD's,
Classic FM

Art – Monet & Impressionists

Reading – for a few years
could not stop

**Passions and
Interests**

Newness

Self

Practices

Ideas

Reincarnation v. orthodox
Christianity

Astrology v. views of friends who
reject it

Quantum physics v. old ideas of
material reality

Meditation – opened up doors
within me

Gradually ceasing formal
religious practice

Guiding by inner voice

Sense of unfolding

Personal development
workshops

Fig 13: A "Newness" Mind-map

Points of breakthrough, or "Aha's," can bring you both joy and the most pain. Joy comes from a meeting of minds. The pain may come from clashes with others with different views or a fixed view of a faith tradition. Although it looks to some as if the world is moving toward a global connection to Spirit, to others it may seem a time of disintegration.

The traditional faiths have been criticized by some for becoming fossilized over the centuries. Just as you may explore new dimensions, so do the religious traditions and many within each of the traditional faiths are finding renewal. For some this has centered on a search "not only in themselves but also in relation to one another, so that a cosmic universal religion can emerge." Father Bede Griffiths (1989), who wrote these words, was among a growing number of people who suggest: "This is a task for the coming centuries as the present world order breaks down and a new world order emerges from the ashes of the old."

In 1982 Fr. Bede Griffiths, calling on his deep experience of the traditions of Christianity and Hinduism, first explored *The Marriage of East and West*. His words still speak clearly of the reflection needed to integrate change and newness:

> "In every person a certain balance or harmony has to be achieved, but in the west today the masculine aspect, the rational, active, aggressive power of the mind, is dominant, while in the east the feminine aspect, the intuitive, passive, sympathetic power of the mind is dominant. The future of the world depends on the marriage of these two minds, the conscious and the unconscious, the rational and the intuitive, the active and the passive. In India and all over the world today these two minds are meeting."

Activity: Breakthroughs And Resolutions

Look back at the activities relating to newness (pages 79, and 81).

- *What can you see as your major breakthroughs or "aha" experiences?*
- *Where have your new ideas clashed with previously held beliefs?*
- *Where have they clashed with the viewpoints of others?*
- *What, if any, have been your points of crisis, newness, or resolution?*
- *Can you identify ways in which you are finding balance or harmony between the foundations of your faith and the challenge of newness, or a marriage of your two minds?*

YOUR EVOLVING FAITH

So far in *Changing Faces of Faith* you have considered the foundations of your faith and re-examined them in the face of contemporary critiques of religious belief. Next you look at how your faith is evolving; where it is today in the light of the impact of other faiths, your image of God, and understanding of Spirit.

ENGAGING WITH OTHER FAITHS

Eck (1994) wrote of the religious landscape in America: "what grounds us spiritually isn't necessarily confined to membership in our own birth tradition." This pluralist view is not synonymous with syncretism – cherry-picking a one-off religion of choice from elements of different traditions – but engages in dialogue to enrich and enlarge understanding. "Because the one we call God is too vast to be fully comprehended by any human construct," she argues, "all the great traditions are necessarily partial and incomplete." We will "increasingly recognize God in other faiths, precisely because we have experienced God's presence in our own."

In recent decades an explosion of travel, migration, and media coverage has led to greater exposure to other religious traditions. Teachers and books introduced Eastern and Middle Eastern traditions to the West. Many people now gain inspiration through the Bhagavad Gita or the meditation, incense, and rituals of India. Others find meaning in the Kabbalah, the Eightfold Path of the Buddha, the Qurăn, or Sufi dance from the world of Islam. Still others appreciate the serenity of Taoism and other Chinese/Japanese philosophies. The face and teachings of the Dalai Lama are respected worldwide and Gandhi and Martin Luther King bear witness to non-violence in both Hindu and Christian religions.

Traditional faiths also inspire through religious texts, music, art, architecture, and dance. They are associated with symbols that represent expressions of belief about spirituality. The next activity gives you an opportunity to reflect on the meaning that symbols have for you, reminding your non-verbal memories of the impact of traditional and newer images of spirituality on you. It also provides opportunity to reflect on the influence of other faiths in your evolving faith.

Activity: Symbols And Images As Inspiration

Below are some symbols and images associated with spirituality.

- *Look at each one and reflect on what significance and meaning it might hold.*
- *Select an image from among these, or find or sketch another of your choice that*

is meaningful for you.
- *What does it represent in terms of your expression of spirituality?*
- *What impact have other faiths had on your evolving faith?*

Fig 14: Symbols And Images Associated With Spirituality

Despite increased awareness of the different ways of faith, some of the differences in belief cause separation, and even war. This has been true in the past – the bitter legacy of the battles of the Crusades between Christendom and Islam still echoes down the centuries – and today – religious bigotry caused civil strife in the Balkans and Northern Ireland and tension in parts of Asia and Africa.

Yet not all messages about and across the faiths are messages of difference and separation; there are also common threads. The Dalai Lama identifies the strength in diversity of the variety of religious and wisdom traditions across the world – necessary to meet the diverse spiritual and ethical needs of human beings. Thinkers, such as Hans Kung, draw out the common threads of ethics and values. One such thread has been called "the Golden Rule" which recognizes kindness as the common root of an ethical and spiritual practice. Below are examples of sayings taken from different faiths with a common message of kindness grounded in mutual respect.

Bahaism: "Lay not on any soul a load which ye would not wish to be laid upon you, and desire not for anyone the things ye would not desire for yourselves."
(*Gleanings from the Writings of Bahá'ulláh,* 66, 127, The Bahá'í)

Buddhism: "A state which is not pleasant or enjoyable for me will also not be so for him; and how can I impose on another a state which is not pleasant or enjoyable for me?"
(*Samyutta Nikaya* V, 353.35-342.2, Bodhi, trans 2002)

Christianity: "And as ye would that men should do to you, do ye also to them likewise."
(Jesus of Nazareth, *The Gospel According to St Luke,* 6:31,)

Hinduism: "One should never do that to another which one regards as injurious to oneself."
(*The Mahabharata,* Anushana parva, 113:7, Dharma trans, 1999)

Islam: "No man is a true believer unless he desireth for his brother that which he desireth for himself."
(Muhammad in the *Hadith Ibn Madja,* Introduction, 9, Clarke trans, 2000)

Jainism: "A man of religion should treat all beings as he himself would be treated."
(*Kritanga Sutra,* I, 11:33, Jacobi trans, 2003)

Judaism: "What is hateful to yourself do not do to your fellow man. That is the whole of the Torah."
(*Babylonian Talmud,* Shabbath 31a, Epstein trans, 1985)

Native American: "Grandfather Great Spirit, all over the world the faces of living ones are alike. With tenderness they have come up out of the ground. Give us the strength to understand, and the eyes to see. Teach us to walk the soft Earth as relatives to all that live."
(*Sioux prayer,* in Roberts and Amidon, Earth Prayers, 1991, p184)

Sikhism: "As thou deemest thyself, so deem others. Then shalt thou become a partner in heaven"
(Source unknown).

Taoism: "Regard your neighbour's gain as your own gain, and your neighbour's loss as your own loss."
(*Tai Shang,* 3, Li Ying-chang *trans,* 1994)

Zoroastrianism "That nature only is good that does not do unto another whatever is not good for its own self."
(*Dadistan-I-dinik,* 94:5, Muller and West *trans* 1996)

Fig 15: The Golden Rule

Activity: Your Golden Rule

The examples opposite of a golden rule show that statements appear in similar terms in the world's major religions.

●*Consider how far you agree with these statements. You might begin by identifying any with which you feel in sympathy.*
●*Can it be written in words that express your understanding of it and which you can support?*

IMAGES OF GOD AND SOUL

As your faith developed you might have been aware of some of the things that influenced you and have consciously chosen to accept or reject them. Other influences may have been so subtle that you remained unaware of how they were shaping you.

Such images and metaphors are important. For all those who find the images from their childhood comforting, others find them alien and inhibiting. In the Judeo-Christian tradition, many people experience the image of God that they received in childhood as a stumbling block to the continuation or the development of their faith today. Borg (1997) suggests that in the Judeo-Christian tradition, there are two primary models of God. The "monarchical model" – God as king, lord, and father, a male authority figure who rules the universe – gives rise to what he calls a "performance model" of spiritual life, couched in the language of obedience, guilt, and sin. The "Spirit model" is a cluster of images of God to do with intimacy, relationship, and belonging – God as a non-material reality pervading the universe as well as being more than the universe – in which God is near, compassionate, and nurturing.

The next activity helps you explore images and metaphors you may have held, drawing on a dialogue between two leading characters, Celie and Shug, in Alice Walker's novel *The Color Purple* (1991).

Activity: Images of God

Celie and Shug had been brought up to believe in an image of a God who was responsible for all the good and bad things in their lives. They start to talk about their images of this God.

Celie derived her image of God from "the one in the white folks' bible". "He big and old and tall and graybearded and white. He wear white robes and go barefooted".

Shug observes this God looks like the people in the "white folks' church." She explains how she moved away from her own early view: "My first step from the old white man was trees. Then air. Then birds. Then people. But one day when I was sitting quiet … "

● *When you sit quietly, what images, perceptions, metaphors, feelings, bodily sensations come to you of God, Spirit, a Presence, or Ultimate Reality? How does it represent itself to you today?*

● *What do you associate with your images and metaphor, giving you insight into the nature and attributes of your God, Spirit, Presence, or Ultimate Reality?*

● *Become aware of conversations, events, ideas, or things that either confirmed the images and metaphors of your childhood or helped you move on from them.*

● *Try to note down these and other key stepping stones; they may have been meeting new people, being exposed to different ways of looking at something, a new dawning realization that there are other ways of being.*

Image and metaphor allow you to access your images and impressions of spiritual experience in ways that can be free of form and language. But you cannot avoid language and concepts altogether and terms like "soul" or "a sense of soul" need to be examined too.

The idea of an individualized soul appears in most cultures and there are many names for it. Its nature is mysterious and shadowy and reveals itself in diverse ways, such as intuitions, flashes, whispers, sudden urges, and maybe a sense of inner radiance and meaning. For some people it is linked to conscience; in Hebrew the words for "conscience," "compass," and "the hidden truth of the soul" all have the same root. In *The Quest* we have imagined that you are aware of something of this kind within you. Because it means different things to different people *The Quest* adopts the phrase "a sense of soul" to indicate that this diversity can be cohesive rather than divisive. The next activity, however, collects together a number of descriptions and views about soul itself; reflecting upon these descriptions may help you to take a further look at your sense of soul.

Activity: Recognizing Your Soul

The descriptions in Fig 16, pages 89-90 present different images of soul. Some are quotations and some are compiled for this activity. Read through them all, comment on those that mean something to you, and perhaps add your own ideas.

● *What does "soul" mean to you at this point?*
● *Can you add other ideas and quotations of your own?*
● *Collect together your thoughts and musing on the meaning of soul; allow yourself time to dwell on them for a day or two. Then return to this activity and record – draw or write – the connections and associations between "soul" and "your sense of soul" that are most meaningful.*

Many people continue to derive comfort from images, beliefs, and values

	Your Comments
"A sense of personal calling, that there is a reason I am alive" (James Hillman 1996)	
"I don't develop; I am" (Picasso)	
A feeling for the totality of things and the inner bonds between them	
The soul is your inner experiencing	
Paradoxical in nature: omnipresent and scarcely discernible; wide open and fairly closed; powerful and delicate; can harbour eternal thoughts and transient desires	
Part of the universe that lives in a personal form in us	
That place in us where the inner world meets the outer world. The soul mediates between and relates one world to the other	
The inner world of soul is not perceptible by the senses but by an inner capacity for perceiving what is present within us	
"The soul has two eyes, one looks at time passing, the other sends forth its gaze into eternity" (Angelus Silesius)	
Your soul is your consistent, innate sense of who you are. It acts as your guide, giving a sense of direction and purpose	
"Laughing and weeping are the two inward movements of the soul that make visible the opposite poles of feeling"(Rudolf Steiner, 2003)	

Continued over

Fig 16: Table Of Images Of Soul

Continued from previous page

	Your Comments
My soul is invisible; it is not measurable; it is my dimension of connectedness with others and with the cosmos	
The soul has "spiritual authority within as inner life and inner light" (Heron, 1998)	
Everything in the soul is in process, in continuous movement	
In the soul past and future are dynamically present	

that are familiar from the tradition in which they grew up. Their legacy is supportive. However, others carry varying measures of distress from the images and attitudes they encountered; women who felt demeaned by patriarchal forms or young people who experienced authoritarian, repressive, or abusive behaviors. For them, the religious experience of their past has been damaging. Before moving on, therefore, the next activity gives you time to reflect on your evolving faith and an opportunity to reflect on rifts or discomfort you may feel.

Activity: Review Of Your Faith

You will need two sheets of paper for this exercise.

Take one sheet of paper and divide it into four boxes. In the top left-hand box, write "Images and practices of the faith/tradition of my past: what was life-affirming for me?" In the box alongside, write "Images and practices of the faith/tradition of my past: what was limiting or difficult for me?" In the bottom pair of boxes write "Images and practices of my faith today: what is life-affirming for me?" and next to it "Images and practices of my faith today: what is limiting or difficult for me?" Fill in these boxes with your responses and recollections.

Take the second sheet of paper and divide it into two boxes. Give one box the heading "Affirmations, Crises and Resolutions". In this box, compare and record what you notice about your past and current images and experience of faith.

Give the last box a heading "What I would like to move toward" and use this box to note down both the broad outline of a faith that you hope to find and the steps, both of discovery and healing or reconciliation, that will help move you toward it.

MOVING AHEAD INTO THE UNKNOWN

The faces of faith are changing and the foundations of your faith may have been shaken. We see examples around us of a longing to avoid the challenge and uncertainty of such profound change. Fundamentalism is one reaction: the Chief Rabbi in the UK, Jonathan Sacks (2002), describes fundamentalism as "The attempt to impose a single truth on a plural world." Some respond with determination: Rudolph Bahro, a leader of the Green movement in the former East Germany wrote: "When the forms of the old culture are dying, the new culture is created by a few people who are not afraid to be insecure."

In the mythic hero's journey, refreshed by Joseph Campbell for modern times, the hero (or heroine) is called to leave behind the known and journey into the unknown: "the old skin has to be shed before the new one can come." This involves crossing a threshold of some kind – a potentially risky experience – to seek out new treasures to bring back home. Most of us cross thresholds in life and engage in new journeys. Some are life changing, e.g. leaving school, becoming a parent, changing a job, moving house, retiring, dying – the last of the thresholds in life. Both outer and inner things have changed; after such thresholds life can never be quite the same again, which is why many societies devise rituals or rites of passage to mark threshold experiences.

Campbell (1995) suggests that: "the goal of the hero's journey is yourself, finding yourself." Deepak Chopra (2000) suggests that: "The aim of spirituality is to learn co-operation with God." Whatever the definition of the spiritual journey, much of spiritual and personal growth is about becoming more fully who you truly are. This may involve a willingness to go deeper within, to churn new ideas within you, to share more of yourself with others, to search for new meaning, to pursue a path of discernment with a more open mind. It may involve going on an outer journey or pilgrimage. Shirley Maclaine says at the start of *The Camino* (2000), the story of her outer and inner pilgrimage to Santiago de Compostela: "I was ready for a new understanding that would carry me forward for the rest of my life."

The journey may involve a willingness to discover more of your life purpose. Piero Ferrucci (1982) sees parallels between the way a person's potential unfolds according to an underlying pattern or intelligence and the way nature moves toward a perfect realization of what was previously a potential:

"A bird pecks its way out of an egg.
A bud blossoms into a rose.
A star forms out of the condensation of interstellar gas.
Molten minerals cool into a beautiful crystal pattern."

All patterns have equal dignity and we each have a life-pattern uniquely our own and not someone else's. Ferrucci suggested that each of us should try to "discover the pattern and co-operate with its realization."

Your individual journey may also be running alongside a journey of collective awakening; not just one of us but all of us taking a long, long stride into the unknown. Sir George Trevelyan, one of the forerunners of what might be described as a spiritual renaissance in Britain, used to quote:

"The human heart can go to the lengths of God
Dark and cold we may be, but this
Is no winter now. The frozen misery
Of centuries breaks, cracks, begins to move;
The thunder is the thunder of the floes,
The thaw, the flood, the upstart Spring.
Thank God our Time is now when wrong
Comes up to face us everywhere
Never to leave us till we take
The longest stride of soul men ever took.
Affairs are now soul size.
The enterprise
Is exploration into God.
Where are you making for? It takes
So many thousand years to wake
But will you wake for pity's sake?"

From *A Sleep of Prisoners* (Christopher Fry, 1951)

TRADITION AND TRANSITION: OPEN TO NEW LIGHT

In this chapter you have been considering your evolving faith, how it has formed, the changing paradigms that are a backcloth for your life, and the ways it might be influencing you. The final activity of this chapter is a pause to draw all this together.

Activity: Your Present Religious And Cultural Beliefs, Traditions, And Values

Try to put down, in some form or another, a picture of your faith right now.

●What and who are you, in terms of your present religious and cultural beliefs, traditions, and values?
●What is still of value from the traditions you have known?
●At what point did questions and challenges arise?
●Where has new light entered?
●What do you feel may be just over the horizon of your current faith?
  You might include symbols that you hold dear, images, short texts.

ENCOUNTERING DIRECT EXPERIENCE

"Drop what is imposed.
Find the way that is natural to you.
Your own flow is in harmony with the Tao."

Jasmin Lee Cori (2000)

The founders of the different religions, as well as enlightened teachers who have come before or since, knew what they knew. What we mean by this is that they had direct experience of Spirit. For them, this was like the difference between the <u>theory</u> of knowing that people may drown at sea and a <u>personal experience</u> of being caught in a storm in a small boat. The experience is direct and personal and imprints itself so that you know in a different way.

The faces and experience of faith are changing as many people place less emphasis on traditional knowledge that is passed down to them. Less significance is attached to recorded revelation, the historical experience of others, or particular creeds and beliefs – generally understood as *religion* – and more to the freedom to encounter and trust individual spiritual experience – *spirituality*. But, while direct experience may feel alive and powerful, it comes with a health warning: in the religious traditions there are priests, imams, and rabbis who mediate your experience and provide a check on its authenticity whereas today, if you journey outside a faith community, you have to discern for yourself the content and nature of your encounter. *Encountering Direct Experience*, therefore, raises such questions as:

○ What has been your experience of 'something more'?
○ What were you encountering?
○ What maps might help you understand what is happening?
○ How can you approach and anchor direct experience of Spirit?

EXPERIENCE AND SPIRIT

Encountering direct experience of Spirit or "something more" can be as tantalizing as it is transformative. All too often it is experienced powerfully and fleetingly, leaving you with the feeling that something important has happened but you can't re-create it, bring it back, or hold on to it. People's experiences of encountering Spirit vary widely too; such experience may be felt, heard, seen, come in ecstasy, be a bodily sensation, be a metaphorical understanding of phenomena such as light and myriad other forms. The contrast ranges from Moses' experience of a burning bush, recounted in the Bible, to one recounted by Richard Moss (1987). Moss was watching two butterflies dancing and mating when suddenly one of them, a black butterfly, flew to him and landed right between his eyebrows.

> "In that moment, all of creation became a single consciousness, a state of indescribable glory and unspeakable peace. The fear that existed when I stood rooted in egoic consciousness was now the most exquisite nectar. I was suffused with a current of aloneness so transcendently blissful that there was no analogy within ordinary experience that even approximates it. It was living bliss, but it was also the most profound intelligence. There was a flood of knowing, of understanding as though all of existence stood before me in its totality with its secrets uncovered and revealed."

A different example, from Janice, one of *The Quest* co-authors, recounts a direct experience arising unexpectedly in the very ordinariness of a daily activity:

"One day, when I was sitting quietly at the top of our garden, suddenly my perception of the world shifted. I could see the whole of creation as dancing and shimmering with the same one energy flowing through everything and manifesting in different forms – a bush, a flower, a wasp. I was overawed by the beauty and by the certain knowing that this energy was both beneficent and loving. The experience only lasted a few minutes and then returned to normal. But the memory of it has stayed with me. I used to be scared of wasps and kill as many as I could but I have never touched one since that moment!"

The experience that Moss recounts was brought about by a shock, a discontinuity in his experience that took him out of the ordinary consciousness of watching butterflies. Janice's direct experience just happened in the course of a familiar activity. Whatever precipitates the encounter, a direct experience of Spirit is frequently characterized by a shift in perception accompanied by a different kind of knowing – a *gnosis*. It can be a shattering or even life-transforming experience. For others, however, it grows slowly until, one day, there may just be a clear awakening: "Why didn't I see it this way before?"

The ways of experiencing Spirit in the examples above are not restricted to thinking. Thinking, using left-brain activity, has always been emphasized in Western educational and religious traditions. Indeed some commentators suggest that "the culture in which we live tends to make a virtue of severing our cognitive understanding from the experience of our hearts" (Loring, 1997). In the next activity you recall your own experience of "something more" and explore some routes to direct experience that may be known to you, including your heart and body.

Activity: Your Experience Of Spirit Or Something More

You may find it useful to look back at your response to the first activity in **Telling Your Story** *and the activities on spiritual experience in* **A Growing Sense of Soul.**

1. Look back at any experiences of something more you have had. Pick out one or two that were significant. If nothing comes to mind immediately, reflect on your childhood, any dreams you have had or moments of awe or deep joy.

2. How did you register your experience? Was it feeling, hearing, seeing, tasting, smelling, bodily sensation, presence of the "other," an awareness of the heart, seeing light or a shimmering energy, etc?

3. What was the experience connected with? For example:

- *Nature*
- *Relationship*
- *Inner connection or inner voice*
- *Far memory of some past or future time*
- *An inspiration or idea you reached alone without having heard it from anyone else.*

4. Describe as best you can the quality and nature of the moment. For example:

- *Filling you with wonder or awe?*
- *A sense of connection to something other?*
- *An overwhelming sense of inner knowing?*
- *In some way different to any of these descriptions?*
- *Of course it may have been ineffable or impossible to put into words.*

This activity may generate significant memories and insights; find an appropriate way to record them for later reflection.

One Questor recounted an experience that came as a vision of light. She described a nearby bush that briefly appeared to be completely suffused in a translucent light. This came at a time when she was considering how she could have the kind of personal relationship with Spirit as God, in the way that many other people experience. She said

"Although the experience was quite ephemeral, it told me that this kind of relationship is possible within my understanding of God as Spirit or as an energy. I haven't always been able to recreate this relationship but since then I have never doubted that it exists and this alone has fundamentally marked a shift for me."

WHAT ARE YOU ENCOUNTERING?

In *Getting Started* we defined Spirit as "a powerful dimension, encompassing more than your sense of soul...widely perceived as an energy or force that can change individual lives, society and the planet" (page 15).

There are two particular, and linked, interpretations of Spirit or something more that call for reflection: that it is all-encompassing and wider than your immediate experience – *transcendence* – and that you find it within yourself and deep within all life – *immanence*. For some people, there is no gap between the transcendent and the immanent aspects of Spirit; it feels more like one seamless encounter. In the earlier accounts by Richard Moss and Janice, the transcendent – "all of creation became a single consciousness" and "I could 'see' the whole of creation as dancing and shimmering with the same one energy flowing through everything" – and the immanent – "I was suffused with a current of aloneness so transcendently blissful" and "I was overawed by the beauty and by the certain knowing that this energy was both beneficent and loving" – meld into one totality. This kind of knowing derives primarily from insight, or inner wisdom, and can be enhanced by passed-on experience or insight of others.

The next activity gathers definitions of Spirit and something more from various sources of passed-on experience and insight. Clarifying your own definitions of Spirit and something more will help you reflect on what you are encountering.

Activity: Your Own Definitions Of Spirit And Spiritual Principles

Read all the descriptions below to see the range of views. Put a tick in the first column of boxes for those descriptions that immediately strike you as close to your

own view or that have some meaning for you. Put a tick in the second column against any that have no meaning for you.

Now go through them again more slowly. This time, use the third column to jot down any thoughts, ideas, recollections or experiences that the descriptions trigger. Don't worry about trying to give responses that are consistent with each other.

Finally, review all the statements and your responses to them. Use the box at the end to add further responses of your own. You may find some that fit well together and you may find some that seem incompatible with each other.

Box: A Description with much/ some meaning for you
Box: B Description with little/ no meaning for you

	A	B	Your views
Spirit is accessible to us all and we each have our own valid experience of Spirit			
There is a presence, called by many names, but which is everywhere; it is both within and external to each person and can be interpreted as pure energy or in a particular form or shape			
Our experience of Spirit is deepened and the connection constantly nurtured by practices that incorporate silence and stillness			
The universe was created by God. He is greater than and distinct from it.			
Spirit dwells deep within and I embody Spirit in my being			

Continued over

Fig 17: Your Own Definitions Of Spirit And Spiritual Principles

THE QUEST

Continued from previous page

Box: A *Description with much/ some meaning for you*
Box: B *Description with little/ no meaning for you*

	A	B	Your views
My connection with Spirit needs to be embedded in daily life			
Spirit leads to a transformative learning/living process which is a reference point in living			
There is a relationship between my spiritual life and my emotional/ psychological life. My work on the psychological is focused on eliminating the obstacles to Spirit			
Spiritual growth includes being open to a dimension that is greater than myself			
There is an ongoing, fresh revelation every time a person has an encounter with God; both God and the person can be changed by the encounter			
A divine presence inhabits every particle of nature and the universe			
I need to be aware of how I experience and interpret Spirit in daily life; where I flow or get stuck			

Continued from previous page		**Box: A** *Description with much/ some meaning for you* **Box: B** *Description with little/ no meaning for you*	

	A	B	*Your views*
I experience God as an ultimate creative force			
Awareness of Spirit involves consciously experimenting with ways of embedding it in daily life and activity			
Spirit can be visible through the love, truth and wisdom of my inner being and through my outer actions			
I experience Spirit as a longing to be connected to something that protects me and leads me through, no matter how difficult or impossible; it feels like a desire for coming home			
As I pursue an inner journey (into feelings, values, self-awareness, thoughts, assumptions etc.) I can, in the right circumstances, begin to open to an awareness that is larger than myself			
The universe is a part of God but God is more than just the sum total of the universe			
Spirit is a being 'out there' with whom I can have a personal relationship and communication			
			Continued over

DIFFERENT WAYS OF KNOWING

Jung (1921) suggests that you come to knowing through four key functions: thinking, feeling, intuiting, and sensing. We have added creativity as a fifth way of knowing in the diagram below; creative expression is placed at the center as the potential culmination of the other four ways of knowing.

To be alert to new possibilities in your spiritual experience, you may wish to experiment with being open to Spirit each day in a range of different ways. The next series of activities, based on Jung's model of different ways of knowing, explores ways of knowing and engaging with Spirit that correspond to thinking, feeling, intuiting, and sensing. Record your responses to the series of activities in a way that allows you to collect them together. The first activity presents a skill of spiritual reflection that primarily employs thinking.

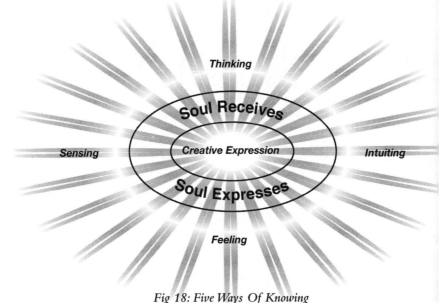

Fig 18: Five Ways Of Knowing

Activity: **Skills of Spiritual Reflection:**
The Way of Knowing Through Thinking

This activity introduces a new skill of spiritual reflection associated with Observing and Reflecting

CRITICAL INCIDENT ANALYSIS

WHAT DOES IT MEAN?

Critical Incident Analysis is a structured and analytical way of reflecting on events. The analytical nature of the practice allows you to stand back from your reactions to, and emotions about, the experience, so that you are able to learn from it. It helps you to break down barriers to reflection, particularly those which cause you to be defensive about your decisions, or to make excuses about your actions.

STARTING OUT

Choose any incident from your experience that is significant or critical; an argument with someone, a family wedding, an interview. To begin with, try some incident or event that was relatively recent.

1. Describe the incident or event as factually as you can.

- *What was the situation? Where were you, who else was involved, what was going on?*
- *What happened? What did you do? What did other people do?*
- *What was significant or 'critical' about the incident?*
- *What were your thoughts at the time? What have you thought about it since?*

2. Try to distinguish between fact and your interpretation of facts.

- *What were you trying to achieve?*
- *Why did you act or react as you did?*
- *What were the consequences of your action, both for yourself and for other people?*
- *What were your feelings at the time?*
- *What are your feelings now? Are there any differences?*

3. Analyze your responses.

- *What factors influenced your decision/actions?*
- *What was the reaction of others involved?*
- *How do you know how they felt?*

4. Consider alternative actions.

●*With hindsight, how might you have dealt differently with the situation?*
●*What other choices might you have made?*
●*What might have been the consequences of those choices?*

PRACTICING

●*How can you best make sense of the experience?*
●*What have you learned from the experience?*
●*How might you apply this learning in the future?*
●*What might you do differently if it happened again?*
●*Has it alerted you to any further knowledge you might need or skills that you might usefully develop?*

Next, you turn to knowing as feeling. Heart-based feeling is a primary way of knowing. Science is now showing that around our heart are receptor cells, much like brain cells, which can receive and respond to information. Doc Childre (1996) has been setting up a worldwide system for "Heart-maths" which encourages children to learn through their heart rhythms as well as their brains.

Activity: The Way Of Knowing Through Feeling

Try different ways of experiencing through feeling:

(a) Response to visual images such as icons, stained glass, paintings, etc. has long been part of religious experience. Find an image that evokes an instinctive response in you. Gaze at it with your heart rather than your mind and let it speak to you. Be aware of the impact the image has on you, and what you feel.

(b) Go somewhere where you can be surrounded by the natural world, somewhere you find beautiful. Try to feel nature's energies, and pay them your full and loving attention. Actively explore a feeling relationship with the rhythms of life through this connection.

> *"And I have felt*
> *A presence that disturbs me with joy*
> *Of elevated thoughts; a sense sublime*
> *Of something more deeply interfused,*
> *Whose dwelling is the light of setting suns,*
> *And the round ocean and the living air,*
> *And the blue sky, and in the mind of man;*
> *A motion and a spirit, that impels*

All thinking things, all objects of all thought,
And rolls through all things."

(Wordsworth, Lines written a few miles above Tintern Abbey, 1798)

The next activity focuses on Jung's third way of knowing, through intuiting. Intuition is an important channel for encountering Spirit and most of us already use our intuition to a far greater extent than we realize; later in *Encountering Direct Experience* you will reflect specifically upon the kinds of intuition that are naturally open to you. Meanwhile, here are some things different people have said about what intuition feels like to them.

"I have a gut feeling."
"An idea comes into my head in a flash."
"I get a niggling feeling."
"I have a kind of picture inside my head."
"It is just a sense or impression."
"I hear an inner voice."
"My dreams give me messages."
"I just wake up with a new knowing."
"Apparently unrelated ideas suddenly come together to a pattern."
"A sense of acceptance comes over me, then I know I've got the right answer."

Activity: The Way Of Knowing Through Intuition

(a) Hold a current question in your mind and heart. For example, a person with whom you have a difficulty, a challenging situation, or a need to reconcile apparently conflicting ideas or beliefs.

   Move into silence with this question in your heart and mind and be open to ways that an answer might come: a flash of inspiration, a gut feeling, an inner voice or prompting, an image. If nothing comes immediately continue to hold it in your awareness over the next few days, open to the possibility of new insight. Note any occurrence or synchronicity that seems meaningful to you or any dreams you can recall.

(b) In a group of four or so people, ask one person to describe an issue or challenge he or she is facing. In silence, each person asks for an insight or image to help clarify the issue. Share any insights and images sensitively in the group. Allow the person asking for intuitive insight to decide what is /is not helpful and how to interpret it.

Jung's fourth way of knowing is through sensing. Part of the delight of having a body is our ability to hear, see, smell, taste, touch at physical levels and possibly, as our senses become more refined, at inner levels as well.

"Heard melodies are sweet
But those unheard are sweeter."
John Keats

There are so many ways that you can experiment through the senses. The activity focuses on listening and sounding as two possible ways of knowing through the senses; you will probably be able to think of others. Use the activity as a model for experimenting with each of the senses to work out those senses you feel at home with and those you wish to develop further.

Activity: The Way Of Knowing Through Sensing

Each part of this activity needs to start and end with silence. It is often through silence following a period of activity that you come into contact with your deeper self.

(a) Actively listening to music can help you be more receptive to the present moment. If you can do this activity at a live performance of music then so much the better, if not, select a piece of music that you feel drawn to and listen to it. Set time aside for really listening and, starting from a moment of silence, let the music speak to you in a new way. What does the piece evoke in you? What experience does it give you of Spirit or something more? Feel the place where you respond most deeply.

(b) Voicing as a way to connect has been part of many traditions, from chanting "Om" in the Eastern tradition to hymn singing or choral works in the West. Try chanting alone or with others and see what insights or shifts might occur. If you are not used to chanting, try to listen to chanting on the radio, CD, or tape first.

Louisa, a music teacher, says that "voicing immediately touches a deeper part of our brains from where the magic of our humanity starts to emerge. When people voice they begin to harmonize; their cellular structure changes as though, often for the first time, they are massaging the inside of their bodies."

Finally, creative expression can also be a way of knowing. Having worked through the previous activities, you could draw together your experience through the fifth way of knowing, creative expression.

Activity: **The Way Of Knowing Through Creative Expression**

Choose a mode of expression you have not used before such as drawing, painting, clay modeling, writing in a different form such as poetry, embroidery, composing music. Use flowers or greenery from a garden or vary a familiar medium, e.g. if you draw, find colored rather than white paper, or use ink if you usually draw with color.

Set aside plenty of time to do this creative activity. Allow your creativity to express your current experience in any way that spontaneously emerges, working in as uninhibited a way as you can. Explore and express all the sensuous details, delight in color, shape, or form.

A MAP OF YOUR ENCOUNTER

As you read *Encountering Direct Experience* and work through the activities, you may be gathering many memories and new experiences. Do you feel that you have encountered something more? Is this Spirit? Now is a good time to take stock and gather your experience, reflections, insights, and questions into a more coherent shape before your next steps on your spiritual journey.

Within the different religious traditions there are maps that symbolically represent the changing perspectives of a spiritual journey as different stages of faith. For example, in the Zen Buddhist tradition there is a series of ten ox-herding pictures that depict the stages of enlightenment. In the Hindu tradition there are maps that are based on the *chakra* – or energy – system of the body, depicting seven evolving levels of consciousness. These can be contrasted with the more recent ideas, for example, of Lawrence Kohlberg, who devised a map of moral development, and James Fowler; these relate more to the Judeo-Christian tradition.

In 1981 Fowler carried out research on nearly six hundred people aged from four to eighty-eight, including Jews, Catholics, Protestants, agnostics, and atheists. From his research, Fowler defined faith as a person's way of making sense of life and made a connection between the outer events of our lives and our struggle to fulfill our potential and find higher order values and meaning. He analyzed six stages from childhood experience, influenced by fantasy, stories, and imitation of adults, through stages of literal beliefs to a stage of conventional faith. Beyond this he identified a more reflective stage, open to our own "deeper self" and a final "unitive" stage, based on an underlying sense of the one-ness of all creation and embracing all approaches.

These maps identify stages of discovering Spirit. You may be able to recognize stages in exploring your sense of soul and discovery of Spirit or it may be enough of a struggle to build up a map of your current position. Piero Ferrucci (1982) calls maps a visual representation of our inner territory. He adds: "these are impoverished, static versions of the actual territory. Nevertheless, they are useful tools to facilitate exploration ..."

In *Telling Your Story* you told your life story; many writers, starting from their own experience, depict their stories in maps or visual representations that facilitate exploration. You look next at three maps from different writers' perspectives – one quite straightforward, the other two more complex – before drawing your own. You may find these maps challenging, so the next activity helps you see how any particular map sheds light on your life. You can also rely on your gut response to them, taking into account physical as well as emotional reactions, thoughts, and any sense of being inspired or excited as well. Sometimes the maps refer to transpersonal rather than spiritual; transpersonal is a broader term including subtle realms, such as the psychic and paranormal.

Activity: A Critical Approach To Maps

Take a critical approach to the maps that follow. Use the questions below to work out whether or not any particular map is useful for you.

- *What is your immediate gut reaction to it?*
- *Be more analytical and look for (a) what makes sense, (b) what you do not understand, and (c) the point where your eyes glaze over or your mind goes blank.*
- *What in this map relates to your experience?*
- *How could you explain to someone else what the map-maker is trying to convey?*
- *What seems to you to be true in the map-maker's ideas?*
- *Are there any implications for your life map and how you perceive yourself?*
- *What does not seem to fit and why?*

FRANCES VAUGHAN

The first map comes from Frances Vaughan's book *The Inward Arc* (1985). She suggests that achieving growth is part of becoming "whole"; we do not grow effectively whilst some aspects of us get left out or left behind. She says:

"From an existential point of view, the self seems to grow like an organism, rather than being constructed by adding qualities or attributes like building blocks ... Patterns of growth are discernible, but the process is not rigidly determined ... When viewed as an organising principle, the self is not exclusively identified with any particular stage or component of psychological development. It may be experienced in moments of unitive consciousness as being one with the larger whole of which it is an integral part. Whatever we think we are, we are continually engaged in a process of relational exchange at all levels of awareness: spiritual, existential, mental, emotional and physical."

The circles in her map represent different levels of yourself. In order to grow you must experience and transcend each different level, starting from 1, and incorporate it into your larger self. To become whole you must address all levels and any associated distress and turmoil, so becoming fuller and more integrated. As you become less dominated by painful memories or experiences you are more able to give a central focus to the spiritual/transpersonal level.

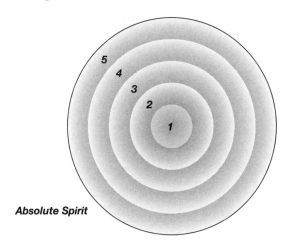

Fig 19: Vaughan's Map Of Becoming Whole

At each level, you may be saying:

1. *Body / Physical aspect*: I identify with my physical body and basic issues of survival and security, e.g. I am defined by what I look like, my physical strength, my need for physical comfort, etc.

2. *Emotional aspect*: I identify with my desires and needs, being dominated by my prevailing emotion or desire of the moment until that is satisfied and the next one takes its place.

3. *Mental aspect*: I am caught up with thoughts and preoccupied with my ideas about who and what I am. I may be "stuck in my head", unaware of how I feel or what is happening to others.

4. *Existential aspect*: I have to engage with the realities of human existence. This includes things that are both painful and difficult, e.g. death, pain, and illness. I may be blocked by my incapacity to accept and live with human suffering. A healthy existential self is necessary for a coherent and integrated acceptance of what is going on around me, and for trying to create meaning in the world.

5. *Spiritual / Transpersonal aspect*: my previous, narrower identity is broken down to allow for an encompassing sense of myself as an organizing principle within a larger system of relationships. (adapted from Frances Vaughan, 1985)

Activity: Relating Vaughan's Five Aspects To Yourself

First settle yourself in a quiet and relaxed way. Use the questions in the previous activity: A Critical Approach to Maps *to reflect on Vaughan's map.*

Take another look at the way Vaughan has constructed her concentric circles. Do you notice that she puts the physical in the middle and the spiritual in the outermost ring?

● *Why might she do it that way?*
● *Would you nest them inside each other, make them separate or overlapping?*
● *Try putting the circle for your spiritual aspect in the middle instead of on the edge. Does that feel different? You might come up with a completely different map from Vaughan but one that reflects you far more accurately.*

ROBERTO ASSAGIOLI

Psychosynthesis, founded by Roberto Assagioli, is a major influence in transpersonal psychology. Assagioli says:

"On the psychological level it aims to build a personality which is free from emotional blocks, has command over all its functions and has a clear awareness of its own centre. On the transpersonal level, it enables the individual to explore those regions full of mystery and wonder beyond our ordinary awareness, which we call the superconscious: the wellspring of higher intuitions, inspirations, ethical imperatives, and states of illumination. This exploration culminates in the discovery of the Self, our true essence beyond all masks and conditionings."

(Whitmore 1990, quoting Assagioli)

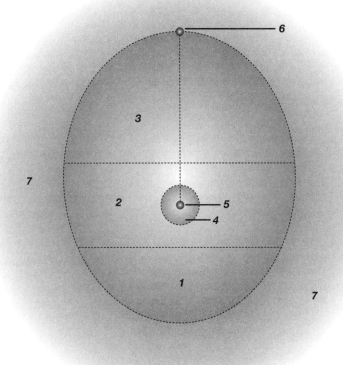

Fig 20: Assagioli's "Egg" Diagram

In Assagioli's map (1991) – the "egg" diagram above – the lines are dotted to show that they are not rigid boundaries and there is a flow between them and in each aspect you may be aware of:

1. *The Lower Unconscious* – my past in the form of long-forgotten memories and repressed parts of myself, e.g. anger where it stores repressed action, controlling my actions, keeping me a prisoner of my past.

2. *The Middle Unconscious* – my recent memories, thoughts, and feelings of everyday life. Although I may still <u>su</u>ppress thoughts or feelings (such as hunger in mid-afternoon!), this is different from <u>re</u>pressing them as I do in my lower unconscious.

3. *The Higher Unconscious or Superconscious* – the seat of my higher aspirations, intuition, and spiritual energy, including artistic, philosophical,

scientific, or ethical insights and the impulse to altruistic action. This is the source of flashes of inspiration and where I experience a feeling of connection with who I really am. It is always present in me, both actual and potential.

4. *The Field of Consciousness* – my immediate images, thoughts, feelings, desires, and impulses that I may observe, analyze, judge, and act upon in any one moment. It is constantly changing and influenced by the surrounding *Middle Unconscious* (2). This is akin to my capacity to be present in the experience of each moment.

5. *The Conscious Self or "I"* – this is my center of consciousness, where I am aware of myself as an "I" and which remains unaltered whatever changes around/in me. Most of us do not experience this "I" in a very clearly defined way but the more I work on myself, the more I am in contact with this "I".

6. *The Higher Self* – the point of my pure Being unaffected by any conscious experience. The "I" of the *Conscious Self* (5) is a reflection of this transpersonal self or Spirit. I may be unaware of it or I may access it through long spiritual practice or spontaneous spiritual experience.

7. *The Collective Unconscious* – this is the collected experience of my family, culture, and humanity in general. It influences me in subtle ways, such as through archetypal images, and current fashions and movements.
(Adapted from Ferrucci, 1982, and Whitmore, 1990)

Activity: Relating The Egg Diagram To Yourself

First settle yourself in a quiet and relaxed way. Use the questions in the activity:
A Critical Approach to Maps *to reflect on Assagioli's map.*
   Does Assagioli's egg diagram suggest anything meaningful to you about yourself and your journey?

The final map is adapted from one of several presented by John Heron (1998). We use it to suggest that Spirit can be experienced through exploring four different areas:

- ○ *Transcendent consciousness* – spiritual consciousness, beyond all name and form (top left)
- ○ *Subtle realms* – invisible processes and presences (top right)
- ○ *Everyday world* – human society, nature and the visible cosmos (bottom right)
- ○ *Awareness of indwelling life* – spiritual life immanent within all things and ourselves (bottom left).

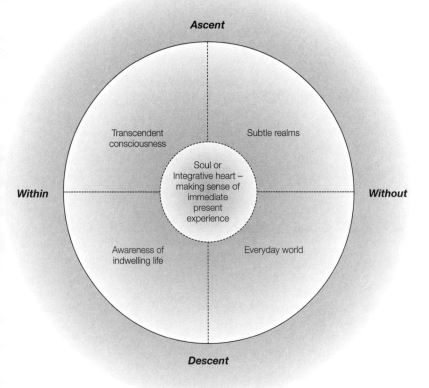

Fig 21: Our version of Heron's Map Of Experiencing Spirit

Activity: **Relating Heron's Map To Yourself**

First settle yourself in a quiet and relaxed way. Read Heron's descriptions of the parts of his map. Write into each section anything from your own experience that you relate to his description. Then use the questions in the activity: A Critical Approach to Maps *to see what you make of Heron's map.*

Before looking at the three maps, we briefly explained the ox-herding and chakra maps from the Buddhist and Hindu traditions. Heron (*op cit*) says: "the beliefs and practices of the various mystical traditions constitute a huge data-bank, a massive resource which, when treated with due caveats, can be drawn upon, modified and revised in framing the maps which guide the examined life and co-operative spiritual inquiry." You may encounter other such maps on your spiritual journey. The questions in *A Critical Approach To Maps* may be useful again, offering a useful reflection on your own map when you have drawn it!

The next activity is a significant undertaking. Whether you just sketch a hazy response at present or draw a detailed map, you are likely to return to add to it over the next days and weeks – or you may re-draw it altogether.

Activity: Your Map

Get paper, pens, and colors together. Think back over the maps you have looked at and jot down what has been useful in them and what has not been useful.

Using minimal analytical thought, draw a map, diagram, or picture that represents you, your sense of soul and image of Spirit now. Pay attention to images, colors, shapes, location, and relationship of the various elements of your map.

WAYS OF CONNECTION – COMMUNION – UNION

You have been exploring your encounter with direct experience, reflecting on your perception of Spirit, experimenting with Jung's different ways of knowing, and drawing a map that helps you picture your image of something more. You have done a lot of active digging! Hopefully, you have met or recollected experiences that connect you with your sense of soul and the radical aliveness of Spirit.

In early times people experienced a sense of aliveness in the universe. This kind of connection was then largely lost in Western civilization, until it was re-discovered through such ways as creation spirituality, the rituals of earth-centered traditions, and celebration of lunar and solar rhythms. In those early times, people had felt and interpreted this aliveness as a Presence or Ultimate Reality they could be in communion with.

"An unchanging One-ness
An ever-changing Presence.
An indefinable original totality
It is impossible to give it a name,
but I call it the Tao."

Lao Tze, (in Hodge, 1992)

As time went on, the sense of almost continuous communion with a Presence was replaced with a perception of the same Presence as being "out there." Connection with it then was through prayer, devotion, or contemplation. For many people, within and outside the religious traditions, this is still true.

What is felt as a Presence or Ultimate Reality has been experienced across traditions, in both orthodox and unorthodox interpretations; people consistently experienced it as accessible. Below are three ways in which it is expressed in different styles.

> "Be still and know that I am God" (Psalm 46:10)

> "Closer I am than your jugular vein" (The Qurăn, trans. Arberry, 1998)

> "Simply know and accept that I AM with you, that
> I AM guiding you and that all is very, very well" (Caddy 1986)

The search for experience of Presence or Ultimate Reality continues. The next diagram is compiled from one individual's experience and shows some of the many ways in which experience of Spirit may be encountered.

You may not have experienced many of the ways of connecting with Spirit shown in this diagram. You may have experimented with other ways of connecting or established a rhythm of spiritual reflection that you hold dear and may have gone more deeply into that. However, the possible ways are vast and many writers emphasize the benefit of variety, being drawn towards a rhythm and habit that matches your needs and changing life situation.

Fig 22: A Personal Map Of Encountering Spirit

Finally, therefore, in *Encountering Direct Experience* you return to the central question: how do you find a way to encounter Spirit or something more that feels right and works for you? Loring (1997) reminds us that: "It can help us develop the habit of referring the events of our inner and outer lives to the divine." The final sequence of activities in *Encountering Direct Experience* uses the framework you met in *Heart of The Quest* and *Developing Your Skills* to introduce fresh skills appropriate to this question:

○ *Meditation and Contemplation* – an example of *Stillness and Being Centered*
○ *Journaling* – an example of *Observing and Reflecting*
○ *Using Intuition* – an example of *Opening*
○ *Going With The Flow* – an example of *Integrating*

These new skills are first practiced, then all the work you have done in *Encountering Direct Experience* is brought together in an activity that helps you consider the way you can best continue and develop your direct experience of Spirit at this time. For each activity, practice the skill over a period of time and keep a record of your experience that you can call on.

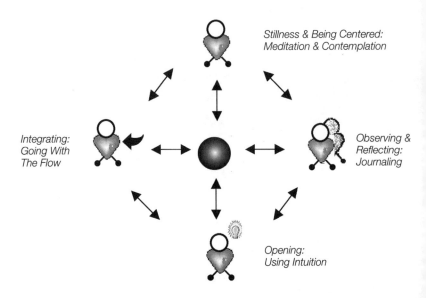

Fig 23: **The Quest** *Framework: Developing Your Skills*

Activity: **Skills of Spiritual Reflection:**
Encountering Spirit – Stillness And Being Centered

This activity introduces a new skill of spiritual reflection associated with Stillness and Being Centered

MEDITATION AND CONTEMPLATION

WHAT DOES IT MEAN?

Most faiths have a tradition of meditation or contemplation designed to reach the point of silence and stillness where awareness unfolds. We use both terms as they embrace similar practices in all traditions. All are methods to suspend preoccupation with everyday life and enter a state of heightened awareness and inner peace. Some of the many techniques are simple and some require long and rigorous training. Many people begin meditating by finding a teacher or joining a group.

STARTING OUT

Begin from the method described in Finding Inner Stillness *(page 25). Set aside 15-20 minutes in the morning or a period in the evening. Choose one of the following examples of practicing to move more deeply into a still, deep place within. Regular practice is more effective than occasional sessions.*

PRACTICING

*1. **Reflecting on a quality**, such as love or peace. Use an image to help the mind focus, or think of a person who embodies the quality such as the Buddha or Christ, or someone with spiritual significance for you. The aim is to integrate a particular quality in your own being, so that you too embody the quality.*

*2. **Repetition of a mantra** uses a sacred word that has a special resonance to help still the chatter of the mind. Common mantras repeat one of the names of God; examples might be the Muslim call to Allah or a call to Jesus Christ in the Christian tradition. A powerful Hindu mantra is "Om" or "Aum", thought to vibrate in your body to the same resonance as life itself. A Buddhist mantra is "Om Mani Padme Hum" (Oh the jewel in the lotus).*

*3. **Meditation on sacred texts**, as in the Christian practice of* lectio divina, *brings to the texts the deep consciousness cultivated in other forms of meditation. Read the text aloud and use your imagination to unlock the wisdom in the words. Unlike straightforward reading, you enter into the text, perhaps imagining yourself playing a role in the situation and deepening your understanding of the words.*

4. **Prayer** is best likened to an intimate relationship in which you open your heart to God through dialogue. There is no best way to pray and it is not limited to particular formulas you learned as a child; Dom John Chapman advised, "Pray as you can, not as you can't". Reading, meditation, or journaling may open into prayer as you move into addressing God about what is in your heart and life, your deepest longings and intention for a relationship with God.

5. **Walking** meditation is done slowly, if possible outdoors in a beautiful place, aiming to enjoy the walking, not to arrive anywhere. Walk more slowly than usual, coordinating your breathing with your steps, e.g. take three steps as you breathe in and three as you breathe out. Pay attention to the contact between your feet and the ground, stopping when you want to look at something more closely. Even when you stop, keep the rhythm of the breathing as before. Then go on walking.

6. **Alignment** brings your consciousness to a central point, such as a point between the eyebrows, known as the third eye. In eastern tradition, this is the seat of the soul, and is linked to the pituitary gland, which works with impressions from the inner self. Other traditions focus on the heart center – 'the cave of the heart' – or seat of love and wisdom linked to the thymus gland near the root of the neck.

7. **Inner listening**, placing yourself in a state of deep consciousness, with the intention of hearing the 'still, small voice' or divine voice. It is important to learn to discern the origin of the still small voice and distinguish it from the many other internal voices, e.g. the voices of our desires and beliefs.

8. **Watching the breath**, keeping your focus on the end of your nostrils or the movement of breath in and out of your lungs, counting 5 inhalations and exhalations then counting another 5, throughout your mediation time.

Stillness and being centered – whatever method you use – essentially tills the soil. It prepares and opens you to awareness of the movement of Spirit. It provides raw material, which is treasured and nourished. As you observe and reflect on the raw material it becomes the ground of your conscious spiritual life. The next activity, therefore, introduces the skill of journaling, one of the most widely used skills for working with the raw material of your life.

Activity: Skills of Spiritual Reflection:
Encountering Spirit – Observing And Reflecting

This activity introduces a new skill of spiritual reflection associated with Observing and Reflecting

JOURNALING

WHAT DOES IT MEAN?

The purpose of journaling is to suspend the rational, the linear, and the logical, and open to your unconscious and intuitive side. Journaling is far more than keeping a regular diary of events. Ira Progoff (1992), who created an intensive journal process, emphasizes that the content of your life – the things that happen – is simply the raw material through which you create the work of art that is your life. Your inner relationship to the content, how you experience it and the process that unites the content, can all be clarified through journaling.

STARTING OUT

If you are new to journaling, start in a small way, perhaps by trying to do a little writing at the end of each day.

1. Make sure that you are comfortable, calm, and relaxed. Think about the day you have just had, just noticing, without censorship or judgment, all the thoughts, emotions, and images that pass through you. Don't worry if your mind drifts off in lots of different directions. Unlike meditation, this is fine.

2. Write down some of the things that have come back to you. Write by hand, not on a computer. Don't worry about writing proper sentences. At this stage, a stream of phrases, images, or just words is fine. There does not need to be any order or reason to your recording.

3. When you've finished, don't immediately read what you've written. Leave it for a while. Try the same exercise every evening for a week.

4. After that first week, return to your writing and read it through. From the distance of a few days, you will view it with more detachment and neutrality. Let yourself feel the movement and the tempo of your life, notice tensions within yourself, themes and patterns emerging in your writing. Whatever you become aware of, notice it, without evaluation, calculation, or judgment. After a time, there may be one particular element in your writing which beckons to you, requiring further attention.

5. Write about that item now, letting the words just flow. Afterwards, read aloud to yourself, without editing, interpretation or embellishment. Read it aloud to experience what you have written in a different way. Then sit in silence for a while.

PRACTICING

1. Trust in the process. The results of journaling are cumulative, and you may find nothing much happens for while. Generally, consistency and trust in the process bring results. If you take up the practice of writing daily pages, you will find increasingly that you can lose the habit of engaging in qualifying, judging thought, and connect more with your own inner wisdom.

2. Try capturing the sensations of a particularly meaningful spiritual or emotional experience in a brief story or word picture. Focus on imagery, sensations, feelings, and qualities. Identify a symbol for this experience if you can, and write about it. Try to re-experience the moment in depth.

3. If you are feeling deep emotions — great joy, intense sorrow, huge anxiety — journaling may help you to see a broader picture, and to integrate those feelings into the larger meaning of your life.

As you observe and reflect, it is important that you do not fall back into too much analytical thought (though that has its proper place too), evaluation, or judgment. Brain research has shown that different lobes of the brain carry out different functions. The left lobe is where your rational, analytical, and sequential processes are located. The right lobe governs your more symbolic and imaginative processes. While Western educational systems have often over-emphasized the left-brain functions, more holistic approaches value both sides equally. The third new skill addresses using your intuition.

Activity: Skills of Spiritual Reflection:
Encountering Spirit – Opening

This activity introduces a new skill of spiritual reflection associated with Opening

USING INTUITION

WHAT DOES IT MEAN?

We are beginning to recognize how much of our knowing comes in ways that are unconscious and intuitive rather than at a conscious level. Taken literally the word in-tuition can be taken as tuition from a source within.

History provides some famous examples of the results of intuitive processes:

●Archimedes' cry of "Eureka" while bathing as he realized water displacement gave the possibility of measuring irregular volumes.
●Kekulé's dream of intertwined snakes providing an image of the structure of the molecule benzene.
●Einstein's claim that he thought in images and perceived the nature of light

while lying in a field watching beams of light from the sun, only later working out the mathematics which led to his famous equation.

Archimedes, Kekulé, and Einstein had been working on their respective problems for a long time but it was in moments of quiet contemplation or dreams that the solutions to their problems emerged.

What intuition feels like is personal and individual. Some people describe a gut feeling or a hunch. Others hear inner voices, get messages from dreams, notice a sense of rightness or instant knowledge. A characteristic of intuition is that it allows you to perceive the whole of a situation rather than see a part of it.

STARTING OUT

1. You probably already use your intuition to a far greater extent than you realize. For example, you may have experienced an inner knowledge that you have solved some problem, or know how to do something. You may have trusted your 'gut feeling' about something, and acted according to that feeling. The first major step in developing your intuition is to learn to trust it more. Notice the intuitive signs to which you respond e.g. an idea comes into your head in a flash, a niggling feeling, a sense or impression, an inner voice, dreams, waking up with a new knowing, apparently unrelated ideas come together in a pattern, 'rightness', a lurching movement or sensation inside.

2. To encourage your intuitive wisdom to surface from within, try working with symbolic images. While meditating, ask for an image that represents wise use of your intuition. Wait for an image or symbol to emerge, then reflect on the image or symbol, or dialogue with it.

PRACTICING

1. Relaxed attention. Intuition can rarely be hurried. You have to wait for it to take its course, but it seems to be easier for it to emerge if you are in a state of relaxed attention, open to whatever comes up, rather than prejudging ideas. Practice putting a problem or issue on the back burner, allowing insights to emerge in your consciousness in a way that your mind can hear them.

2. Recording impressions. Intuitive insights can be fleeting, so some people find it helpful to carry a small notebook in which to capture ideas as they emerge. Try keeping a record of any intuitions or hunches that you have and notice how you recognized them. You might also record any intuitive decisions you make. A few weeks later, look back to see how those judgments turned out.

3. Applying intuitive insights to your life. Learning to read your own intuitive system takes practice. Intuition may bring you the seed of a completely new idea. Remember also to engage your rational mind. "The right co-ordination of intuition and mind seems to be the best way in which the riches offered can be correctly interpreted, connected with everyday reality and communicated" (Ferrucci, 1982).

The final activity in this series of skills of spiritual reflection is *Going With The Flow.* The quotation at the beginning of this chapter (page 93) reminds us that experience of Spirit is not necessarily special and different (though it may be); what is special or different in a conscious life is your capacity to integrate your profound experiences and their learning into your daily life. In the tradition of the Tao, this is expressed as a natural part of being who you are.

Activity: Skills of Spiritual Reflection:
Encountering Spirit – Integrating

This activity introduces a new skill of spiritual reflection associated with Integrating

GOING WITH THE FLOW

WHAT DOES IT MEAN?

Many of us recognize times when everything flows harmoniously; we feel as if this is the right thing at the right time. Those times, when we lose touch with the rest of the world and are totally absorbed in what we are doing have been identified and researched as "creative flow experiences" (Csikszentmihalyi, 1990).

Such times seem to involve merging with "the flow" and may be accompanied by a sense of discovery, accomplishment, and joy. There seems to be a universal current, or Spirit, and "going with the flow" involves plugging into this so we get a clearer sense of direction and more energy in a synergistic, or creatively harmonious, way. We need to take care that we do not mislead ourselves either!

STARTING OUT

Those moments of feeling "with the flow" may seem to be intermittent, and impossible to predict and plug into. However, you can begin to become more aware of universal energy, and engage more actively with it.

1. Looking for Potential. What is "being in the flow"? Is there any yardstick to look for? One way of familiarizing yourself with finding the flow you are going with is to reflect on potential. If "flow" is a manifestation of a universal current or Spirit you might expect it to lead towards harmony and the highest good. So at any moment, stop and ask, "What is the best that can happen now and what can I do to help bring that about?"

2. Sensing the Flow. *Awareness of universal energy is creative and dynamic and we can experience ourselves as "creative participants in a universal wholeness" (Spangler, undated). Encourage your ability to sense the flow by noticing the times when you feel totally absorbed in what you are doing, highly creative and full of energy, attuned to a greater energy.*

3. Engaging and Staying in the Flow. *In* The Celestine Prophecy *(Redfield, 1993) the hero is instructed to "keep his energy high in order to engage the flow of evolution and receive the information he needs to make decisions." Keep a check on your capacity to engage in the flow by building your energy and keeping it strong, asking for answers, staying alert, noticing coincidences, and trusting the process.*

4. Merging with the Flow. *Think of a moment or experience when you have been so involved in what you were doing that you lost a sense of individual consciousness and instead had a sense of being one with some greater energy or consciousness.*

PRACTICING

1. Allow yourself to be more impulsive. If you have a sudden urge to do something, as long as it cannot harm you or others, act on it. Notice what happens to you.

2. Notice when you are feeling "out of sync" with your surroundings. Perhaps you feel flustered or pressured, quite the reverse of the way you felt when you were absorbed and plugged into the universal energy. At these times, try to let go and practice returning to that place of silence and stillness at your center. Try to notice if feeling stressed or under pressure includes resistance to what is happening.

3. Try asking yourself what is the best that can come out of any particular situation. Seek the potential, and bend your effort to what is possible.

4. Trust the process. Give up your own expectations of the outcome, and allow the process to work with you. Trust that it will turn out right, even if it is not the right that you expected.

YOUR WAY OF CONNECTING

You have covered a lot of ground in *Encountering Direct Experience*, much of it deep and searching. What, after the work you have done, is the habit, way, or rhythm of spiritual reflection that best helps you explore your sense of soul, stay in connection with Spirit, and ground your experience at present? As a way to draw together your work in *Encountering Direct Experience*, the activity below re-visits the concept of spiritual intelligence that you met in *A Growing Sense of Soul* as a way to check this out for yourself.

Activity: Your Way Of Connecting

This activity is relates to Zohar and Marshall's (2000) characteristics of spiritual intelligence (page 66).

Review your experience so far with the skills of spiritual reflection in The Quest. *Also include any previous experience of spiritual practice you have had. Then consider:*

1. How you might look more keenly for the connections between things.

2. How you might be more reflective, more self-aware, and more honest with yourself.

3. How you might enhance your willingness and will to change.

4. How you might reflect on your own center and deepest motivations.

5. How you might commit to a path whilst remaining aware that there are many paths.

●Which of the skills of spiritual reflection you have used so far are you comfortable with? Include an example from each of the types of skills of spiritual reflection: Stillness and Being Centered, Observing and Reflecting, Opening, and Integrating.
●How do they help you connect with your sense of soul and Spirit?
●How do they enable you to integrate what you are encountering?

When you have used this rhythm and plan for a month review how you are getting on.

John Habgood, a former Archbishop of York, writes of the journey of faith as:

"a liberating thing, a breaker down of barriers, a refusal to accept fragmentation as the last word, a stimulus to look beyond our own relative, partial, blinkered standpoint, an encouragement not to be frightened and overwhelmed by mysteries beyond our understanding, a promise held out to us that truth is one, and trust is great, and will prevail. (Howatch, 1999)"

PASSION AND CHANGE

*"Follow that will and that way that experience confirms
to be your own."*

(Carl Jung, 1921)

As you come to understand and trust your inner knowing, your sense of soul can be expressed more clearly in everyday life. So it's important to consider what you might find changing as you move in this direction. There are times in your life when you are acutely aware of change – things are no longer as they were. This chapter, *Passion and Change*, and the one that follows, *Dark Nights*, explore different facets of change.

Some kinds of change fill us all with excitement and joy – passion – and some seem to take us into a dark place with no obvious way out – pain. Sages tell us to approach both passion and pain as different phases of the same phenomenon; it's just that we differentiate between them on the grounds that one – passion – is generally more appealing than the other – pain. In *Passion and Change* you look at the process of change before delving more deeply into your passion and purpose. This builds up a toolkit to use in *Dark Nights* as you look at the kinds of change encountered through anger, despair, spiritual crisis, and dying. However, you should not treat passion and pain as if they are separate things; joy and grief, elation and distress, march closely together in your life and change offers a perspective on working with them.

Passion and Change, then, focuses on questions such as:

○ How can you be more at ease with change in your life?
○ Does everyone other than you know their purpose?
○ What helps you pick yourself up when you stumble?
○ How can you use what arises in your life as a springboard for growth and compassion?

THE BUSINESS OF CHANGE

Jack Kornfield (1994) sums up his approach to dealing with all sorts of changes in a way that makes a lot of sense to us. He writes:

> "the purpose [of spiritual life] is to work directly with the most primary elements of our body and our mind, to see the ways we get trapped by our fears, desires, and anger, and to learn directly our capacity for freedom ... The practice is to use all that arises within us for the growth of understanding, compassion and freedom."

At the Findhorn Foundation, a spiritual community in north-east Scotland, a long standing co-worker, Judi Buttner, says:

> "Each life experience helps me develop qualities in myself that lead me closer to a state of mind that is peaceful or still and more centered and uncluttered. This leads me towards an experience of one-ness rather than of separation from other people and my surroundings that helps me to feel connected to Spirit as the "ground of all being." With this as my base, I feel less drowned in the drama of the form and shape that events and circumstances seem to take on. The key to life experience is how I use it to learn."

These statements ask a lot of you as you go about your daily business. What is more, some life changes are big and obvious, while others, just as important, are subtle and barely noticed. You take for granted the way your cells break down and are replaced, and you hardly see how experience impacts gradually and changes you, altering how you respond to people and situations. You can, however, be sure that nothing stays the same, even when you don't notice the difference. Change is not restricted to occasional and significant events but is a daily part of living.

Activity: Change And Life

●*What is your first reaction to the statements by Jack Kornfield and Judi Buttner?*
●*What changes have taken place in your life in the last 5 years?*
●*What changes have taken place in the last few days?*
●*Do you immediately see any change that represents what Kornfield called "our capacity for freedom"? Can you see any change representing "our fears, desires, and anger"? Are there any ways in which you used "all that arises within [you] for the growth of understanding, compassion and freedom."?*
●*Have you any general thoughts about how change has affected you?*

The purpose of the questions in the activity is for you to think about how life always changes, sometimes bringing inspiration, joy, and fulfillment, sometimes leading into some of the darkest passages you have known. But, whatever the circumstances, similar stages and feelings accompany all change – disorientation, confusion, beauty, stress, despair, elation, sensitive feelings, insight, loss of security, love.

If there are such similarities between different types of changes then it may be possible to regard passion and pain as demonstrations and signals about change rather than events in themselves. In the next activity you re-visit two changes that were significant to you to see what validity this possibility has for you.

Activity: Your Response To Change

Pick out two significant changes in your life, one that was welcome and one that was not welcome. Try to recall them in as much detail as you can, then complete the chart.

	A change you welcomed	A change you did not welcome
What was the change?		
What were your feelings, both initially and as time passed?		
Could you influence anything about this change?		
What helped you manage?		
What was most difficult?		
Consider whether you learned from this change. Note it down. What helped/would have helped you move on?		

Fig 24: Your Response To Change

> *When you have completed the chart, look back at the two examples you used and ask yourself:*
>
> ● *What similarities and differences were there in your responses and feelings to the two changes?*
> ● *Can you pick out anything you notice about your attitudes to change and your way of responding to it?*
> ● *Are there other things you learned that you want to add?*

Some of us find change difficult to cope with; it readily produces feelings of fear and drowning. Other people seem to thrive on the edge of the chaos of change. Generally, your response to change is a combination of passion and pain. The important thing is to see it as just that – a response. Bringing flexibility into your response gives you a greater degree of choice over the way you perceive and face change. Nevertheless, we wouldn't want you to think it is simple or straightforward, or that the writing team have dealt with the changes in our lives easily. We haven't.

It is widely acknowledged, however, that finding meaning and purpose in change can help you perceive its opportunity for growth. So the next activity experiments with searching for meaning through story-telling, using the heroic journey as an analogy that corresponds to some broad characteristics of change, helping you re-frame it and see it in a new light.

ANALOGY OF THE HEROIC JOURNEY

"The hero's journey explains the human experience of change. First we are called to adventure either by personal choice or forced into it by an external event. When we must leave the known world we experience a sense of loss. Next is a series of struggles (and challenges) as we step into the unknown and meet our own demons and dragons; this causes anxiety and anguish even if we have chosen and willingly pursued the change. However, eventually we are rewarded; we have gained a new identity. Now we must return and share what we have learned."

Susan M Drake (1993)

In this quotation, Susan Drake picks out four of the main stages on the heroic journey: the call to adventure, leaving the known world, meeting demons and dragons, and reward and return. Joseph Campbell's work on the heroic journey included the stage of "the supreme ordeal", which is too important to leave out. Here then is a simplified version of Campbell's model, using five stages of the heroic journey and their meaning:

The call to adventure: whatever arrives from outside your ordinary known world and disturbs it, either by inspiration or catastrophe. The challenge you face is whether to follow the call or not.

Leaving the known world: the moment of commitment to follow the call represents the crossing of a threshold; after this there is no turning back until the call is resolved in some way. At the same time, your commitment opens up the possibility for all kinds of magical things to happen that could not have happened before.

Allies, demons, and dragons: these are the inner and outer allies, demons, and dragons that move you on or hold you back. They may appear as either positive or negative aspects of the situation.

The supreme ordeal: this is the point in the journey, or process of change, where you face what you fear most. It often involves some form of death and resurrection (real or symbolic) of yourself, your relationships, or your dreams.

Reward and return: you are rewarded (often in unexpected ways) for accomplishing the journey or achieving the object of your quest and return to share your experience with others.

Activity: Re-Visiting Change

The purpose of this activity is to use a well-known story, the heroic journey, to reframe a change in your life.

Choose one, or both, in turn, of the changes in your life that you used in the previous activity (or choose a completely different change in your life if you prefer). Below are the 5 stages of the heroic journey. Take each one and see if, and how, it might be applied in this change in your life.

In the change you have chosen, what represented:

- *The call to adventure?*
- *Leaving the known world?*
- *Allies, demons and dragons?*
- *The supreme ordeal?*
- *Reward and return?*

Try being the illustrator of your story and make some drawings of the 5 stages of you on your heroic journey. As you do so, consider what looks different from this perspective.

Take a break after this activity, giving yourself time to let it sink in.

Change brings opportunity. And opportunity is potential – though it may not feel much like that. There is opportunity and potential because in that moment both events and aspects of your personality are in flux; they are more fluid and flexible until boundaries and constraints move back in place.

PROMPTINGS OF PASSION

So, what might this opportunity or potential open up for you? The experience is unique for every person and yet it can be hard to tell what has really changed. Peak experiences are memorable and unforgettable, but is passion limited to such peaks? Many of the changes you undergo – particularly as you explore your sense of soul and connect more clearly with Spirit than before – will be subtle, so subtle indeed that you might not even notice they are taking place.

It is also worth remembering that there are many different gateways to Spirit. While some people are attracted to a reflective or contemplative way, others are attracted by paths that work through ecstasy and beauty or kinesthetic dimensions such as dance, music, or sport, where new levels of performance may echo peak experiences.

One example is the Way of Beauty, in which the meaning of beauty is far wider than we commonly use. The Navaho Indian people bid those they meet to "go in Beauty" when they part from them. Beauty has long been understood as an aspect of the divine, an inner quality that is ordinary, life-sustaining activities, community with others, and the natural environment. This echoes the activity in *Encountering Direct Experience* where "going with the flow" was identified with finding harmony and the highest potential. Thomas Merton, the Trappist monk, wrote: "One of the most important – and most neglected – elements in the beginnings of the interior life is the ability to respond to reality, to see the beauty in ordinary things, to come alive to the splendor that is all around us."

Activity: Appreciating Beauty

Spend a while reflecting on the way of beauty in your life.

- *What does beauty mean to you?*
- *Try to notice beauty in ordinary and extraordinary things, with the eyes of a child.*
- *Tonight, as you lie in bed, remind yourself of Merton's characterization of beauty. Recall those ordinary things in the day that had value and beauty in them in any way. Do not restrict yourself to visual beauty but draw widely on the beauty of sound, being, and relationship, everything you can recall.*

• *Over a period of time, observe to what extent practicing a Way of Beauty brings you "alive to the splendor" and prompts your passion.*

Times when you feel the promptings of passion are often times when you feel most alive physically. Your appreciation of beauty is more acute. You awake to the physicality and energy of the planet on which you live. Many wisdom traditions emphasize working with this Way of Life-Force in the earth and in the human body. For instance, in the Hindu tradition it is called *prana*, and it flows through seven *chakras* or energy centers; *prana* is said to be the source of all life and the evolution of the universe.

A residential program at the Findhorn Foundation offers an example of a Way of Community based on a conscious attempt to be guided by Spirit. The development of students' sense of soul is supported through learning to listen to their inner knowing, community service, and the rhythms of daily life. Below are some of the statements the students made about the subtle shifts they noticed in themselves whilst they were on the program:

○ I can give more of my attention to other people
○ My self-esteem and self-confidence have increased and I am more accepting of who I am
○ I am more familiar with my inner and subtle worlds
○ I feel more authentic and I am more true to myself
○ I can recognize, and work with, my intuition
○ I am able to be the observer of myself as well as the actor
○ I am able to make more conscious choices
○ I feel more fulfilled and at peace
○ I do my work with a clearer sense of purpose
○ I am more aware of my resistance to my potential
○ I am more open to the full range of my experiences

Activity: Keeping A Check On Yourself

• *As you work through* The Quest, *do you notice any changes in yourself similar to those the Foundation students noted? Are there other changes of which you are aware?*
• *Do you notice which gateways to Spirit are more available to you? Nature, gardening, quiet reflection, care for others, outdoor activity, beauty, arts, movement, construction, organizing, community work – the possibilities are many.*
• *Look back at your responses to (a) Your Edge (page 52) and/or (b) Spiritual Intelligence (page 66). Has anything changed since you did those activities?*
• *Use your journal – or whatever is your ongoing way of recording and reflecting – to carry out a review every three or four weeks and track what is happening. Notice where your passion is engaged.*

Passion can evoke strong feelings. Many people believe that living in alignment with passion – what Joseph Campbell called following your bliss – is living in harmony with the Ways of Spirit. You may feel more integrated and more aware of your sense of soul. It may be accompanied by hearing "the still small voice" by an inner prompting of inspiration, or learning to put your trust in the sense of flow practiced earlier (page 120).

But responding to passion is not necessarily straightforward. Following your promptings of passion can lead to conflict with the expectations of family and friends. While it can be hard to live with other people's disappointment it is still harder to live with your own. When you are prompted by the force of passion you have to decide whether to pay attention to this force and how you can work with it.

LIVING YOUR TRUTH

Exploring your sense of soul may deepen into a growing identity with a much bigger picture of your life. Living this kind of truth, prompted by passion, is a threshold calling you to tap into your soul's sense of your gifts and directions. The next activity uses a technique of dialogue to gain a clearer picture of this truth; it is followed by an activity that pays attention to any replies you receive.

Activity: Letter To Your Soul

In this activity, you will be writing a letter to your soul, however you understand it. Write the letter simply and honestly, as if you are writing to a most trusted and compassionate friend. There is nothing that can shock or disturb your friend. The friend is there to hear your questions, thoughts, feelings about your soul, problems, crises, joys, up and downs, hopes, and dreams.

For example, write about:

- *How you are feeling with life at present, the ups and downs …*
- *From the perspective of your soul, what is prompting your passion now is …*
- *What you see as needing to change is …*
- *The qualities that would be most helpful to you are …*
- *You would appreciate insight into what is not clear about …*
- *You recognize that you need to heal …*
- *Your insight about what the situation is teaching you is …*

Your questions might be general or you might want to make them very specific:

- *What is your truth …?*
- *How can you live more closely to your truth at this point?*

- *What are your unique gifts for?*
- *What is being asked of you?*

Before finishing your letter, it is helpful to ask very open-ended questions such as:

- *What would be appropriate next steps for you?*
- *Is there anything else you need to know now?*

Then end your letter however you wish.
When you have finished writing your letter, put your paper and pen aside. Sit comfortably and bring your attention back to your center. Take a few moments to appreciate yourself then just stay still and quiet, becoming aware of your body, the noises and life around you, your surroundings. Then open your eyes and gently move yourself so you feel grounded.

If this has been an intense activity remind yourself of today's day and date. Make a gentle transition back to daily life and ground yourself thoroughly again.

When you have finished writing your letter, you need be to open to any reply you get and give attention to the form in which it comes. You might get an immediate sense as you finish writing of a response to your questions. Over the next few days, though, while the letter is fresh in you, stay alert and listen for the replies, noticing synchronistic meetings, ideas, and whispers that you come across. These replies are important. In the last activity, you consciously opened a channel of communication with your soul, switching your attention from outer to inner listening. Now you focus on interpreting what is possibly a reply.

Activity: Skills of Spiritual Reflection:
Being Open To Replies

This activity introduces a new skill of spiritual reflection associated with Opening

LISTENING TO THE WHISPERS

WHAT DOES IT MEAN?

You may be familiar with the idea that "God speaks to me", or "my guardian angel taps me on the shoulder", or "every chance encounter has a message for me". These could be interpreted as signs, highly individual and subjective, sometimes called "whispers" or "universal feedback". Messages can come from a situation you are in, or they may come "out of the blue". For instance, a setback can be interpreted as the universe providing you with feedback or hints toward a new direction in your life. However they are received – sensed, heard, seen, or felt – their messages are often very subtle and you need to pay attention to receive them.

STARTING OUT

There is no right way to learn how to hear the whispers, as it is highly individual, but here are some suggestions:

1. You can receive whispers in many forms. You might feel a sense of revelation, insight, a feeling that a piece of jigsaw has just locked into place. You might get physical sensations, like a shiver or a tingling. Be aware of what happens and talk to someone or record it in some way.

2. Play with the possibility that mundane events, normally dismissed, may hold a real message for you. Gill Edwards (1991) says: "Everyday events constantly mirror our inner world, offer guidance and provide opportunities to develop personal qualities, skills and talents. Our everyday world is truly a magical oracle."

3. It is essential to test the validity of whispers, to question their truth. Considerable self-awareness and honesty are needed to check whether what you hear or experience is just ego, "spiritual inflation", or a way to make yourself important. Be self-critical; test the message with someone you can rely on. One yardstick is to check that a course of action will not harm or damage others and accords with your highest values. (A later activity on Discernment, page 139, may help.)

4. Give careful consideration to how you bring any suggested changes into your life.

PRACTICING

*1. **Coincidences or synchronicities.** You may experience events that seem to be complete coincidences. For example, you are thinking about someone whom you haven't seen for a long time and, within a few minutes, that person rings. A book opens to a page where a meaningful sentence catches your eye. Carl Jung (1921) named these events synchronicities, believing that synchronicity is a natural connecting principle, bringing order to the universe. Synchronicities can easily pass unnoticed, but if you are attuned to them, you may begin to trust them to occur when you need them, and then pay attention to them.*

*2. **Questing in Nature.** Some of our ancestors believed that everything in nature is sacred and aware, because the Great Spirit or Mother dwelt in everything. Shamanism, still practiced today by 200-300 million people world-wide, views nature as the manifest form of spirit. Native Americans would set out into nature on a vision quest to seek direction for their lives. They learned to hear what the wind was saying, notice which animal appeared in response to a question, hug a tree and feel its message from deep within. Today we can still listen to the messages the natural world seems to suggest and try to be in harmony with them.*

*3. **Dreams**. This is a huge subject and this summary may just direct you to a deeper study. People have long thought that dreams are messages containing wisdom from your soul. Sometimes the message is clear, transmitting a sign you cannot ignore. Other dreams are less obvious with changing episodes and vague symbols. Experiment with giving direction to your dreams: ask your dreams a question and keep the question in the front of your mind for as long as you can before sleeping. You can dialogue with the elements of your dream to interpret its meaning.*

*4. **Inner guides**. Though it is relatively uncharted territory, increasing numbers of people claim to be in touch with an inner guide. Many people connect with angels, power animals, or devic (elemental) forms. Others are communicating with friends and relatives who have died or with children before they are born. Your perception of guidance, whether it appears to come from outside or from within your own thinking, depends on your belief systems and your psychological development. It is a huge subject, too important not to include and care is needed in following it up.*

You may find it useful to re-read the letter to your soul from time to time. You can also write another at any time, changing the questions and prompts, and checking out your inner listening with someone you can confide in. As you develop inner listening and open a channel of communication with your soul, clarity and a sense of purpose grow.

A SENSE OF PURPOSE

Right now, though, you may be thinking that you lack clarity about your purpose; you thought that's what *The Quest* might help you find. But the kind of indications or whispers you have been alert to since the previous two activities may be helping to awaken you more fully to a sense of purpose.

Wondering what you're doing here, and whether there is really any purpose to life, is quite normal; many of us spend much of life exploring the issue. Often your idea of purpose centers on making a difference although that does not have to mean being famous or saintly. Your purpose may be right here and now, bringing your deepening sense of who you are into your life exactly as it is. It may also take a lifetime's struggle to achieve this, with setbacks along the way that are hard to contemplate. Purpose, and the way it manifests Spirit, is very much about the values and principles you bring to how you live your life. If your purpose is worthy, and you uphold your values and principles, you will be living your truth. Remember that you probably can't do it all today or this week either, and the rest of the world may even resist your ideals and vision!

What does it mean to experience and live your purpose? David Spangler (2004) writes:

"I know from my own experience that when I am doing what I most love to do in a way that uses my capacities fully and allows me to feel effective, capable, and contributing, then I feel as if I am one with everything. I feel in the flow, in the groove; I feel connected to all that is, part of all that is, giving and receiving to and from all that is. I am in a state of joy."

Although you may have an idea of your sense of purpose, putting it into words can still be difficult. The next activity offers one way to help you clarify a personal purpose statement. The point of such a statement lies in consciously harnessing your life-force to the way you can best express your unique skills and gifts. In this activity don't feel you must stick rigidly to the outline suggested if it doesn't suit you; just use it as a springboard to find your own way of expressing (whether in words or pictures) what you believe your purpose to be.

What is a purpose statement? It could be a statement about what you think you're doing here, and where you hope to move on to in the future. It could be about staying where you are but – from your inner perspective – doing it differently. Everybody's purpose statement is different. Don't forget that what you write now isn't carved in stone. Your understanding and interpretation of your purpose is likely to change as your circumstances change, and your knowledge grows; growth and development require change.

Activity: Your Purpose Statement

The intention of the activity is to give you your own reference point. It is a shorthand way of affirming many things you have worked on up until now in The Quest.

1. Recap on what you've identified as being important to you. Make a list of the values that matter most to you. (You might refer back to your responses to the activities on values in **Telling Your Story** *page 47.) Pick out one or two that stand out for you most now and note them down.*

2. Take a moment to imagine the world as you would like it to be. Imagine your ideal world in as much detail as you wish. What would it be like? Find three words or short sentences to describe it and note them down.

3. Mull over the things you have noted down and consider their significance to you.

4. Now read the following sentence and complete it so that it rings true for you: The essence of my purpose in life is to express and apply my (fill in one or two words from your list of values in no. 1) in order to create a world which is ... and where ... (fill in with the words or short sentences from your second list).

5. Do you see opportunities to be/do this now? How could you bring more of the essence or intention of the purpose statement into your current life? Over what period of time might it come about?

But purpose, however small or large, needs to be brought into being. Otherwise it stays as a nice idea that never quite made it. In the light of the last activity, you may find it useful to reflect on this quotation ascribed to Goethe:

"Until one is committed there is hesitancy, the chance to draw back, always ineffectiveness. Concerning all acts of initiation (and creation) ... the moment one definitely commits, then providence comes too. All sorts of things occur to help one that would never otherwise have occurred. Whatever you can do or dream you can, begin it. Boldness has genius, power and magic in it. Begin it now."

Your act of initiation may be big or small. The important thing is to do it.

Activity: Beginning It Now

This activity introduces a process of intention, setback and insight that you can apply to many other situations.

●*Intention*: Look back at your purpose statement. Based on your notes from the last activity, identify a step that you can accomplish within the next 7 days that confirms, or moves you in the direction of, putting your purpose into practice.
●*Setback*: As you read your statement, jot down the first thing that could happen or that you might do that will get in the way of accomplishing your intention.
●*Insight*: Reflect on the setback(s) and find an insight − an action, thought, or positive step that is realistic and that you will take to overcome the setback you identified.
●*Keep your intention, setback, and insight together to support you over the coming days and weeks.*

Sometimes, though, with the best of intentions and however hard you try, you falter or feel you are going off-track. On every journey, even if it's just a walk from home round the corner, you can stumble, drop something, or stub a toe. Your life journey is no different as you falter over unexpected crises and obstacles on the way.

Mistakes are one part of this learning process. And some mistakes are less simple than they seem. The following description of faltering rooted in unconscious resistance to the demands of your next step is popularly attributed to Nelson Mandela, in his inaugural speech as President of South Africa in 1994:

> "Our deepest fear is not that we are inadequate. Our deepest fear is that we are powerful beyond measure. It is our light, not our darkness, that most frightens us. We ask ourselves, who am I to be brilliant, gorgeous, talented and fabulous? Actually, who are you not to be?"
>
> **(Nelson Mandela, quoting Marianne Williamson, 1992)**

Then again, you may stumble because you over-estimate the progress you have made. St John of the Cross in *The Dark Night of the Soul* calls you to test yourself against the temptations of spiritual inflation – times when you imagine that a little progress on your spiritual journey has taken you farther than it has.

Susan Drake described such faltering as part of the heroic journey (page 126). She drew attention to "a series of struggles (and challenges) as you step into the unknown and meet your own demons and dragons; this causes anxiety and anguish even if we have chosen and willingly pursued the change." She continued: "eventually we are rewarded ... now we must return and share what we have learned." This is the juncture at which *The Quest*, following Joseph Campbell, adds a stage of asking for help and finding allies. Whenever you encounter a hiccup or an obstacle, it's likely that you will turn to a trusted source for assistance and support.

ASKING FOR HELP, FINDING ALLIES

The great spiritual traditions teach that help is always there. However strong you are you need, or probably welcome, support. There are a variety of places where you can find it, both inwardly, as in the activity of writing to your soul, and externally, through spiritual companionship. You may already be following *The Quest* with one or more friends and find companionship a joy and a help. Rufus Jones (1937, in Vining 1981) wrote: "I pin my hopes to quiet processes and small circles, in which vital and transforming events take place." Alternatively, you may find that from time to time you are able to talk about your journey with someone else. You will find some resources for help and support on the Resources page in *The Quest* (page 237) and on our website (www.thequest.org.uk).

Ultimately, though, you will find the support you require from your sense of soul, and beyond that through your connection with Spirit, as you develop your inner wisdom and trust it more and more. You can consciously expand and encourage your natural knowledge and understanding so that your capacity to tap into your sense of soul is strengthened. In the activity *Letter to*

Your Soul (page 130) you practiced calling upon this wisdom. The next activity strengthens this capacity through a visualization addressing it as a Wise Being; the activity uses the visualization as an example of a further skill of spiritual reflection.

Activity: Skills of Spiritual Reflection:
Your Wise Being

This activity introduces a new skill of spiritual reflection associated with Stillness and Being Centered

VISUALIZATION

WHAT DOES IT MEAN?

Visualization combines stillness and being centered with imagination. Your mind has a natural facility for working with symbols and metaphors; even if you do not normally see in pictures you may be able to sense sound, color, smell, bodily or a felt-presence. Symbols and images are the language of the imaginative mind and allow you to explore and appreciate personal experience. Visualization makes sense of it through access to the unconscious.

Visualization can be used as a tool to guide many different aspects of life. If you are troubled, requiring support, needing to be refreshed, needing reassurance or confidence, visualization may help you to tune in to or be receptive both to images that can guide you, and also to new symbols created in your imagination. All visualizations have common features, but they are extremely personal and individual. You are very unlikely to experience exactly the same images as somebody else, although the language you use to describe them may be similar.

STARTING OUT

This is a specific example of using visualization to connect with your Wise Being.

Read through this visualization, pausing as you go through it. Alternatively, you can record it or ask some one else to read it to you as a guided visualization; if you are in a group, partner each other to take it in turns to guide and to reflect. Have paper and a pen handy during the activity.

Spend a few minutes relaxing and feeling centered, then bring your attention inwards.

Imagine it is a warm summer morning and you are in a green valley full of flowers.

You can see a mountain in the near distance and you start to walk toward it. Between you and the mountain is a forest through which you must pass. It is fresh in the shadow of the trees and you feel cleansed.

As the path begins to emerge from the forest, it starts to climb the mountain.

The path becomes steeper and steeper and you need all your effort to climb up. You might need to reach out and hold on to the smooth granite boulders.

As you climb higher you enter a cloud of mist but you can feel the rocks beneath your hands and you keep on going.

You come out of the cloud and see the sky again as you breathe in the fresh pure air.

You are nearly at the summit and the climb is easy now. As you reach the top look around, all the world is beneath you.

You become aware of a presence there with you, the warm, humorous presence of somebody who loves you very much and who will always be there for you. Look into the eyes of this person. Feel his/her wisdom and love.

You can ask any questions you wish or say anything you want. Listen carefully for the answers.

Once you have completed your conversation, thank your Wise Being for what you have learned. Return by the path you came along until you find yourself back in the green valley.

Take some moments to become aware again of your body, and gently become aware of the noises around you and your surroundings before opening your eyes.

Note down, if you wish, any answers or insights from the visualization before you move on to doing anything else.

(*Adapted from Diana Whitmore (1990)*, The Joy of Learning)

PRACTICING

There are many different ways of using visualization techniques, although all use the imagination, with imagery and symbols. Audio tapes that lead you through guided imagery can be helpful. Some variations, which you might like to try at different times, are as follows:

1. **Energy of the chakras**. *This visualization works with the colors associated with each of the seven chakras or energy centers in the body. Concentrate attention on each of the chakras in turn, imagining its color spreading out through the body, and bringing warmth, energy, and well-being.*

Start with the color red for the chakra at the base of the spine. Go on to orange for the chakra in line with your navel, and yellow for the chakra at the base of the ribs. Next is green for the chakra at your heart, then blue for the chakra at the base of your neck. The chakra at the brow, located midway between, and slightly above, your eyebrows, is associated with the color purple, and finally, for the chakra at the crown or top of the head, imagine silver-white.

2. **Visualization for specific purposes**, *either using a guided visualization or experiment with being receptive to whatever your imagination produces. For example, you can renew energy levels, seek help in making decisions, get guidance in relationship matters, or look for aid in starting or continuing a particular project.*

3. Visualization techniques for health and healing used successfully in cases of ill health in recent years. Cancer patients in particular may benefit from imagery that helps facilitate healing. Healers of all kinds, from many different traditions, have always used imagery to aid the natural healing process.

In many of these kinds of activities you are declaring your intention to receive a reply, a message, an insight that will guide your actions and behavior. However, you need to use discrimination to decide whether you are receiving a true message or just hearing what you want to hear. Already in *Passion and Change* you have been discriminating where whispers come from and used good sense about the messages you receive. A further skill, therefore, to add to your skills of spiritual reflection is discernment.

Activity: **Skills of Spiritual Reflection:**
Discernment

This activity introduces a new skill of spiritual reflection associated with Integrating

DISCERNMENT

WHAT DOES IT MEAN?

An assumption of a faith based on experience is that you can listen and receive whispers and guidance from Spirit. Your responses to the activities in The Quest *are individual and highly subjective. However, once they are received you must discern their source.*

Even if they are authentically from Spirit, you must reflect on their meaning. Paradoxically, while finding your truth is important, you must also test your experience to ensure it is not a convenient distortion that serves or reinforces your habits or patterns. Discernment probes the messages, discriminating between what you are hoping, or would like, to hear and the message itself.

STARTING OUT

Discernment seeks truth and requires a questioning attitude:

1. If someone else was describing your visions and messages to you, how might they appear from a different point of view?

2. Are your personal interests, feelings, etc, engaged in any message? Check how clear you are of attachment. Do you feel a "charge" around it? Is it serving your personal agenda?

3. Take responsibility for your message. Does it come from Spirit, your subconscious, or elsewhere? Take responsibility for your interpretation of the message; even if it is from Spirit, it has come through you and you should assume it is subject to the unintended distortion of your unconscious.

4. Test your meditation, whispers, or intuition; mull it over, check it out with a friend who will not just collude with your particular perspective.

PRACTICING
1. Probing questions to ask in any situation, new thought, reading, and so on

- *What is really happening here?*
- *What new light, insight, or understanding does it give me?*
- *What are the implications or possible effects?*
- *What are the possible problems and pitfalls?*
- *How can I use or adapt it for the good of all?*

2. Exploring personal issues

- *What is the real issue of growth here?*
- *What lessons have I learned here?*
- *What is the purpose for me in doing ... ?*
- *If I act on this, is it congruent with my highest values?*

3. Strategic questioning

Explore an issue by asking questions that dig deeper into the reasons behind the matter, and help to open up the options available. Open questions should be used here, as well as "What if ... ?" and "How about ... " questions.

- *Which issues has this experience brought up?*
- *What impact might this have in the future?*
- *What would be the effect on those around you?*
- *Can you imagine any other options?*

4. Children's questions

Notice the kind of questions that children ask. Exploring a sense of soul is partly about retaining that sense of mystery and wonder that some children have. The questions they ask are often directly associated with that profound mystery which is life. You may find that they take you deeper into the wonder.

5. Test your insight, inspiration or whispers with one, or a few, trusted people, asking their help to churn, or thrash this around, and test your inner knowing. (Refer back to the activity The Way Of Knowing Through Intuition *part (b) page 103.)*

WHAT HAS CHANGED?

At the beginning of this chapter you set out to consolidate your ease and skills in handling change, reflect on your purpose, and find ways to support yourself in the face of faltering and setbacks. The underlying premise, however, of perceiving change in this way is that you can use what arises in life as a springboard for growth and compassion; if you can find this in the changes prompted by passion then you can turn with more heart to the *Dark Nights*. The closing activity of *Passion and Change*, therefore, reviews your relationship with change at this point.

Activity: What Has Changed?

Sit down and breathe evenly before beginning this exercise. Try to clear your mind of thoughts. Then picture yourself as you started this chapter **Passion and Change**.

●*Recall how you felt inside: your strong feelings about particular issues, your general emotional state, etc.*
●*Remember how you re-visioned a change in your life as a heroic journey. What did that mean to you?*
●*Review how you looked at passion and purpose in your life and consider if you have shifted at all.*
●*Have the activities suggested any other strategies that might help you face change in your life in the future?*

Now take a piece of paper and either (a) draw and color any images, shapes, or colors that tap into your current relationship with change or (b) draw a shape on the paper that represents the limits of your ease with change. Put inside the shape all those aspects of change with which you feel comfortable. Put outside the shape aspects of change, past or possible, which would be difficult to flow with.

   Consider how you can use what you have learned about yourself and what you can use to help you extend your comfort zone with change.

DARK NIGHTS

"Pain is but the breaking of our shell of understanding."
Khalil Gibran, 1926

In *Passion and Change* you focused primarily on changes characterized by passion and purpose. But not all change can be surfed on waves of inspiration! There will be times when your sense of soul dries up, when you lose direction and times when you seem to be in an abyss of crisis and despair. Such discomfort and distress are as much part of life as joy and inspiration.

St John of the Cross wrote a timeless guide, the title of which gave a name to these experiences – *The Dark Night of the Soul*. One example of the dark night of the soul is a depth of distress that cannot be accommodated within your current understanding of Spirit, when your sense of soul can hardly come to terms with profound anguish, hardship, or injustice. It can also describe a spiritual desert, when your spiritual life is dry and arid with no sign of life or abundance.

However, the dark nights also contain light; behind the clouds stars still shine. Whether you experience the abyss or the desert, it is a time to hang on, trusting that the inevitability of change will bring relief, new meaning, and insights as it unfolds. Your willingness to embrace pain facilitates transformation.

In the dark nights you may experience a kind of death as your identity or assumptions about life no longer suffice. A space opens between what has been and what will take its place. This space can seem chaotic but contemporary theories of chaos recognize the potential for transformation in it. William Bridges' advice, in his book *Transitions* (1980), is to resist the desire to escape as soon as possible but stay in transition and chaos as old forms die and new ones emerge. The Psalms in the Old Testament of the Bible are eloquent testimony to the discovery of hope and wisdom in chaos whilst the Hindu Upanishads point to the movement that can be released by transition:

"From delusion lead me to Truth.

From darkness lead me to Light.
From death lead me to Immortality."

The Brihad-aranyaka Upanishad (Mascaro, 1965)

In *Dark Nights* you continue using change as a lens for reflection, but turn to your own dark nights and what you push away out of sight. Throughout this chapter, the activities encourage you to keep some key questions in your awareness:

○ How can I balance dark with light?
○ What kinds of crisis might I encounter?
○ What helps me move on?
○ Does focusing on the change help me deal with pain?

BALANCING DARK AND LIGHT

Some changes are forced upon you and you have to make the best of the situation you are in. Nevertheless, we suggested that help – the light – is present even in the midst of difficulty – the dark. When you see only the dark you are limited to things that hinder you; when you keep this in balance with the light you are reminded of things that help, such as relationships, friendship, security, and feeling held by your sense of soul. In the next activity you choose a time in your life to re-visit the dark and look for the light that was also present.

Activity: Seeing The Dark And The Light

Recall a change, or a series of changes, in your life that you found hard to cope with at the time and that you feel able to look at again now. It may be helpful to look back at your notes from the activity Your Response To Change, *page 125.*

● *Make a note of the things that represented the dark.*
● *What caused your distress?*
● *What was most difficult to cope with at the time?*
● *Don't be surprised if you find old feelings surfacing again. Allow them to remind you how difficult this time was and see yourself with compassion. After a while you will know when you can move on to do the rest of the activity.*

Next look at where in the same situation, you found light; resources of help, support, acceptance, new strengths, whatever they may have been.
   Now take a closer look at both the dark and the light.

● *How far did the light support you through the darkness you experienced?*

●*Did those sources of help lead you to any long-term growth or insight?*
●*Were there any sources of light you might find in other dark nights of your soul?*

Without underestimating the length and depth of your struggle, it is possible to find the most amazing sources of help in the darkest moments. You may even come to a point where you can appreciate a particular situation because of what you gained or learned from it.

CRISIS

SPIRITUAL CRISIS

Any crisis challenges your accustomed perceptions and ways of being. While each crisis has particular characteristics, symptoms, and determinants, they all affect your spiritual life. It may immediately strengthen your sense of soul but it is equally likely to shake it up before you reach a new resolution or clarity.

In the view of Caroline Myss (1996), a medical intuitive who shows links between emotional and spiritual stresses and specific illnesses,

"the <u>symptomology</u> of a spiritual crisis is almost identical to that of a psychological crisis. In fact, since a spiritual crisis naturally involves the psyche, a beginning mystic may be unaware that the crisis is spiritual in nature and may describe his or her dilemma as psychological.

The symptoms of a spiritual crisis are distinct, however, and threefold. The crisis usually begins with an awareness of an absence of meaning and purpose ... secondly ... strange new fears ... make a person feel as if he or she is losing touch with a sense of self or identity. "I am no longer sure of who I am and of what I want out of life" ... the third symptom is the need to experience devotion to something greater than oneself.

The many psychological texts available today that describe human needs rarely mention our fundamental need for devotion, yet we all biologically and energetically need to be in contact with a source of power that transcends human limitations and turmoil. We need to be in touch with a source of miracles and hope.

The crisis usually begins with an awareness of an absence of meaning and purpose that cannot be remedied merely by shuffling the external components of one's life. One feels a much deeper longing, one that cannot be satisfied by the prospect of a raise or promotion, marriage or new relationship. Ordinary solutions hold no attraction. Those who are in a spiritual crisis ... have a feeling that something is trying to wake up inside them. They just don't know how to see it ... The absence of meaning, the loss of self-identity, and the need for devotion are the three strongest symptoms indicating a person has entered into the dark night."

Interestingly, Myss adds: "The inadequacy of the external components of the person's life is a consequence of the spiritual crisis, not the cause."

Crisis can assault you in many different ways. Experiencing fear, panic, confusion, a curious elation, as if you are working on automatic, are common reactions to crisis. Often crisis forces you to confront significant challenges. It is widely accepted that the positive potential of crisis is that it brings you face-to-face with things you prefer not to look at. At some point you have to walk through the fire. Crisis can also be an opportunity for spiritual growth. So it becomes especially useful to find ways of working *with* – rather than *against* – crisis so that your spiritual and psychological emergence is supported rather than ignored or repressed until it becomes an emergency. A growing number of psychiatrists and psychotherapists work with the spiritual dimensions of crisis; they can be found by asking around, or by looking for those trained in transpersonal psychologies such as psychosynthesis or professionals belonging to the Spiritual Emergence Network founded in 1978 by Christina Grof.

THE SPIRITUAL DESERT

As you explore your spiritual path, you may well encounter a dark night, a period when you seem to lose connection with your sense of soul, when you doubt your faith and experience, and your inner life is dry. This can be hard to endure. It may be precipitated by an existential crisis, a traumatic event, or simply a diminishing return during your time of spiritual reflection and practice. The dark night of the soul in a spiritual desert is well documented in the lives of saints and sages in religious traditions. It may be full of profound apprehension at separation from your sense of soul and Spirit; in spiritual literature it is seen as a time of purification. The very aridity of your practice and seeming futility of living by spiritual values jolts you out of familiar and complacent rhythms. Any change in life – loss of job, ageing, aimlessness – may force a shift in your identity and you are vulnerable to doubt and uncertainty.

However, you can use this as a time to re-visit your earlier beliefs and ways of experiencing Spirit as you search for fresh understanding. It can be used as an opportunity for sitting in the desert, accepting it as your present place, seeking new ways and ideas, and using all your inner and outer power of discernment to deepen those things that speak to you and laying down those that don't.

Activity: Sitting In The Desert

Use these times of crisis to experiment and draw more widely on different traditions and ideas, seeking out some that are new to you and some you already know. Below are some suggestions to help you.

● *Turn to the list of references to skills of spiritual reflection in* The Quest *(page*

259) and practice some that are less familiar.

●*Look in your library, read magazines, articles and book reviews, listen to the radio, watch the television, search the Internet always alert to the whispers – what spiritual writing, practices, or teachers attract or draw you right now?*

●*Trust, being willing to just sit and acknowledge the desert, asking for help in whatever ways come naturally to you.*

●*Write another letter to your wise being, describing how you are feeling and your current situation.*

●*Question, gently, what is happening: what feelings, questions, and concerns are coming up, what is resonating, what is challenging you, what are your thoughts and intuitive hunches, what do you notice and what is the learning?*

●*As you practice just sitting, with unconditional holding, become aware of what ripples through you or attracts your attention.*

●*Seek out spiritual friends and companions, those who can listen and support you to allow this period to pass, whether that takes a month or a year.*

EXISTENTIAL CRISES

Many challenges cause you to deeply question the point and nature of human life. They are crises of meaning and times when you are vulnerable to repeating patterns of defensive or negative attitudes, feelings, and behavior. Crises of meaning are also openings to opportunity as they cause you to question the very basis of your existence. As we wrote *The Quest*, we noticed that our encounters with such crises initially pulled us into chaos and confusion. Through experience we learned not to panic but to pause, reflect inwardly, trust that a step forward would emerge and that, ultimately, we would find a way through to a new resolution.

You will know from your own experience and reading that there are certain key and significant life issues. We don't get through life without meeting them along the way. These life issues recur in myths, poems, stories, films, and other media. Have you ever watched a film, read a story, myth, or poem, and felt that it exactly mirrored your situation?

Activity: Crises Of Meaning

Turn back to the Activity Telling Your Story on page 39.

Pick out some of the major crises of meaning or turning points you have faced. Don't just pick out the big events, rely on your "whole-feeling-sense" about your life to pick out things that may appear minor but which you know represented really significant turning points for you.

You may identify these challenges as times when you felt confused, that something was changing but you couldn't put your finger on exactly what. You may have been aware of reacting strongly, feeling disoriented, unsure how to proceed.

Alternatively, the crisis of meaning or turning point may have been very evident, such as loss of someone you loved, major decisions about a job or place to live.

Choose one or more of these crises of meaning to apply to the exercises and questioning strategies that follow.

Victor Frankl was a psychiatrist whose book *Man's Search for Meaning* (1959) was based on his experiences in a concentration camp in World War II. Frankl developed his experience into a theory of "logotherapy" asserting: "Man's search for meaning is the primary motivation in his life." He speaks of existential frustration as both the struggle to find meaning in personal existence and what that meaning is. He says: "To be sure, man's search for meaning may arouse inner tension rather than equilibrium. However, precisely such tension is an indispensable prerequisite of mental health."

In such moments of crisis, there is tension between opening up and closing down. In the context of your personal development, you have a choice between staying where you are and repeating the patterns, feelings, reactions, and behavior of the past or choosing to work through the origins and defenses of your patterns, learning to respond differently and move on. In the context of your spiritual development, you may use the opportunity to experiment; to see these episodes as the "breaking of the shell of our understanding" (Gibran, 1926) and being alert for emerging new understanding.

When we began to gather ideas for *The Quest* we spent a weekend telling our stories, collecting all this material together and sifting it to see what common themes and signposts emerged. We found we had experienced many common crises of meaning and all of them were rooted in key life issues:

○ Questioning your identity, purpose, and meaning
○ Facing fear, abandonment, pain, and despair
○ Living with choices and change, uncertainty and doubt
○ Facing illness, ageing, and death
○ Dealing with resistance and letting go
○ Experiencing love and feeling connected
○ Managing your power, authority, influence, self-discipline, and autonomy, and that of others
○ Needs and desires for material things
○ Living through chaos and crisis
○ Your experience and understanding of Spirit.

Sometimes we could see which crisis of meaning we faced, other times it was less obvious. We reviewed this in the light of our experience and found that each kind of crisis was associated with certain questions. If we observed the questions we were asking we were better able to identify the nature of our crisis.

Activity: **Identifying The Crisis**

Look at the mind-map What's Happening to Me? *(page 149). Each heading names one of 10 common existential crises. Beneath the heading are questions frequently associated with this type of crisis.*

Using one of the turning points or crises you chose in the previous activity, read the questions under each heading on the mind-map and pick out any that are relevant to you. You might find that questions from more than one heading apply.

•*Look at the headings associated with the questions that "spoke to your condition". How far, if at all, do the headings correspond to the crisis you faced? Was it clear to you what kind of crisis you faced at the time?*
•*Does it shed any light on the situation to see it as an example of a common existential crisis now?*
•*Is there a different way that would help you to identify the kind of crisis of meaning that you faced?*

Repeat this exercise for any turning points or crises in your life for which it may be useful.

Of course, identifying and naming the nature of the challenge may help but it doesn't necessarily enable you to engage with your challenge or the struggle to move through it. In the next topic, you will find some tools to help you address these challenges.

ANGER, DESPAIR, JEALOUSY, AND REVENGE

There's a place that opens only to tears.

Danah Zohar, 1990

When you face a crisis over a major life issue, you may experience a depth and extent of feeling, such as anger, despair, jealousy, and revenge, which you have never met before. You may feel betrayed and your sense of self and confidence are shredded. Such feelings bring up complex issues and reactions and it is hard work to reach a point where you are able to recognize them, let them go, and move on. Sometimes you find you cannot resolve your feelings and then it is wise to seek face-to-face support from a trained person.

Almost certainly such feelings stir deep-seated ideas and assumptions about how things are, or should be, in your life. Ram Dass, a contemporary writer of Jewish origin who studied and taught clinical psychology before working with a Hindu teacher, talks about the ego as "our software for functioning on this planet. It is who we think we are." He then writes about

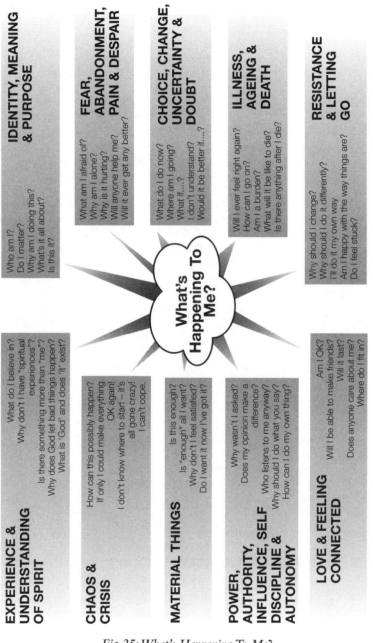

IDENTITY, MEANING & PURPOSE

Who am I?
Do I matter?
Why am I doing this?
What's it all about?
Is this it?

FEAR, ABANDONMENT, PAIN & DESPAIR

What am I afraid of?
Why am I alone?
Why is it hurting?
Will anyone help me?
Will it ever get any better?

CHOICE, CHANGE, UNCERTAINTY & DOUBT

What do I do now?
Where am I going?
What if....?
I don't understand?
Would it be better if....?

ILLNESS, AGEING & DEATH

Will I ever feel right again?
How can I go on?
Am I a burden?
What will it be like to die?
Is there anything after I die?

RESISTANCE & LETTING GO

Why should I change?
Why should I do it differently?
I'll do it my own way
Am I happy with the way things are?
Do I feel stuck?

EXPERIENCE & UNDERSTANDING OF SPIRIT

What do I believe in?
Why don't I have "spiritual experiences"?
Is there something more than "me"?
Why does God let bad things happen?
What is 'God' and does 'it' exist?

CHAOS & CRISIS

How can this possibly happen?
If only I could make everything OK again!
I don't know where to start – it's all gone crazy!
I can't cope.

MATERIAL THINGS

Is this enough?
Is "enough" all I want?
Why don't I feel satisfied?
Do I want it now I've got it?

POWER, AUTHORITY, INFLUENCE, SELF DISCIPLINE & AUTONOMY

Why wasn't I asked?
Does my opinion make a difference?
Who listens to me anyway?
Why should I do what you say?
How can I do my own thing?

LOVE & FEELING CONNECTED

Am I OK?
Will I be able to make friends?
Will it last?
Does anyone care about me?
Where do I fit in?

What's Happening To Me?

Fig 25: What's Happening To Me?

his ongoing experience of his own anger:

> "Most of our spiritual work has to do with extricating ourselves from
> ego and moving to Soul – going from an identification with our
> thoughts ... to the cultivation of the witness ... Yet the ego level is
> always at work. Take anger, for instance. I still get angry ... Anger
> comes from holding a model of how you think the world ought to be
> but isn't." (Ram Dass, in Shapiro and Shapiro, 1999)

You also need to be able to distinguish this kind of unproductive anger from
that which is the righteous anger needed to change the ills and injustices of the
world.

Facing unproductive anger or your despair, desire for jealousy, revenge, and
similar feelings is hard. In the immediate moment, being aware that this is how
you feel may be as much as you can do. Certainly don't underestimate how
important it can be to say to yourself "I feel angry/afraid/jealous/frustrated ...
now" and how it can lead you to view things differently. Sometimes you may
be tempted to try to dispel the emotions very quickly; you may be frightened
by, or ashamed of, your emotions. As Bridges (*op cit*) reminds us, such
transitions are fruitful times. You can learn much while you are in the chaotic,
uncomfortable place on the edge of, or far beyond, your comfort zone. He
advises that you stay with the churning discomfort long enough to discover its
message.

But, in the moment, any other feelings and thoughts are crowded out.
Profound emotional responses to a crisis can't be worked out swiftly by means
of reason and logic. Other areas of the brain have to come into play, and they
may not be immediately accessible. "Reason and logic are fine but you need
another tool here to open up the area of the mind which deals not in words
but symbols and images," says a character in Susan Howatch's novel *The High
Flyer* (1999). In working with these feelings, working from a perspective
focusing on change, there is a knack of waiting, noticing the moment when a
small space opens up and you are not completely taken over by the feeling
itself. When you can feel a small – however small – drop in the temperature of
your feelings, you may be able to look into it. If this is difficult you might first
try to release some of the tension that is created by externalizing it.

RELEASING FEELINGS SAFELY

The principle of the next activity is that your feelings can be released, at least
to some extent, by externalizing them, getting them outside instead of staying
inside where they occupy a lot of your energy and attention. It is also an
opportunity to take a closer look at your strong feelings, becoming more aware
of their nature and content. Many strong emotions express hurt, protect your

boundaries, and defend what you value; they serve a destructive function only when they are driven by fear.

Read through the next activity before doing it. If you feel that it is not an appropriate activity for you, try one of the alternative suggestions at the end of the activity.

Activity: Externalizing Feelings

Find a time and place where you can be undisturbed and no one will overhear you. Make a safe space for yourself. If you have a friend or someone you can really trust and <u>who is not involved with your feeling in any way</u>, consider asking them to support and help you. You will need one or two cushions (pillows will do too).

1. Recall a situation, past or present, which aroused strong emotions in you. Take a cushion and put it in front of you. Imagine that on the cushion is the person or thing that is triggering your emotions.

2. Now take the opportunity to tell this person or situation or thing exactly how it is, or was, for you in that situation. Don't try to monitor your language, but allow yourself to clear out feelings that you are holding. Tears may come. If you feel you need to express your feelings physically try pummeling another cushion.

3. If you have a supporter with you, they can help by encouraging you to express yourself fully. Just make sure, however, that you address everything only at the cushion.

4. Notice in yourself when the moment comes to a halt, when the energy has been expressed and comes to a natural end.

5. Take some time quietly to sit and feel more centered back in yourself. You may talk it over with your friend or write, draw, move, or dance to feel that you have completed what you needed to express. Just be careful that you do not re-engage with the feelings again.

<u>Alternatively</u>, you may externalize your feelings by writing, drawing, modeling, or painting everything you are feeling. If it is to be helpful for you, try to get out exactly what you feel, i.e. if you write, write exactly what you feel, and use language as you feel it. Don't imagine that you must censor it first. Do not send the writing (or whatever) to anybody else, especially a person with whom you are angry. Instead, make yourself a little ritual to tear up and destroy the letter at a time that is appropriate for you.

> *Or, go to a place where you can be private — in your car parked somewhere quiet, a beach, a time when your house or flat is empty and you are unlikely to be overheard by neighbors — and shout, scream, or rage until you have expressed what is inside you.*

In releasing emotions by externalizing them, also remember that all your emotions are registered and stored in the physical body. Body-work and grounding exercises can release blocks to your energy flow. There are many techniques for releasing tension and distress through emotional and psychotherapeutic body-work. You can ask around, search the Internet for practitioners or consult a local library to find out about different kinds of body-work therapists and which one may suit you and your situation.

There are many alternative strategies for working on your feelings. Next, you experiment with a very different method based on an exercise from Thich Nhat Hanh, one of the foremost contemporary teachers on peace. Thich Nhat Hanh is a Vietnamese Zen Buddhist who headed the Vietnamese Buddhist Peace Delegation to the talks that ended the war in Vietnam and he has been nominated for a Nobel Peace Prize. His work encompasses all the dimensions of peace, from the intensely personal to world peace.

Activity: Walking Meditation When Angry

Follow the instructions below. If walking is not active enough to channel and dispel your anger, precede the exercise with running meditation, running outdoors, aware of the fresh air until you naturally slow then continue with the breathing and words at a walking pace.

"When anger arises, we may wish to go outside to practice walking meditation. The fresh air, the green trees, and the plants will help us greatly. We can practice like this:

> *Breathing in, I know that anger is here.*
> *Breathing out, that the anger is me.*
> *Breathing in, I know the anger is unpleasant.*
> *Breathing out, I know this feeling will pass.*
> *Breathing in, I am calm.*
> *Breathing out, I am strong enough to take care of this anger."*
> (from *Peace is Every Step*, Thich Nhat Hanh, 1991)

After you have practiced the walking meditation, consider:

- *How do I know "that anger is here"?*
- *What does it mean that "the anger is me"?*

- *In what ways do I experience anger as unpleasant?*
- *What happened before in my life to reassure me that the feeling will pass?*
- *What can I do that helps me to feel calm?*
- *Where in me is my strength to take care of this anger ...... and of myself?*

This activity can be adapted for feelings other than anger.

Take care of yourself when you are doing these sorts of activities and be compassionate both for yourself and for anyone else with whom you follow *The Quest.* This poem, by Yoko Ono, epitomizes this kind of compassionate friendship – with yourself and others.

REVELATIONS

Bless you for your anger,
For it is a sign of rising energy.
Direct not to your family, waste not on your enemy.

Bless you for your sorrow,
For it is a sign of vulnerability.
Share not with your family, direct not to yourself.
Transform the energy to sympathy
And it will bring you love.
Bless you for your greed,
For it is a sign of great capacity.
Direct not to your family, direct not to the world.
Transform the energy to giving.
Give as much as you wish to take
And you will receive satisfaction.

Bless you for your jealousy,
For it is a sign of empathy.
Direct not to your family, direct not to your friends.
Transform the energy to admiration
And what you admire
Will become part of your life.
Bless you for your fear,
For it is a sign of wisdom.
Do not hold yourself in fear.
Transform the energy to flexibility
And you will be free
From what you fear.

Bless you for your search for direction,
For it is a sign of aspiration.
Transform the energy to receptivity
And the direction will come to you.

Bless you for the times you see evil.
Evil is energy mishandled and it feeds on your support.
Feed not and it will self-destruct.
Shed light and it will cease to be.
Bless you for the times you feel no love.
Open your heart to life anyway
And in time you will find
Love in you.

Bless you, bless you, bless you
Bless you for what you are.
You are a sea of goodness, a sea of love.
Count your blessings every day, for they are your protection
Which stands between you and what you wish not.
Count your curses and they will be a wall
Which stands between you and what you wish.
The world has all that you need,
And you have the power
To attract what you wish.
Wish for health, wish for joy.
Remember you are loved.
I love you!

ADAPTING TO CHANGE

In your dark nights you can draw on change as a way to approach personal issues of pain and anguish within an underlying context of spiritual development. In *Getting Started* we said that we see the *personal* and *spiritual* strands of *The Quest* as complementary. The *personal* aspect deals with the content of your personality and working on this helps you move towards independence, individuality, and autonomy. The *spiritual* aspect offers a route to meaning and purpose through a sense of being part of something greater than yourself. In *Passion and Change* you addressed passion through the perspective of change to clear the way for expressing your sense of soul. As you work with adapting to change, you face the constraints to your spiritual growth arising from the issues and challenges of personality.

When *The Quest* writers compiled the list of existential crises and associated questions above, we began to wonder what kinds of things we had done that helped us meet the challenge or take the opportunity. We found that we were often helped when someone else came along and asked "Have you thought of … ?" or "Have you looked at it this way … ?" The questions on the next mind-map *How Do I Deal With What's Happening?* (page 156) were compiled from what had been said to us, plus some questions we wished someone had asked us!

While some of us are happy to take quite an analytical approach to life, others of us are not. When we suggest questions, you should not imagine you must respond as if you are in school. What we do ourselves much of the time is read the questions, let them give us a flavor, and then touch into our "whole-felt-sense" response, and our associated feelings, intuition, physical reactions, and highest intentions as well as our thoughts.

Activity: Moving Through, Moving On

Pick one of the crises you looked at for Activity: Identifying The Crisis *(page 148), which you could identify as a particular kind of existential crisis.*

Turn to the mind-map How Do I Deal With What's Happening? *(page 156) and try out the sequences of questions. Test the questions to see if they help you (a) sense a shift in your response to the challenge, (b) see it differently.*

Try applying the questions to a current challenge.

You may notice that often you experience being pulled by your call to love, inspiration, joy, and creativity at the same time as you are held back by your repeating patterns of negativity, alienation, separation, and distress.

Love is pulling you to a greater wholeness and deeper expression of your sense of soul, while *fear* is holding you back, restricting you to patterns and responses that are within your comfort zone, even when this limits you and damages your relationships. The quality of your experience is affected by the extent to which you are pulled by love or held back by fear, even though your actual circumstances may stay the same. The grid below combines a model of love and fear with the 5 levels of self that you met in Frances Vaughan's model of wholeness (*Encountering Direct Experience* page107); the purpose of the activity is to help you become more aware of both love and fear as you work through an issue.

Activity: Continuum Of Love And Fear

Choose a challenge, current or recent, that you have found difficult, but choose one that is not so overwhelming that you cannot work on it.

Recall the different aspects of the situation and how you acted. Review the ways it engaged your capacity to love – where you felt pulled to put your highest

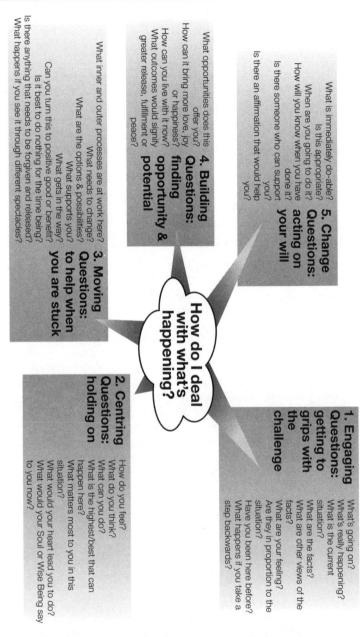

Fig 26: How Do I Deal With What's Happening?

values and ideals into practice – and your concerns for survival, mortality (yours or someone else's), and you felt held back or limited by your fears. See if you can name the root of your fear.

Next reflect on where you register love and fear whether on the physical plane or through your emotions, thoughts and ideas. Consider where you can stay open to your sense of soul and connection to Presence and where this is more difficult. Try to sort out how your love and fear are present at each level.

Write or draw on the continuum to map out where love and fear, as described above, are present. Map how you move between them as the situation unfolds.

ASPECT OF YOU	LOVE <············> FEAR
Physical	
Emotional	
Mental	
Existential	
Spiritual	

Fig 27: Working With Love And Fear

Joycelin, one of the Quest co-authors, gave an example of perceiving love and fear as forces at play:

"When my younger daughter told me she was planning a six-month trip to Africa, my first reactions were dominated by my fears. I feared she would have an accident and this was a real physical fear in my stomach. Then my emotions took over, and I cried. I couldn't stop thinking about it. I imagine that, unconsciously, it recalled all my fear-based assumptions around death and loss. After a little while, remembering some of my own experiences at her age, I realized I did not want to impose my fears on her and cause a rift between us. I felt that I wanted to help her take her next steps in life. Over the next while, I worked with my fears. I talked with her because I knew that I found my own emotions easier to deal with when I really understood why she was going and her hopes and dreams. I made a point of talking, sharing her plans with her. By the time she went off, I was sad to see her go but also proud and delighted and followed her adventures with great excitement."

Of course, all these things are going on inside, seemingly all at once. It takes time to separate them out. At the time, it seemed that the experience just happened. But it helped to take time to reflect, observe, try to unpack some of what was happening inside – look at the part played by fear and how this could, with effort, be turned into the very same actions but more loving, less fearful. As you become more skilled in identifying your fear, you notice that fear can lead you to over-react and it is an obstacle between yourself and the expression of your sense of soul. Love, on the other hand, expands.

"It can act with courage, resolve, and toughness if need be, but, as in the martial art of Aikido, it does so with an intent to redefine and re-imagine the nature of the conflict so that everyone, including the attacker, is protected while the energy of the attack is redirected into harmlessness. (Spangler, 2004)"

This may help you to pinpoint some of the ways you are thrown back into habitual ways of meeting situations. Your awareness is important because difficult emotions that are not released usually recycle and arise again in some other form. The next activity can help you appreciate the steps you take to try to live differently and act from your sense of soul, putting your highest intentions into practice.

Activity: Facing The Fear

Close your eyes and recollect a difficult issue that you have had to face. Choose the first one that comes and spend some time re-entering the situation, recalling it in as much depth and detail as you can.

- *Where were you?*
- *What were the surroundings, people, smells, colors, sounds?*
- *What was happening?*
- *What did you feel or do or think?*

Move slowly through the stages as the issue unwound and played itself out. Note where you registered the issue, in your physical body, your feelings, your thoughts, your attitudes, beliefs, and concerns about being alive, your highest intentions and values.

- *Where is/was fear present?*
- *What is the underlying fear?*
- *How did facing the fear change your perceptions of fear and of yourself?*
- *Were there aspects where love was present also?*
- *Are there any ways in which you can work on your fears so they can be faced in the future and you can move towards replacing them with loving?*

Before finishing this activity, take time to appreciate yourself for your courage in facing your fears, and your willingness to change and move towards being loving.

YOUR READINESS TO GROW

Some kinds of change appear to push you from within, as if your sense of soul is prompting your growth. You are obliged to review attitudes, habitual patterns, and aspects of personality you prefer to ignore. You face your "shadow" that, according to Robert Bly (1998), is "the long bag that we drag behind us." It includes all those parts of your personality it is hard to acknowledge, even to yourself. You repress them – sweep them under the carpet – only to find they pop out unexpectedly and distort your behavior. Have you ever been surprised at the force of anger or blame that suddenly erupts from you? Your shadow may also show up when you are overly negative about the faults in others, projecting your shadow characteristics onto them. Mahatma Gandhi said: "The only devils in the world are those running around in our hearts – and that is where the battle should be fought." Recognizing in yourself the fundamentals of destructive anger and hate that in others fuel extreme acts of violence and terror, is one of the most challenging preludes to transformation. Working with your shadow from a spiritual perspective involves recognizing it, accepting it, and trying to work to resolve and integrate it. Frederic and Mary Ann Brussat (1996) wrote: "Give up trying to hide, deny, or escape from your imperfections. Listen to what your demons have to say to you."

As you work through *Dark Nights* try to recognize your own shadow. What do you least want other people to know about you? What are the thoughts, feelings, desires, and intentions that are known only to you? Invite them into your awareness to reflect on the message they have for you: a message of something in the past that needs to be healed or released. Integrating your shadow may require healing for you as well as forgiveness and the courage to offer reconciliation with others. Above all deal kindly with yourself and others.

A Catholic priest, Richard Rohr (1999), who directs a center for contemplation and action, says:

> "God calls us to take the path of the inner truth – and that means taking responsibility for everything that's in you; for what pleases you and for what you're ashamed of … In the spiritual life, nothing goes away. There is no heavenly garbage dump. Everything belongs."

Andrew Cohen (2000) puts it differently:

> "Very few of us face anything. Without being aware of it, we are in the grip of a fear-driven habit, a habit of avoidance and denial. That habit is the movement of ego. The movement of ego is a compulsive need to remain separate at all times, in all places, through all circumstances."

Tony Parsons (2000), speaking of fear, also wrote:

> "The things I can be afraid of are endless, because if one fear is
> overcome I can put another one in its place ... If I cease to label
> suffering as "bad" and "mine" and simply allow it as energy in a certain
> form, it can then begin to have its own flavour, which can take me
> deeply into presence."

Your readiness to grow is connected with your willingness to take
responsibility for all of your life. Once you take this responsibility, no longer
blaming any one else or expecting some one else to sort things out for you,
you will begin to notice changes in your attitudes and perceptions.

Activity: Focus On Your Attitudes And Perceptions

*Can you recall any occasion when you were able to deal with a difficult situation
by changing your attitude about it or finding a way to see it differently?*

*Did you learn anything about your responses that you might use in another
situation?*

Joycelin, one of *The Quest* co-authors, says that she does not find change
easy. In a book by Ayya Kheema (1987) she found advice she has found useful
ever since. Ayya Kheema suggested that it might be impossible to change your
mind completely about something – too big a step all at once – but it is
possible to "loosen around the edges." Joycelin gradually worked out for
herself ways of "letting go" just a little bit. That gave her sufficient breathing
space to change her mind a bit more. She went on to say:

> "Changing the way we look at something is hard. I seem to need a
> way to create some space inside around my distress that allows change
> to come in. If I'm completely filled up with resistance and distress then
> I haven't got room for anything else. So I have first to find a way to
> loosen around the edges."

Activity: Coping With Change

*Have you a strategy for helping yourself cope with change or see it differently? If
so, note it down and notice how and when it is most helpful.*

LETTING GO AND DYING

Death of the body is the ultimate image of letting go, of transition and
transformation. It is a change that many of us resist, finding it difficult to

loosen around the edges of our perception of death. In the words of the venerated Indian saint Ramana Maharshi, death asks you to question "*Who* or *what* is it that dies?" However, you experience a kind of death whenever you experience change; accepting loss, dying to old ways, days past, and the self that has changed. If you can accept the "little deaths" of life with more ease – seeing the potential transformation they hold – you can begin to face other unresolved grief and denial of bodily death so you can live more fully now. Only then is death accepted as a natural part of living, with fewer regrets for the life you did not live. Elisabeth Kubler-Ross, a Swiss physician renowned for her groundbreaking work with people who are terminally ill, puts it this way: "Our only purpose in life is growth. There are no accidents" (1998).

In *Telling Your Story* you explored what might be an edge for you. Contemplating the death of someone you love, or your own death, may be an edge. The groundbreaking work of people such as Kubler-Ross and Stephen Levine has helped to change many attitudes to dying and death. Their pioneering work has shown how important it is to come to terms with the change from life to death. As long as you fear death and try to avoid looking at it, then the energy that it takes saps your capacity to appreciate the gift of life and live it fully.

Why? There are three principal answers to this question. Firstly, until you look at what dying means, you may not embark on completing unfinished business in your life; making your peace, telling your loved ones what they mean to you, forgiveness, releasing guilt and judgment on yourself. Making such completion, whether when approaching death or earlier, releases you to live more fully now. Secondly, when you fully accept the finite length of life and the unpredictability of the time of your death, you become more appreciative of the gifts of life. Thirdly, contemplation of your death may help you to consider who it is that dies. The next activity calls you to live life fully now and face the pains and joys of life as you approach death.

Phyllida Anamaire (2001), a yoga teacher with a background in theology and in humanistic psychology, trained and worked with Elisabeth Kubler-Ross before going on to run her own workshops in Europe. Her work is influenced by her personal experience of living and bringing up children in Northern Ireland; she has continued to work there with those who are terminally ill and on forgiveness and reconciliation with those traumatized by the long struggles or loss of their loved ones in the Troubles. In the passage below, she summarizes what she has learned from her experience and her work in sitting with many people as they die.

"When we fully live the *now* of our lives, dying is simply the next step. What does it mean to live life fully? To live the *abundance* of our lives, the bounty-full dance of life? For many people, it means being grateful for all that life brings, being present to pain and to joy. For others it could be defined as taking risks and challenges along the way, going beyond social conditioning and making dreams happen. Whichever way, the important thing is that there be conscious awareness of the choices we make, and that we live life from a place of self-responsibility and self-respect.

As a Bereavement Counsellor and one who watches and sits with the dying, I see frequently that one of the deepest regrets of the person dying is having not lived life as they wished. One elderly woman confided: "I wish I had married my sweetheart and not listened to my parents who did not approve of him because he was not of my beliefs." I recalled the words of the song: "The heart afraid of breaking never learns to dance" (From *The Rose* by Beth Midler).

Sometimes we have to endure the disapproval of others in order to follow our own heart's song. Sometimes, we have to risk alienation if we want to live our lives fully and with integrity. If we caretake another's feelings instead of following our own inner knowing we invariably carry resentment and remorse later on: "If it hadn't been for you, I could have had a richer life." So I am prompted to ask: "What delights your heart and feeds your soul?"

Activity: Catching Up With Your Life

- *What, for you, "delights your heart and feeds your soul"?*
- *What are the ways, now or in the past, in which you suffered the loss of your own soul?*
- *If you were told that you had one week or one year left to live, what would you do and what changes would you make?*

The next activity focuses your attention on contemplating your own death. It is doubly hard to come to terms with the death of those you love if you have not examined your feelings around your own death. However, the activity can be adapted to reflect on the death of someone else, changing it to enter into dialogue and reflection on their life rather than your own. But we recommend you use it for your own reflection first.

Activity: Your Life Review At Dying

Before beginning this activity, gather together the pens, paper, and other things you may wish to use to record your thoughts and feelings. It would also be helpful to try to set aside a time when you can be undisturbed and when you can give yourself time afterwards quietly to absorb its meaning for you.

In this activity you will be contemplating some of the circumstances surrounding your own death. You may find it easier to read the activity into a tape recorder and play it back. Alternatively you might prefer to read it through and then go into the contemplation asking yourself the questions that have most clearly remained with you.

Settle yourself comfortably and take a little time to center, letting go of whatever else you have been doing before beginning the activity. Breathe deeply and relax, bringing your attention to your inner being.

As you do so, allow an image of your own funeral to appear before you. See your family and friends, colleagues and those who have come to your funeral. See the flowers and the place where your funeral takes place. Hear the sounds, music, rites of passage said over your body, the talk among those present. When the ceremony finishes and the people present leave, you remain there. From your new perspective beyond your death, you are able to look back and revisit or reconstruct some occasions in those last weeks before your death.

There may be a few people that you gathered around you; they may still be alive or they may have died before you. You talk with each of them, explaining why you asked them to be with you. What do you say to each of them?

You are able to have a few minutes on the phone or write a short note to any other persons you chose. Who do you choose? What needs to be said? Do you receive a response from them?

You are able to reach out to those whom you have disliked or ignored or with whom you have been in conflict. As you near death, what might you say to any such person?

When you are asked if you have a final wish, what do you reply?

As you plan your funeral with those close to you, you ask a person dear to you to speak of you at your funeral. What would you like them to include in what they say about you?

Later, when you are alone, you look back over your life. What are the things of which you are especially thankful or proud? What mattered most to you? Next, turn to things you regret or wish had never happened the way they did? For what do you need to forgive yourself? Are there apologies or regrets you send to others?

One night, as you fall asleep, your guardian angel comes to sit with you. Your angel tells you how deeply they appreciate and respect you for the life you have lived. What do you imagine the angel means? What does your angel tell you they mean?

In your final hours, you have the chance to extend your life, in a state of wellness that has been normal in your life. Who would be in your life with you? How would you choose to spend your time? What would you most value and appreciate?

As you die your attention gently turns back to the self that remained after your funeral earlier in this activity, the one that stayed behind after everyone else had left. And you ask "Who am I and who is it that dies?" You listen to any reply or insight that comes.

As you prepare to leave this contemplation, pause to gather any thoughts, *feelings, insights, or understanding that will be helpful to you. Take time gently to rouse yourself, wriggle your toes, move your body, breathe in and out, and then open your eyes.*

Before moving on, ground or record this activity in whatever way you wish to bring about a feeling of completion. Then stand and shake yourself and move, make some sounds to ground yourself back into your everyday life.

You may find this activity has a powerful effect on you and its impact may make itself felt for a while. You may have dreams that are connected with the activity or find that people who figured in your contemplation come into your dreams. Be gentle with yourself as the continuing impact of the activity unfolds. The purpose of such work is to help you to release your energy more fully into life.

In *The Prophet*, Khalil Gibran (1926) wrote:

"You would know the secret of death.
But how shall you find it unless you seek it in the heart of life?
The owl whose night-bound eyes are blind unto the day cannot unveil the mystery of light.
If you would indeed behold the spirit of death, open your heart wide unto the body of life.
For life and death are one, even as the river and the sea are one."

TAKING STOCK AGAIN

While life and death are one, don't forget that life doesn't work in straight lines! You may work in circles and spirals, repeating processes, issues, and cycles over and over again. Hopefully, though, at each turn you can use something that you have learned from before, gradually gaining insight. Sometimes you can see a specific place or way in which you have changed and grown; but it keeps on happening as change is a lengthy – if not life-long – process.

As you reach the end of this chapter, we imagine that working on change has taken you to your edges many times. So the final activity helps you take stock, considering whether you feel as though you have made any progress in your personal and spiritual dimensions during the time you've been working on change in both *Passion and Change* and *Dark Nights*.

Activity: Your Relationship With Change

Spend time doing this activity; it is a detailed review that works at a number of levels. At this important point of your journey with The Quest, *you revisit the skills of spiritual reflection, your relationship with change and the changes that are taking place. You may feel your sense of soul shifting.*

It may be helpful to look through the notes, journal, or record you have made from the activities in this chapter. (You can also reflect more comprehensively on your work since you began The Quest if you wish.)

As you work through the activity, pause and take a break between the different sections, to allow new images, insights or reflections to emerge.

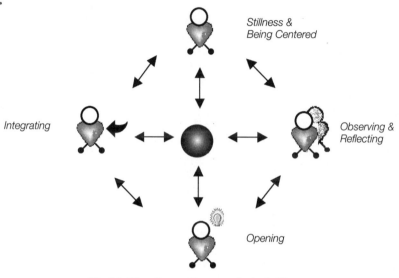

Fig 28: **The Quest** *Framework And Change*

Stillness And Being Centered
Settle yourself down and feel centered and balanced. Take time to bring your attention fully into this moment. Notice how it feels to you now to be quietly present to yourself, your situation and your surroundings.

Observing and Reflecting
Pause for a few moments to recall your journey through **Passion and Change** *and* **Dark Nights.** *Remember where you started from, and consider where you are now.*

- *What memories stand out for you?*
- *What prompted your passion?*
- *What was most challenging?*

Opening
Recall what has moved, touched and inspired you as you worked through these

last two chapters.

- *What has had meaning and value for you?*
- *What makes your heart sing or sink?*
- *Were there any times when you found the stars still shining behind the clouds of your dark night?*
- *What do you see as 'peak experiences' or key insights at this point?*
- *What prompted these peak experiences or key insights?*

Integrating
What have you been able to bring more fully into your life?

Aspects of Change:
- *Where/how are you noticing change in yourself?*
- *Where have you been most resistant?*
- *Where have you found that you accepted change with ease or realised that a change was not needed?*
- *How do you see your relationship with change at the moment?*

Your Sense of Soul
What may be shifting? Where is your sense of "your essence, a core within that holds your wholeness and potential, perhaps infused with connection to a Presence or Ultimate Reality understood as the ground or fabric of existence, or something that feels radically alive"?

- *What words, images or symbols best represent your sense of soul now?*
- *What has remained unchanged and true for you?*
- *Do you have any new or different understanding and experience now of your connection with the sacred?*
- *What practices of spiritual reflection are most helpful to you?*
- *What most re-affirms your sense of soul?*

This activity reviews your work with change in **Passion and Change** *and* **Dark Nights**, *but it can equally well be used for a general-purpose review at any time by substituting appropriate words for the titles of these two chapters.*

WHOLENESS AND CONNECTION

"I take the spiritual life to be a life which aims to discover human wholeness, the integration of all aspects of our humanity – body, soul, mind, emotions and the connection of the self to all of creation."

(Paul Lacey, 1999)

At the beginning in *Getting Started* we said that *The Quest* uses the phrase "your sense of soul" to mean "your essence, an inner core that holds your potential and wholeness and is a vital, living source; for some, it is also infused with connection to a Presence or Ultimate Reality, the ground or fabric of existence that feels 'radically alive'." So far much of your exploration has been inward, rather than outward, looking; you have addressed body, soul, mind and emotions in various ways, although, of course, this task is never complete.

In *Wholeness and Connection*, therefore, you consider wholeness and connection looking outward, your place amidst "all of creation" through questions such as:

○ What is wholeness?
○ How can I understand and experience connection?
○ Are there ideas and concepts that explain reality from a whole and connected perspective?

LOOKING AT WHOLENESS AND CONNECTION

One way to approach wholeness is through its absence. John O'Donohue, in *Anam Cara* (1997), tells a story of some African people helping an explorer through a journey in the jungle. They hurried along together for about three days but then the Africans refused to go any further. They explained that they had traveled too fast and needed to wait a while and give their spirit time to catch up with their body. They are describing a state of disconnection in which they temporarily feel less than whole.

You may recall times when you have felt fragmented, vaguely disconnected, and less than whole, without necessarily knowing why. You may feel you too have been rushing through something that felt like a jungle. Feeling that you need to let some part of yourself catch up may indicate a loss of integrity – in the sense of wholeness – and a desire to bring all aspects back into one whole.

Activity: Exploring Wholeness And Connection

●*Can you recall times when you needed to stop and let all the different parts of yourself catch up or something like this?*
●*What does 'wholeness' mean to you?*
●*Can you recall a time, or times, when you have felt whole in this way?*
●*Is there any connection between wholeness and your sense of soul?*
●*What might help you experience yourself as whole and part of a larger whole?*

Many of the activities in *The Quest*, particularly the skills of *Stillness and Being Centered*, help you find and build up a sense of wholeness (for references see page 260). The next activity, however, provides a focused opportunity to experience yourself as whole and reflect on the association between wholeness and connection, both individually and in relationship with your environment, whether that is a bubble a few feet around you or encompasses the whole Earth.

The activity is informed by a technique called bio-spiritual focusing (Gendlin, 1981 and Campbell and McMahon, 1985). Gendlin and McMahon had been students of Carl Rogers, the father of humanistic psychology. They became intrigued by Rogers' notion of wholeness, in which a therapist tries to be with their client in an open manner, and by being present to their own feelings and attitudes enables their client to see themselves as whole too.

Activity: A "Felt-Sense" Of Wholeness And Connection

Read the activity then do it without referring back to these instructions as you do so.

Settle yourself in a chair and relax, breathing into your body and taking time to let yourself let go of all that has been occupying you. Take your attention gently inside.

When you feel ready, ask yourself, how you are in relation to wholeness and connection. Then wait for a 'felt sense' to arise – a whole body sensation that takes stock of how you are now. You may register this 'felt sense' in your abdomen, chest, throat or it may be more vague, elusive, and subtle. It represents something that you cannot yet put into words.

Notice where you feel disparate or scattered. Ask this 'felt sense' how you might best move from whatever feelings represent lack of wholeness to you into a caring, peaceful presence of wholeness and inner connectedness. Wait in an open, gentle way for any shift or settling that happens or any image or insight that comes.

Allow a peaceful presence of wholeness and connectedness to come alive in you. Let it first fill you and then the space around you as if it is creating a bubble. Hold your hands open on your lap as if you are sitting with this bubble.

On this occasion, or a later one when you feel ready, imagine reaching out beyond this bubble to connect with the wholeness in the world around you. Take time to experiment with noticing your wholeness in the context of the wholeness around you.

When you are ready, gently bring your awareness back to where you are sitting and feel grounded and balanced.

This exercise can be repeated whenever you wish to re-connect the scattered parts of yourself, let your spirit catch up with you, remind yourself of your wholeness and the connection that is wholeness between yourself and the wider whole.

In the last activity you explored wholeness and connection in a structured and deliberate way. You may experience also similar feelings of wholeness and connection when you are engaged in contemplation or taking time to be present in the moment or when you are in the midst of actively doing some task. Whether you are busy *doing* something or not, you may come to recognize characteristic features of your experience of wholeness and connection.

Activity: Recognizing Wholeness And Connection

●*How do you experience times of wholeness and connection?*
●*Are they similar to, or different from, the times you noted in the activity:* Exploring Wholeness And Connection?
●*What characteristics might help you recognize such times in future?*

CONNECTION TO A GREATER WHOLE

One characteristic that many people associate with wholeness and connection is awareness that they are not an isolated body but part of a greater whole. Deepak Chopra (2000) describes connection with a greater whole as follows:

"Everything that we experience as material reality is born in an invisible realm beyond time and space, a time revealed by science to consist of energy and information. This invisible source of all that exists is not an empty void but the womb of creation itself. Something creates and organizes this energy. It turns the chaos of quantum soup into stars, galaxies, rain forests, human beings, and our own thoughts, emotions, memories and desires ... we will see that it is not only possible to know this source of existence on an abstract level but to become intimate and at one with it."

It can be difficult to be clear on your connection with a greater whole and find a comfortable language to talk about it; so many images and assumptions, negative and positive, are associated with the names that identify particular representations of a greater whole. In the next activity you are asked to reflect afresh on your connection and the images and assumptions you make.

Activity: **Your Connection With A Greater Whole**

Consider whether you feel there is "a greater whole" and what that might be for you, using the following lists of names to reflect on this:

- *There are names traditionally used in the major faith communities for Spirit, such as God, Tao, Great Spirit, Brahman ... ?*
- *There are contemporary names such as Gaia, Mother Earth, the Goddess, God/Goddess, the Divine ... ?*
- *There are more abstract names based on qualities or principles such as Love, Energy, Light, Wisdom, ... ?*
- *Perhaps it's more like a larger version of "an essence, an inner core that holds our potential and wholeness and is a vital, living source" or an image of Wholeness or One-ness or a Void or the Beloved?*
- *You may be aware of it simply as "the Unknown" or Mystery*
- *You may experience connection with a greater whole but one that has no abstract or tangible existence; simply relationship or being part of the Earth, planet, or reality.*

1. What is your experience of connection with something beyond yourself and how can you describe it?

2. If the words are difficult – and it is hard for many people – in what other way can you describe or identify connection?

INNER AND OUTER

As you explore wholeness and connection you may encounter an existing assumption that separation, between you and others and between you and your environment, is the norm. A fundamental plank in this wall of separation is the unconscious assumption of personal separation in which your inner world and outer behavior are divorced from each other. The prevailing paradigm still favors the image of the body as a biological machine. This is consonant with a belief that you can behave in ways that ignore or over-ride your inner feelings and thoughts or that you can divorce what happens from how you feel and think about it.

This is increasingly understood to be false. External stresses, such as heavy work commitments, family distress, poor housing, and environmental pollution, can be a cause of mental and emotional breakdown; the outer affecting the inner. Inner attitudes and beliefs also affect outer physical well-being; scientists such as Candace Pert and research in fields such as psychoneuroimmunology demonstrate there is a connection between body biochemistry, endocrinal and nervous systems and well-being.

David Peters (2004), Professor of Integrated Healthcare, Westminster University and chair of the British Holistic Medical Association, explains:

"Rather than reducing the body to its component parts (organs, cells, tissues, nuclei, genes), we can see the body in context with its biosphere, culture, community, family. We can see the whole living person. The human body/mind is potentially self-regulating. Instead of diagnosing disease x, and prescribing pill y, we need to understand our lived experience of the body and how it affects thoughts, feelings, and impulses. We also need to understand our inter-relatedness to one another and to Gaia. The new science of consciousness recognises that brain states and body states correlate with thought, feelings, and intuitions. Sensation, language, emotions, and behaviour affect physiology. Being loved makes a difference to mortality. Individual states and traits impact on health outcomes. We can use the mind to heal the body."

He also cites evidence that bears this out at the cellular level.

You may also recognize how your inner attitudes, thoughts and feeling can affect the circumstances of your outer life. As one Quest writer put it:

"There are days when I get out of bed feeling grumpy, and don't want to have anything to do with anyone. So, of course, my family is upset, and things happen all day that add to my bad mood. The way I feel shows up in what I do, and the world seems to react back. Conversely, if I'm happy, the world seems to be happy too. I don't suppose anything is different really; it's just my way of seeing it."

Activity: Connecting Inner And Outer

Recall a recent stressful, tense situation at work, within your family, etc.
•How did this outer situation affect your inner world in terms of emotions,

attitudes, and thoughts?

●*Think of the opposite case. Has there been an experience you can recall when you being grumpy, fed-up and critical on the inner affected the outer situation?*

●*Now recall yourself in another situation at work, within your family, etc., when you were feeling happy and content on the inner.*

●*How did your happy inner world affect the outer in terms of your relationships at work, in the family, etc.?*

●*Finally, has there been a parallel situation when a happy external situation affected or changed how you felt inside?*

You will need these notes for the next activity.

In the next activity, you translate your notes from the previous activity onto a grid and add any other examples you can think of.

Activity: Mapping Inner And Outer

The grid opposite helps you to distinguish between inner and outer in yourself and your life situation and mark the flows between them.

First, look through your notes from the previous activity and think about the connections between what goes on at your inner and outer level.

Now, enter one example from the previous activity in a relevant row on the grid. Put an arrow in the middle column to indicate which way round the connection works, i.e. if inner affects outer use the —-> arrow and vice versa. Use the columns headed inner and outer to add any notes or insights you wish.

Add more examples to include both outer affecting inner and inner affecting outer. It might be hard to distinguish the direction that the impact flows in some examples because inner affects outer which then impacts again on the inner and so on.

You can investigate this further by asking someone you trust to tell you if they notice you being affected by what is going on around you (outer affects inner) or if your mood affects what happens around you (inner impacts on outer).

Before leaving this activity, look again at the examples in your grid and think about how far the situations you noted were your personal inner and outer world and how far they were influenced by your culture, community, work environment and other external factors. Jot down anything you notice.

Keep this activity, as you will use it again later.

When you focus on your individual experience, inner world, and feelings, it can be easy to forget that you usually spend most of your time in a state of your own individual awareness, relating to everything that is outside you from your own sense of self. You unconsciously assume that you are seeing the world as it really is, overlooking the fact that you may be seeing this outer world as a reflection of the current state of your inner reality. On the other hand, the

	Inner	or	Outer
At work			
Family			
Relationships			
Leisure			
Other			

Fig 29: Mapping Inner And Outer

view that the world outside is the real and objective truth and your inner world is a subjective illusion is similarly limited. These assumptions are so ingrained in the old Western paradigm that you may forget they can be just a view, not absolute truths, and that they can be challenged by both ecological evidence and models and non-dualism in the mystical streams in religions.

In order to probe this further you need to put yourself inside an alternative world-view that helps you question whether or not "you" and "it" are as separate as you assume. The next section uses a variety of ways of understanding wholeness and connection, and then outlines the integral theories of Ken Wilber and Spiral Dynamics before exploring how a holistic paradigm may cast light on your perception of spirituality.

EXPERIMENTING WITH CONNECTION

"We cannot separate the healing of the individual from the healing of
the planet. They are one and the same, because the consciousness of
each individual is connected to the collective consciousness. Although
we are individuals, we are also part of the whole."

Shakti Gawain, 2000

Your total connectedness to the world and its total connectedness to you can
be difficult to grasp. Read the examples below of various ways in which
people have tried to explain it so you get a variety of pictures of connection.

(i) Make 5 holes in a sheet of paper. Place the fingers and the thumb of one
hand through them. Rotate your wrist until your palm faces upward and the
paper is between your eyes and your palm. Your fingers now appear to be five
separate chunks of flesh. There is no apparent connection between them, *except
your knowing that this appearance of separateness is an illusion.* When you turn your
hand over the connections – that they are all part of one – are obvious.
(Barrett, 1995)

(ii) Jung once remarked that when humans could first see the Earth from
outer space, the experience would be a seismic moment in our perception of
reality. Until 1961 no humans had been above 60,000 feet into the atmosphere
and space was a mystery. By 1968, Apollo 8 was sending back now-famous
photographs of the earth from space. Edgar Mitchell, one of the astronauts,
later spoke about the overwhelming experience of looking out of the
spacecraft's window at the panorama of stars, moon, sun, and the Earth:

"I had an epiphany, triggered by the realization that the molecules of
my body and the molecules of that spacecraft were manufactured in an
ancient generation of stars. But instead of that being an intellectual
experience – something I had known since my teen days – what was
so powerful and unexpected, was the personal feeling of
connectedness, the notion that the universe was somehow connected,
harmonious and intelligent – accompanied by an exhilaration, a feeling
of wow! … later, in my research around the world with all the various
cultural traditions, I found the esoteric experience, the deep, inner
experience, to be identical in every culture. What is different is the
attempt to explain it." (Mitchell, 2000)

(iii) At a microscopic and planetary level we all breathe the same air. Weather
patterns move the air that we breathe around the globe so each of the breaths
that sustain your life contains atoms of air that have been breathed by each and

every other person on Earth. This mechanism and exchange is extraordinarily fine-tuned in your body and throughout the biosphere, with plants and trees breathing in our used carbon dioxide and breathing it out through their leaves as life-supporting oxygen. Suzuki (1997) quotes Harvard astronomer Howard Shapley: "All people over the age of twenty have taken at least 100 million breaths and have inhaled argon atoms that were emitted in the first breath of every child born in the world a year before!"

(iv) Roberto Assagioli (Parfitt, 1997) put it like this:

> "We are in continuous contact with each other, not only socially and on the physical plane, but also through the inter-penetrating currents of our thoughts and emotions … A sense of responsibility, understanding, compassion, love and harmlessness are all links in the chain of right relationships which must be forged within our own hearts."

(v) Dr. Cornelia Featherstone (2004) argues that we yearn for the healing connection of community and describes the Findhorn Foundation community, of which she is a member, as an example of a full-spectrum model embracing spiritual practice, health and medical care, care in the community, food production, ecology, economy, work, leisure, governance, education, youth, and unity.

(vi) Angela Locke, an author and poet living in rural Cumbria, writes poetically of the landscape in the UK and Nepal, making a link between humanity and the Earth through our ability to be aware of the Earth.

SACRED EARTH

The humanity of Earth
is a woven part
of our consciousness,
and of her Nature.
Without us, we would not 'know'
That Earth is,
And Earth could not know
Herself.

She sees herself in our eyes
As beautiful.
We stand on the sea shore
And watch the waves
And know we are alive,
And Earth through us

Knows her aliveness.
We know the morning birdsong
And the secret night,
And we give Earth back
Her treasures.
So life dreams itself and
We dream Earth
In this unimaginable
Universe,
Where infinity waits
For us to find ourselves.

Angela Locke, From *Sacred Earth*, Pleiades Press, UK, 2001

Activity: What Wholeness And Connection Mean To You

Each of the descriptions is a different way of representing the deep wholeness and unbreakable connections that are flows and links across humanity, the natural world, and planet.

(a) Draw a map or diagram, or write a description or poem that begins to create a picture of what wholeness and connection mean to you.

(b) Add to the drawing or description any pictures, reminders, or mementoes that recall any experiences of your felt sense of wholeness and connection.

FOOD FOR THOUGHT

Think how much food figures in your daily life! Eating is a moment of connection and exchange as you take in food produced on the land and in the sea. You not only eat regularly, but buy food, prepare it, perhaps grow it. Some of your food will come from other parts of the world and you may use recipes from other countries. Eating is often a social event shared with other people. You may have to pay attention to your eating habits because of a health issue, or cultural or religious rules may affect what, how, or when you eat. You may follow debates about connections between human health, the health of the land, farming methods, and animal welfare issues.

Food is also an important part of world patterns of trade, commerce, use of natural resources, cultural diversity, and so on. Each action you take, however small it may seem in the larger picture − such as taking a product off a supermarket shelf − is an essential ingredient in change. Supermarket cash tills are linked to huge on-line databases that calculate ordering and stocking of food in warehouses; every purchase you make affects their moving picture of consumer preferences. It has a small but profound effect on the global economy, sending a tiny but discernible economic ripple around the globe. This ripple, multiplied by billions of consumers worldwide creates new market opportunities for producers. It also creates competition between them, which may bring about changes in employment patterns.

Food-related connections are extensive and complex. But the diagram below illustrates a simple set of the kind of connections you may think about first.

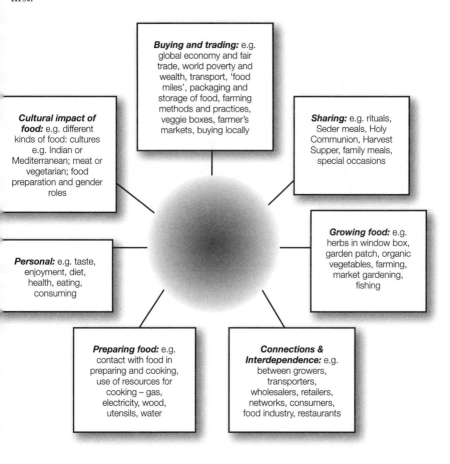

Fig 30: Food For Thought

Activity: **Your Food Connections**

The diagram below reproduces the boxes from the diagram above. Look at it then allow a day or two to pass while you notice the role food plays in your life, including examples not included in this diagram. Then make your own version of the food diagram – you might start with a large version the outline below or yours might look very different.

When you have finished your diagram, reflect on food as a sacred aspect of your life. Consider how you remember and give appreciation of this when you eat.

Are there ways in which food points the way toward wholeness and connection for you?

Keep your diagram handy as you may come across more things to add to it.

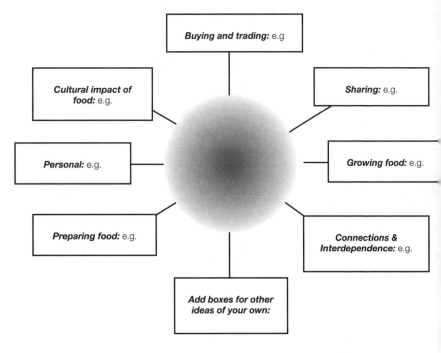

Fig 31: Your Own Food Map

This activity focused on food. You could equally well apply the activity to mapping connections in other areas of your life such as work, family and relationships, money, and community.

MAPS OF CONNECTION

As humanity faces critical problems of violence, poverty, and environmental degradation, many commentators draw our attention to the need to re-shape our perspective of reality, away from one of isolation and separation to a more spiritually alive relationship based on connection and wholeness. Such awareness radically re-shapes how we address the economic, environmental, and social challenges we face, enabling us to see connecting patterns in every area of our lives:

○ Environment, ecology, and care of the planet
○ Community and interpersonal relationships
○ Health and well-being
○ Work, livelihood, money, and economics
○ Creative arts, leisure, sport, passions, and interests
○ Personal and collective spiritual practice
○ Planetary awareness and service.

Ken Wilber (2001), a prolific contemporary writer, has taken wholeness and connection to a detailed and deeper level, developing analyses of a new integral theory. Wilber connects the personal inner and outer with the collective inner and outer in a map that explores links and flows. Wilber maps what he calls the "Kosmos", a word he borrows from the Greeks to mean "the patterned Whole of existence, including the physical, emotional, mental and spiritual realms ... not just matter, lifeless and insentient, but the living Totality of matter, body, mind, soul and spirit."

	Inner	*Outer*
Myself	My inner self. How I see myself. How I think and feel. My values, beliefs, motives, insight, intuition. *(Box 1)*	My outer self. How the world and other people see me. My physical body. What I actually do. How I affect the world. *(Box 2)*
Collective	The culture of the society I live in. Religious and political beliefs and values. Norms, attitudes, etc. that are taken for granted. *(Box 3)*	The environment. Families and relationships. The economic system. The government. Industry and agriculture. World politics and trade. *(Box 4)*

Fig 32: Wilber's 4-Quadrant Map

A simple way to use Wilber's quadrant is to map and conceptualize connection and see wholeness in a new way. This can be built up from the grid you compiled in the activity *Mapping Inner And Outer* (page 172), extending it to link individual and collective and inner and outer. In the next activity you use Wilber's quadrant to explore your intra-personal connections and your connections with the whole that Wilber calls "collective".

Activity: The Four Quadrants In Yourself

Go back to the Activity: Mapping Inner And Outer, *your grid and the notes you made. At the end of the activity we asked you to begin to think about which connections were your personal inner and outer and which were the inner and outer of your environment or the collective.*

Draw a blank quadrant, labeling the rows and columns like the one below.

Work round the boxes in the quadrant by putting one simple thing about yourself in each one. The example below illustrates how you might start with your appearance.

	Inner	**Outer**
Myself	Describe the image you have of yourself and how you feel about your appearance	Describe your appearance or put in a recent photograph of yourself
Collective	What kind of appearance is thought desirable for someone of your age and sex in your society? How are you aware of these images and norms?	Think about and note down how and where you buy things related to your appearance, clothes, facial and body products, exercise, diet etc.

Fig 33: The Four Quadrants In You

Then go round again, adding, describing, or drawing as much as you can, using the example you started with or broadening out to map connections more generally about your life: your inner (Box 1) and outer (Box 2), the family, community, society in which you live and its culture, norms, and values (Box 3) and the social, economic, work, and political ways in which it is structured and organized (Box 4). Begin with descriptions then look for connections and notice where there are flows, links, and impacts between boxes. As you add information the map becomes more complex and powerful.

Wilber says that all four components, or boxes, on the map are active in every experience at any moment. In other words you live in a highly connected and multidimensional Kosmos in which all elements in the quadrant arise together if your interpretation of reality is to be whole. Moreover, Spirit is embedded at the heart and center of the quadrant; in the context of your sense of soul this comes closer to the understanding of wholeness you have been exploring.

The point where the four quadrants meet represents the source or origin of all development

Fig 34: Adding Spirit To Wilber's Map

Wilber identifies Spirit as a primal ground of reality and everything you do as an expression of that Spirit. He also links a gradually broadening sense of self to successively higher levels of human development; these can be superimposed as concentric circles radiating out from the center of the quadrant, with each circle indicating a higher-level expression of Spirit and its attendant individual, cultural, and structural expressions.

Activity: Adding Spirit To Your Quadrant Map

Look back at the quadrant map you made in the previous activity and add Spirit at the center and origin.

• *Remember that all four elements of the quadrant arise together, giving you an example from your life that describes you and your connection to wholeness, all seen as an expression of Spirit.*
• *Imagine Spirit constantly radiating out from the center, whether you are aware of it or not. What intention or impulse might have been trying to express through you?*
• *How might it have been more clearly expressed?*

If Spirit is expressing through you and you are intimately connected to everything, consider if, and how, Spirit might manifest in other ways and other levels.

• *Does this idea make sense to you at all?*
• *Look at the quadrant again and ask yourself whether, how far, and in what ways this possibility fits your world-view.*

Wilber (2001) acknowledges, "we don't just need a map, we need ways to change the mapmaker." Since 2002 his work has been associated with Spiral Dynamics, which offers just such a model. Spiral Dynamics (Beck and Cowan, 1995; Beck 2002) adds an explanatory model of why people, in the same situation, see things differently. Significantly, it adds a theory of transformation by describing how individuals develop and cultures evolve.

Spiral Dynamics grew from work by Clare Graves, whose extensive research data demonstrated coherent swathes of thinking, values, and attitudes within groups of people in society. Spiral Dynamics proposes that these groups can be classed by levels of consciousness, identified as a wave or flow, from older, lower-order values and behaviors to more integral and enlightened ones. Each level has its own aspect and expression of Spirit and is associated with characteristic values and life goals. It incorporates an adaptive intelligence that helps people choose what matters in life. Human beings have a "prime directive" toward more choice, purpose, and greater complexity. At each level, individuals reach a crucial life situation, a point where they are challenged, stuck, or trapped and which offers an opportunity for transformational breakthrough to a higher level. The application of Spiral Dynamics is to craft natural habitats that support people's passage – individually and collectively – through successive waves or levels. Spiral Dynamics has been used in practical situations in various countries, including South Africa when it was in transition from apartheid. Combined with Wilber's quadrant it creates a complex four-quadrant, multi-level model that seeks to explain both connection and transformation.

Wholeness and connection, however, have been known to humanity for many ages and experienced as real. The peoples whose culture and traditions have remained least affected by contemporary changes have long been aware of this preciousness of life and celebrated its richness and importance. More recently, creation-centered spirituality, through thinkers such as Matthew Fox (2000), has developed a spirituality that celebrates wholeness and connection in beauty and abundance, honoring earth and wildness. The next activity invites you to remember this ancient Way of wholeness and connection, adapting rituals that honor the Earth.

Activity: **Honoring The Earth**

Before doing this activity find out which directions to face for North, South, East, and West from where you are.

Put yourself in a centered and reflective state while in a standing position. Stand with your feet about shoulder width apart, your weight balanced evenly between both feet. Have your knees slightly bent, so they are soft rather than locked. Allow your arms and hands to hang loosely at your side.

Feeling the ground beneath your feet, imagine the Earth beneath your feet. Pause to appreciate the Earth, its beauty and abundance. Remember, too, the vastness of the water: rivers, lakes, and seas and the creatures that live in them and give thanks for nourishing rain.

Looking upward, remind yourself of the air around and sky above. Pause for a few moments and wonder at the vastness of the sky, and the dependence on air of life on earth. In the sky, whether clear or in cloud, is the sun, the symbol of Fire, the warmth and power that rises.

Then turn to face the East, the direction from which new light arises each day. Pause to acknowledge what we take for granted, such as the daily rising of the sun, bringing light and the dawn of each new day of living.

Turn to face the South. Appreciate warmth that nourishes seeds of trees and plants, and the seeds of all creativity.

Turn to face the West, remembering the decay of autumn and times when we are often alone with ourselves. Acknowledge the potential for transformation that is everywhere and in everything.

Turn to face the North, and consider winter. Give thanks for the telling of stories in the long evenings and the wisdom that is contained in them.

Stand still, center again in your body, and place your attention in your heart center. Pause to open yourself to your true nature and to the true nature of all whom you encounter this day.

Pause for a few moments to allow the activity to settle within you, then open your eyes and move your body until you feel grounded, present, and ready to move on.

[If you are doing this activity in the Southern hemisphere, you might find it more natural to swap the focus for North and South.]

HOLISM

You have now considered wholeness and connection through both inner and outer experiential methods and more theoretical perspectives. However, your underlying purpose throughout *The Quest* is exploring your sense of soul, which has been explored through wholeness and connection in this chapter. Wilber (*op cit*) argues that

> "we need an integral vision and we need an integral practice. The integral vision helps provide us with insight and thus helps us overcome dissonance and face toward our own deeper and wider opening. And integral practice anchors all of those factors in a concrete manner, so that they do not remain merely abstract ideas and vague notions."

The kind of integral vision and integral practice that anchors a sense of soul needs to be practical and flexible, and, while rigorous, arguably less complex than the Wilber/Spiral Dynamics models. Your emphasis in *The Quest* has been on personal experience, congruent with collective wisdom and flexible in the light of new understanding. *Wholeness and Connection* turns, therefore, to a perception of spirituality that might offer a crucible for the integral vision and integral practice Wilber identifies.

Surveys indicate that in the USA in 1965 a holistic perspective was embraced by some 5 million people. As the new century approached, the number had grown to 50 million (Ray and Anderson, 2000). Other estimates suggest that, when combined with other outward-looking faith groups, the number of "holists" in the USA alone is nearer 158 million (Forman, 2004). Television programs featuring contemporary spirituality regularly attract US audiences in the region of 90+ million viewers (Zolar Entertainment, 2004). Survey evidence suggests similar trends in the UK (BBC poll).

Holism encompasses many contemporary strands and there are numerous organizations and networks seeking ways to express this kind of open spirituality. Forman's (*op cit*) enquiry summarizes the constituent elements as

> "a vaguely panentheistic[1] ultimate reality ... this is indwelling, sometimes bodily, as the deepest self ... is accessed through self transformation and group process ... and not-strictly-rational means ... [this spirituality] becomes the holistic organization for all of life."

The ideas of holism that Bloom (2004) proposes suggest that attributes of a holistic perspective include, for example:

---

[1] **Panentheistic:** a belief that God interpenetrates all of nature but has an identity that is more than, and distinct from nature.

SELF:
O Psychological and emotional literacy
O A self-reflecting and self-managing faith that is authentic and experience-based and congruent with humanity's accumulated spiritual wisdom

COMMUNITY:
O Critically open to change, constant flows of information and abundance of knowledge, making no claim to exclusive nor certain truth
O Upholding diversity and inclusiveness
O Respecting all life and supporting growth towards its potential
O Empowering individuals and locally-based communities demonstrating "low-rise" authority structures
O Espousing a morality and ethics, an example of which might include "non-violence and respect for life, solidarity and a just economic order, tolerance and a life of truthfulness, equal rights and partnership between men and women" (Kung and Schmidt, 1998)

PLANET:
O Perceiving connection
O Ecological/biological models in which a whole is more than the sum of its parts and random elements are continually emerging and self-organizing to form new coherent wholes

SPIRIT:
O Spiritual maturation is a developmental process
O Prioritizing meaning and purpose, cherishing wonder, awe, beauty, and harmony, recognizing many valid ways to explore the mystery that is Spirit
O Deeply rooted in belief and practice of something more than the individual and the apparent world, variously understood as a dynamic, energy, Presence, or ground of existence, embedded in living things, expressed through them and known by a variety of names.

Bloom (*op cit*) describes holism as open-minded and open hearted, embodying common patterns, threads, and relationships. It does not deny traditional faiths, but is critical of narrow and dogmatic formulations. Bloom writes:

"Holism recognises and celebrates the very essence of all religions, perceiving what is best and most useful. In particular, it is aware of the morality and ethics presented by the different faiths, and of the practices that work best to support balanced human development and spiritual growth … It does not bother so much about theology, form and tradition, but is passionately engaged with the underlying and universal principles, skills and precepts. Holism honours the unique cultural form of the different faiths, but gives primary respect to the inner, core message."

Often those studying universality and searching for the core elements of all faiths are accused of syncretism – cherry-picking bits in a way that is shallow and lacks rigor. Bloom argues instead that "It is a wise use of what is available and a clear recognition that the particular traditions are not destinations but are gateways to something deeper and more universal" and adds that many holists are holists within their faith community.

Bloom proposes a holism based on practices, shared across all faith and wisdom traditions, widely recognized principles of personal maturity, and common ethical principles. These are used in the next activity as a way for you to both test out the concept of holism and take stock of your current sense of soul in the light of this exploration of wholeness and connection.

Activity: **Your Sense Of Soul And Holism**

SPIRITUAL PRACTICE

Use Bloom's principles for a holistic practice as a checklist to review your practice as part of **Wholeness and Connection:**

Practice	What does this mean to me? How am I doing with this?
The ability to slow down and come to centre	
The ability to be a kind and detached observer of life and of oneself.	
The ability to connect with, experience and explore the wonder, beauty and mystery of life.	
Honest self-reflection	
What is new or different that you want to add:	

PERSONAL MATURITY

Use Bloom's characteristics to reflect on yourself, remembering that it is not about castigating yourself, but celebrating where this is change towards an expanded and more stable sense of self and compassion where this is still hard.

Characteristic	What does this mean to me? How am I doing with this?
Appreciating and being inspired by the stories and examples of others	
Wise management of one's own spiritual education and development	
Supporting the development and growth of others	
Compassion toward suffering	
Courage to move beyond one's comfort zone to help others	
Willingness to change	

What is new or different that you want to add:

Continued over

Fig 35: Your Sense Of Soul And Holism

VALUES AND ETHICAL BEHAVIOR

Use Bloom's summary of core moral and ethical precepts to review your values.

Values and ethical behaviours	What does this mean to me? How am I doing with this?
Do not harm life	
Be compassionate	
Develop generosity of spirit	
Love	
Recognisimg harmony and beauty	
Enabling and nurturing healthy growth	
Promoting how best to behave and look after myself and those close to me	

What is new or different that you want to add:

THE MEANING OF WHOLENESS AND CONNECTION

- *What is your "felt-presence" of wholeness and connection?*
- *How does this stand in relation to your sense of soul?*

LIVING IN A SACRED WAY

*"Each thought, each action in the sunlight of awareness becomes sacred.
In this light, no boundary exists between the sacred and the profane.
I know that it can take me a bit longer to do the dishes,
but I live fully in every moment, and I am happy."*

Thich Nhat Hanh, 1992

In this chapter you turn to the impact that your inner journey of self-exploration has on the way you live in the outer world. In Celtic spirituality, this is likened to breathing-in as in-spiration from the Beloved and breathing-out as the expression of the Beloved through you. *The Quest* calls it *Living in a Sacred Way*. The chapter explores this in a practical sense by following the thoughts of two or three people, principally one member of *The Quest* team, as they explain their experience and how they see living in a sacred way.

Integrating and embodying the Beloved – your sense of soul – is recognized in all spiritual teachings and metaphors. In the Hindu tradition, it is your "dharma", the expression of your unique talents. On the heroic journey, you have reached the stage of reward and return, where you draw together the personal gains from change and growth to offer its fruits to the community, whether that is your family and friends, your neighborhood, as a global citizen or for the Earth.

As you explore your sense of soul you may experience heightened appreciation of the preciousness of living – like falling in love with life over and over again. You may notice dissonance or discomfort; your changing sense of 'who you are' is at odds with the world in which you find yourself. You may become less close to a partner or friends. Your priorities may shift. You may feel inner pressure to change; some people make major changes in what they do whilst others re-frame their perception and attitudes whilst *doing* the same things as before. There is a Zen saying: "Before enlightenment, chop wood, carry water. After enlightenment, chop wood, carry water".

Living in a Sacred Way, therefore, focuses on such questions as:

○ What does it mean to live in a sacred way?
○ What ideas and methods might help you live in a sacred way?
○ How can you express your sense of soul in a connected and inclusive way?

THE SACRED AND LIVING

How can someone refer to their way of living as sacred? Surely something sacred is extraordinary and set apart from daily life?

Many of us grew up with the idea that something sacred was set apart from routine life; going to church, synagogue, temple, or mosque was special and often on a special day of the week. Something mundane, like doing the dishes, may not occur to you as sacred.

Activity: What Is Sacred?

First, note down your reaction to the title of this chapter. What does the word sacred *mean to you? Now add some ideas about what kinds of things are sacred to you, based on your understanding of the word.*

If the concept of living in a sacred way seems strange, you might find that, like a number of Quest participants, you keep seeing the title as living in a scared way. This is possible too. Different ideas may stretch your comfort zone and take you to – and beyond - your edge; for some people just being alive can be scary.

In the activity above, you may have noted that sacred includes:

○ Something precious
○ Something set aside
○ A special place, like a great cathedral or an ancient monument
○ A special moment, like watching a spectacular sunset.

These examples associate sacredness with being special and this is a familiar interpretation. But that may not be the whole of it. In the poem below a young woman called Jane describes another experience of sacredness as she looks out at night across the waters of the Firth of Forth in Scotland to the county of Fife:

"Every night as I gaze out of the bathroom window
To near far-off Fife
And I see familiar sights;

Every night
Then softly the Spirit of God quietly creeps into my heart
And I see it all anew as the first time –
In quiet ecstasy."

Jane is explaining how something that is familiar and ordinary becomes transformed as she sees something precious and extraordinary each time she looks at the same scene. She seems to have shifted away from perceiving herself as someone separate from the view and just looking *at* it to someone who perceives herself as deeply and meaningfully *connected with* it.

Such moments are an epiphany, a time when the nature of Spirit shows through. Jane, like most of us, probably has an unconscious view of the world based on separation – that things are all isolated and separate from each other. But even in the midst of an ordinary moment this can be replaced by connection and experiencing things as One in which you feel yourself to be part of something much larger. In the Hindu tradition, further exploration of this kind of experience is called *advaita* or non-duality; there is no separate self because it is all one. Teasdale (1999) put it in the form of a question: "How can I speak of God when there is only God?"

Jane has reached a point where things that previously seemed quite ordinary she now *sees differently*. From the evidence of people's accounts of their experiences, *seeing differently* seems to be a key element in living in a sacred way.

SEEING DIFFERENTLY

Pause for a minute and think about times when there's a blurring between what is extraordinary and what is ordinary; Thich Nhat Hahn calls them "the sacred and the profane". You may have experienced moments when you are doing something familiar or simple and found yourself surrendering to a timeless moment in which you felt more deeply connected. The activity *Having An Experience* (page 19) was all about surrendering to such a moment. Judith, one of the Quest team, sees it in a very practical way:

"I think that everything has the potential to be sacred. Whether or not I experience it as sacred depends upon me, the attitude and quality of attention I bring to it. For moments that are sacred to me, I notice that what happens follows this kind of pattern:

○ I am aware in the moment
○ I am able to see the beauty and the intrinsic value in something
○ I appreciate the simplicity, seeing and appreciating the essence of the thing

○ I feel gratitude that this is so

○ I experience reverence, awe, respect, inspiration, joy, delight, peace and contentment

○ For that focused moment, all emotion such as fear and anger fall away, and I feel at one with the thing."

As Judith described this pattern, she also gave examples of such moments – gardening, singing with others, walking, and cleaning the house.

We can sometimes observe a similar sense of the sacred in children. Children may stay close to this kind of wonder and awe for a while as they grow. During this period experiences that seem natural to them include:

○ A sense of an inner life, and of an inner self

○ A sense of the sacred in the infinitesimally small and the cosmically grand

○ A natural sense of morality and justice.

Francis Thompson (c. 1906, reissued 2003) expresses this as: "It is to have a spirit yet streaming from the waters of baptism; it is to believe in love, to believe in loveliness, to believe in belief; it is to be so little that the elves can reach to whisper in your ear." Thompson went on to quote William Blake (1827):

"It is to see the world in a grain of sand,
And Heaven in a flower,
It is to hold infinity in the palm of your hand
And Eternity in an hour."

Activity: Sacred Moments

●*First, recall your own childhood. Was there a moment when you were aware of something that was sacred?*

●*Now think about a time as an adult when you were aware of wonder and awe – perhaps you caught your breath or felt the world stand still.*

●*Describe that moment. What particular qualities define it or make it memorable?*

●*Are there any ways in which you felt as if you were "seeing differently"?*

●*Make a record of the particular qualities or characteristics of that moment.*

●*To what extent were these recollections similar to – or different from – your experience in* Having An Experience?

Many sacred moments demonstrate ways of seeing differently that echo Jane's poem and they are frequently associated with everyday activities:

gardening, making bread, playing a musical instrument, walking the dog, being alone in nature, being in a large crowd at a sports event or music festival. The distinguishing quality of the moment is that it is timeless, imbued with a precious quality, whether that is named as love, peace, beauty, or something else, and feeling part of something beyond yourself.

The word sacred will mean different things to different people. What we invite you to do here is awaken to what you understand by it, exploring it and, through seeing differently, practise the idea of living sacredness in everyday life. This suggests that there is a connection between living and sacred – that you can be both active and alive and aware of the sacred. But this assumption, too, needs to be subjected to the test of your experience and interpretation.

Activity: What Feeling Alive Means To You

Just note down any thoughts, words, pictures, memories, or sounds that come to you as you consider what feeling alive really means to you. Also include notes or reflections on the qualities or characteristics that mark out those times.

If it is difficult to recall such a time, instead consider how feeling alive might be different to what you can recall.

You may have included responses that are commonly given such as:
O Feeling absorbed with what I'm doing in the moment
O Playing with my children when they were small
O When something had meaning or purpose for me
O Looking after my friends or partner when they need help
O When I felt I was making a positive contribution to something
O When I'm in a beautiful place
O Engrossed in a hobby, like painting
O When I see somebody achieve a dream held for a long time
O Feeling excited and energized

Evidence shows that feeling alive is frequently related both to what you are doing and how you perceive or feel about it inwardly. Not surprisingly, many people report that moments when they feel alive are similar to the moments they experience as sacred. They seem to share qualities and characteristics of:

O Living in the moment
O Energy building around the activity with which you are engaged
O A qualitative change in the feeling of the moment or the addition of a 'something more' factor
O Having a sense of purpose
O A sense of being supported by, and serving, something larger than yourself
O Feeling that time has a different reality.

"THE HIDDEN INNER SECRET OF LIFE"

But the kind of experience described above may be in marked contrast to what you may sometimes feel or the sentiments expressed by people whom you know. John Main, a Benedictine monk, who together with Thomas Keating re-established Christian meditation, wrote:

> "There is a great feeling among our contemporaries, I think, of the need, perhaps even the extremely urgent need, to recover the spiritual dimension in our lives. There is a feeling that unless we do recover that spiritual dimension we are going to lose our grip on life altogether. In meeting that feeling we must be perfectly clear that a commitment to spiritual values is by no means a rejection of the ordinary things of life. Indeed the exact opposite is true. Commitment to the spiritual reality is simply commitment to reality and it is the way to really appreciate the wonder of all life. It is the only way to come to understand the extraordinary fact of the mystery of life itself, the hidden inner secret of life that gives it its real excitement." (1984)

The activity below builds on what Main wrote and provides an opportunity for you to reflect further on "the hidden secret of life that gives it its real excitement."

Activity: Your "Hidden Inner Secret"

In this activity you reflect on your "hidden inner secret" through a letter to Spirit, God, or whatever term you use for a Presence that is beyond yourself.

Imagine that you are writing to a Presence that understands you so well, that has immense compassion for your struggles, and respect for your desire to live in a sacred way.

Start your letter however you wish, e.g. "Dear ...

* *Explain how you have been exploring your sense of soul*
* *Your concern that you do not lose your grip on life altogether*
* *Explain your commitment to spiritual values*
* *The ordinary things in which you rejoice*
* *Describe how you see 'reality' and whether this helps you appreciate the wonder of all life*
* *Explain what living in a sacred way means to you and, if appropriate, ask for help and insight*

Finish your letter by writing about the hidden inner secret that gives life its real excitement for you.

Our exploration of living in a sacred way is picked up again by Judith. She explains her hidden inner secret as an enthusiasm that leads her to find ways to make what she does congruent with her sense of sacredness. She says:

"I have come to realise that, for me, things or moments that I respect I also wish to protect, conserve and share. This is stewardship, taking personal responsibility for what is around me. I also wish that good will follow for all beings, and, for myself, I want harmony of thought, word and deed. There needs to be a balance between the wonder – experienced anew through silence and stillness – and meaningful action. I have a choice about how I act, and I choose according to my conscience, my values and my inner feelings."

Activity: Exploring Living In A Sacred Way

●In your letter, what did you write about the hidden inner secret that gives life its real excitement for you
●Re-read what Judith says about her hidden inner secret.

Take a little while to reflect on these things. You might find it helpful to wander outdoors or engage in some other enjoyable activity that gives you space to ponder.

●Describe as best you can what your life would be like and what you would be doing if you were living in a sacred way
●Make a note of times when you have felt closest to living in this way
●What is your sense of soul in these moments?
●What might help increase your awareness of these moments and your openness to them occurring?

We asked Judith more about how she sees living in a sacred way:

"During those times that I think of as living in a sacred way, I have experienced a sense of connection to something larger than myself and it seems like a flow of energy. I felt real, authentic and present in the moment. The experience is simple and profound; it brings me a glimpse of a wiser, more spontaneous and compassionate me. I cease to judge myself; I just am Me, at peace with myself and all around me. Right now, this is the nearest that I can get to what I would call my soul."

Judith links her sense of soul and living in a sacred way with her capacity to be "real, authentic and present in the moment"; being Me is giving her gift to the world.

Peter Goldfarb, a philanthropist, actor and director, likened it to:
"if this is my gift, if this is what I am most capable of doing, then it is
also the way I can most touch other people's lives. Within that context
I experience myself as a kind of vehicle through which something
flows and manifests."

Shapiro and Shapiro (1999) described Goldfarb's process as creative
empowerment

"that emphasised each person's individual and authentic way of being
in the world, getting away from the idea that there is a 'proper way' to
live that we have to learn." Peter Goldfarb puts it that "He is
committed to facilitating everyone with whom he works in
experiencing the fruition of their unique and boundless creativity."

This offers a way to experiment and play with seeing yourself as a partner in
co-creating the world. Meister Eckhart, the thirteenth-century mystic, wrote:
"God is creating the entire universe, fully and totally, in this present now" (Fox,
1983). The "process theology" of Lord Alfred Whitehead suggests that the divine
needs your capacity to co-create in order to complete or know itself fully. In
other words, it is suggested there is scope for your contribution too. In the
activity below, you are invited to apply the possibility a little further and take
some time to reflect on what your creative and unique contribution might be.

Activity: Contributing The Creativity Of Your Life

*The extract below is taken from an interview given by Desmond Tutu,
Archbishop of Cape Town 1986-1996, South Africa:*

*"We were made to enjoy music, to enjoy beautiful sunsets, to enjoy looking at
the billows of the sea and to be thrilled with a rose that is bedecked with
dew... Human beings are actually created for the transcendent, for the sublime,
for the beautiful, for the truthful ... and all of us are given the task of trying to
make this world a little more hospitable to these beautiful things."*

(Desmond Tutu, from The NPR Interviews 1994, ed. Robert Siegel)

*Now reflect on yourself, who you are and what you do as you respond to the
questions below:*

●*In what ways do you dream of going beyond what you take for granted?*
●*Where have you been able to bring about something beautiful?*
●*In all that you are and do in life, what feels most true to how you know
yourself?*

•*How would you describe your 'personal and extraordinary uniqueness'?*

If it is true that your creativity is nurtured when you can be true to yourself:

•*Identify at least three ways in which you have gifts that are true to who you are and that you can offer.*
•*Note them down*
•*Look for quotations or pictures or something that captures their essence. Make yourself a copy of this reminder of your creativity that you can take around with you*
•*From time to time, take out this reminder of your creativity and actively search for opportunities to put your gifts into practice.*
•*Gandhi said that everything we do is insignificant, yet it is of the utmost importance that we do it. How might this be true of your creative contribution to life?*

A similar belief in the importance of the unique contribution that each of us can make is explained by David Spangler (2004). He calls it "incarnational spirituality":

"In the normal Judeo-Christian context, God is seen as the universal and absolute Center around which all creation revolves. But in Eastern religious philosophy, the sense of the sacred is more diffused. It is the "center without a circumference," the center that is everywhere and nowhere, the center that is equally within all things. [The periphery] is the place of engagement and emergence. It is the place of generosity and love, not as a radiance from a single center but as a relationship, a partnering, or an alliance that honors all involved and is generated by all involved."

He describes it as: "a form of co-created, shared wholeness that I feel is our evolutionary edge at the moment." Spangler continues:

"We are all centers of something in our lives. But we are also engaged at our boundaries with others who also are centers. We live in the midst of an ecology of centers, an ecology of suns, a galaxy of everyday life. In this sense, we can think of ourselves as stars as well. It is the emergence of our stardom and learning what this implies in a world of interactive and co-creative partners and systems that is our next step. Incarnational spirituality is a study and a practice to make this process of creative activity conscious and mindful in our daily lives."

In a key sentence that follows, Spangler's concept of incarnational spirituality challenges you to ground the idea of living in a sacred way in concrete action:

> "It is a practice of recognizing how we participate not only in the unfolding of our own particular beings but in the manifestation and emergence of all beings in the world around us, leading to a deeper consciousness of love, blessing, and co-creativity."

ACTING *AS IF*

Both Main and Spangler, like Judith's narrative that you have been following, emphasize the importance of the ordinary things in life as intrinsic to a practice of unfolding – both of your own contribution and participating in the wider emergence of the world around you. So your next step in exploring the idea of living in a sacred way goes back to one of the earliest activities in *The Quest*, one in which you were asked to do something reasonably simple that you enjoy and get absorbed in.

In *Heart of The Quest* one of the earliest activities was *Having An Experience* (page 19) and as you did the activity you were asked to do four actions:

○ Keep your attention wholly focused in the experience – *Stillness and Being Centered*
○ Watch or observe yourself having the experience – *Observing and Reflecting*
○ Reflect on what moved or delighted you or was of value, including any awareness of connection or presence – *Opening*
○ Reflect briefly how you might bring these elements into a similar experience another time – *Integrating*

The Quest framework (page 22) associated these four actions with skills of spiritual reflection and they have been used throughout *The Quest* in one way or another. This is a good point, therefore, to look again at *Having An Experience* and the basic skills of spiritual reflection to see if they can be directly applied in your exploration of living in a sacred way.

Sir George Trevelyan, an innovator in adult education in the 1950s and 1960s, talked about *acting as if.* When you *act as if*, you make an agreement with yourself to try out an idea or a way of looking at things for a period of time (perhaps for four weeks) and throughout this time you *act as if* the idea is true and useful. At the same time you notice what happens and note your experience. After four weeks, you review the experiment, consider whether or not to continue and how you might improve on it for yourself.

The next activity re-visits the basic skills of spiritual reflection in a short form and applies the idea of *as if* to review yourself in daily life as part of your search for an authentic and real approach to living in a sacred way. Read through the activity and decide upon the length of time for which you will try it out. The period of time needs to be long enough to have some impact upon your habitual way of looking at life but not so long that you cannot sustain the experiment.

Activity: Acting As If Living In A Sacred Way

Read through the activity and then write the questions out on cards or notes. Keep them handy while you try out the experiment of acting as if living in a sacred way.

Find some quiet time every day, preferably first thing in the morning, to read the questions and reflect on them. The intention in reading them daily is that they sink into your awareness so they inform your response to situations that arise during the day.

During the day, try to recall the questions and apply them to the current moment. Follow the responses that come to mind providing that they do not appear to be negative or likely to bring harm to another person, animal, living organism, or the Earth.

Each evening, however briefly, review when and how you have used the questions and whether or not they were useful. Over the period of the experiment consider whether this resonates with your sense of soul and if it has any impact upon your perception of living in a sacred way.

The diagram of The Quest *framework for exploring a sense of soul is below the questions. You might find it helpful to make a large copy of it and write in some of your reflections around it as you try acting as if ...*

To act as if *you are **Finding Inner Stillness** ask yourself:*

●How can I be still and centered in this moment in the midst of what I am doing, with whom, and how?

To act as if *you are **Being Your Own Observer** ask yourself:*

●What am I aware of in myself?

To act as if *you are **Opening to Creative Inspiration** ask yourself:*

●What will open my heart and help me touch the heart of others in this situation?

To act as if *you are **Acting With Awareness** ask yourself:*

●What choices can I exercise that would enhance my impact in society or on the environment?

After the period of time that you settled on for "acting as if...." you will need to review your experiment carefully, using your notes, impressions, and insights from the experience. The activity: Critical Incident Analysis *(page 101) might help your review.*

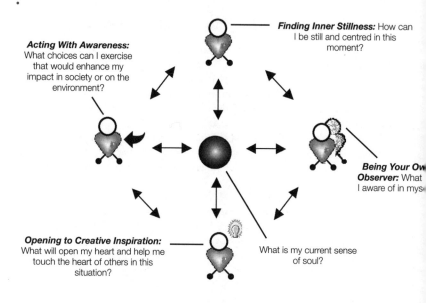

Acting With Awareness: What choices can I exercise that would enhance my impact in society or on the environment?

Finding Inner Stillness: How can I be still and centred in this moment?

Being Your Own Observer: What I aware of in mys

Opening to Creative Inspiration: What will open my heart and help me touch the heart of others in this situation?

What is my current sense of soul?

Fig 36: The Quest Framework And "Acting As If"

By now you have experimented with living in a sacred way in some depth. This has, hopefully, given you a clearer idea of what living in a sacred way means to you and some extended practice in combining this with skills of spiritual reflection. What, though, gives living in a sacred way its "juice"? What might impel you to make conceivably significant effort to follow through and bring your sense of soul more present in daily life?

BEING LOVING

Spangler, a contemporary mystic, wrote of "a deeper consciousness of love, blessing, and co-creativity"; Main, a Benedictine Christian monk, said that "commitment to the spiritual reality is simply commitment to reality and it is the way to really appreciate the wonder of all life"; Thich Nhat Hanh, a Vietnamese Buddhist monk and peace campaigner, wrote, "I live fully in every moment and I am happy". Is there a common theme here that can be extracted and put to use?

Spangler, Main, and Thich Nhat Hanh identify love, blessing, and co-creativity, appreciating the wonder of all life, being happy. These spiritual values, and especially love, are found at the heart of all religions and wisdom traditions. Love, as an idea in itself, is both promising and difficult. Promising because it is attractive and aspirational, difficult because it is an ideal that may be hard to live up to and may lead you into making divisions – creating separation – between what you love and what you don't or can't yet love.

Activity: Love

Note down all those people, animals, things, that you love or have loved.

The Quest writers came up with answers such as:

- ●My partner
- ●My children
- ●My cuddly toys when I was small
- ●An orphaned cat that adopted me
- ●My first car
- ●Nature

These responses suggest special-ness; all the people, animals and things were those that we regarded as special to us.

Sociologists employ the term "operationalize" when they turn an idea or principle into something active. Instead of pursuing love directly, *Living in a Sacred Way* explores love by operationalizing it as "Being Loving"; something that orients you in a loving direction and helps guide your decisions and behavior. But it becomes an active principle rather than an unattainable ideal.

Activity: Being Loving

- ●*What is it like for you to be loving?*
- ●*What emotions and images do you associate with being loving?*

Note down your responses.

The Quest writers responded very differently to the activity on *Being Loving*; the quality of our answers and our images of *Being Loving* were very different to those for the previous activity on love. We noticed:

- ○ Feeling more alive
- ○ Noticing beauty around me
- ○ Feeling very absorbed and focused in each moment

○ Prizing and treasuring the object of my attention
○ Wishing the very best for the loved one
○ Feeling security, comfort, and warmth
○ Feeling more loving in general
○ Feeling opened up
○ Wanting the feeling to expand to include everyone and everything.

The responses on this list are, again, similar to other responses in *The Quest* such as what you may have noted as sacred, your response to *Having An Experience* (page 19), and the experiences that Diana Whitmore identified as characteristics of spiritual experiences (page 57). The next activity, therefore, explores your experience of being loving in more depth, by building on from the last activity and extending your field of view.

Activity: Exploring Being Loving

You will need a large sheet of plain paper and pens. You might find colors useful too. The purpose of the activity is to explore your experience, attitudes, beliefs, and fears around being loving.

To get you started, question yourself around topic areas like:

● *With what and whom can I be loving – now and in the past?*
● *What is it like to be loved?*
● *What are my images of being loving?*
● *What does being loving mean?*
● *Where does being loving happen?*
● *Is there anything I need to be able to be loving?*
● *What have I heard or been told about being loving?*
● *When I've been in love, what was it like?*
● *What are the risks of being loving?*
● *Are there things that I have sacrificed and/or given up in order to be loving?*

Add other questions of your own as they occur to you.
To record your responses to this activity:
● *Start by drawing a shape in the middle of your sheet of paper and writing "Being Loving" in it. You might want to use shapes and colors that represent your ideas about love rather than words (see example on page 203).*
● *As you respond to the questions, and other questions of your own, you can choose whether to put your responses randomly on the paper or whether you want to organize them like branches around the starting point in the center. You can add as many responses to your diagram as you wish so you put onto the diagram all the things that being loving is about for you.*
● *When you have put all the ideas that you wish down on paper we suggest that*

you take a break before completing the activity, then return to it again. When you return to your drawing, take a fresh look at it.

●*What do you see, feel, and think as you review everything that you put on the paper?*
●*Do you see any connections that you had not seen before?*
●*Do you have any new insights or understanding of you in relation to being loving?*

Note down any concluding thoughts, feelings, or ideas that come to you.

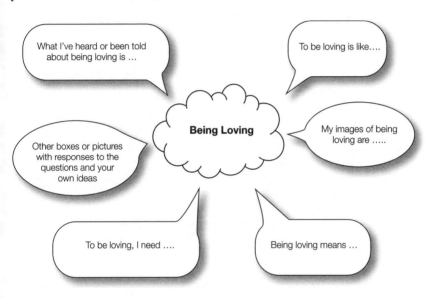

Fig 37: Your Map Of Being Loving

To embrace being loving as an aspect of living in a sacred way is a significant transition for you, and for most of us, to make. You would need to move from perceiving being loving as something special to seeing it as a more natural and common part of daily experience; you would need to expand any simplistic rosy-glow image of loving to one that also deals with the hard realities of everyday situations, hurts, and knocks. So while you are exploring loving, you also need to explore the hardest part of love – to be found in those people, places, things, times, when you can't find a loving response to give.

Activity: **The Edge Of Loving**

For this activity, you will need another large sheet of plain paper, pens, and colors. In the activity you will explore the edge, for you, between what, when, who, and how you love and what, when, who, and how you are least able to love.

Starting in the middle of your sheet of paper, begin by writing or drawing those people or things where being loving arises most naturally and easily for you.

Now move to the outer edge of your sheet and write or draw the people or things where being loving is most challenging. Then, work both inwards from the edge and outwards from the center adding more people and things. See if you can discover a boundary, however blurred, which you might call your "loving edge".

As you work through the rest of this chapter, try to notice when you meet this (or a similar) edge and try to experiment with ways of moving your comfort zone in order to be more open to being loving.

Within the boundary, you are in a zone where being loving seems to be a natural response for you. Outside the boundary is beyond your zone of feeling at ease with loving at the moment. Note that we're not asking you to assume a totally unquestioning loving stance to all life. Although it might well seem to be an ideal to strive toward, few people possess this ability. Paradoxically, it becomes possible to understand love more fully when we have also known and experienced what it is like not to love.

One of the ways in which many of us desert love is when we demonize someone – they are beyond acceptance – or polarize something that hurts or offends us – that is all bad whereas this is all good. We make them separate and treat them as "the other", different and, at its most extreme, not even worthy of dignity or respect. Moreover, we are pretty certain that the qualities we condemn in "the other" are not among those we possess.

Activity: **Testing "The Other"**

You may find this activity hard, in which case it might help to recall the advice of Ayya Kheema to try to loosen a little around your edges, perhaps just to persist in mulling it over rather than dismiss the possibility.

● *Sit quietly for a while and breathe evenly and steady yourself*
● *Bring to mind a person or situation where you feel anger, contempt, rejection, or other negative feeling*
● *Try to see the situation as a whole and identify the ways in which you demonize the person or polarize the situation. What might you not want to recognize or acknowledge here?*
● *Is there a way in which you can remember the humanity of this person or the other possibilities present in the situation?*

- *Try to remain open to the possibility that things can change and the seeds are present now*
- *Sit quietly and find your inner stillness. You may ask for a word or an image that will help you loosen around the edges*
- *Ask yourself what can touch your heart and the hearts of others to hold the prayer that the very highest can come forth*
- *One oft-repeated spiritual epithet is "All is very, very well". If all IS very, very well, ask in what way this is so in this situation*
- *Before you close, return to your inner stillness and release any upset or anger you have felt*

This exercise is more effective if you repeat it a number of times, noticing if there is any shift, however slight, in the intensity of your original feelings.

LIVING LOVINGLY

In this part of *Living In A Sacred Way* you look at being loving with others and in connection with your surroundings. But you start with a new skill of spiritual reflection, one that can be used to bring yourself into harmony and alignment with others, with a task, and even the tools you use.

Activity: Skills of Spiritual Reflection:
Finding Harmony And Alignment

This activity introduces a new skill of spiritual reflection associated with Stillness and Being Centered

ATTUNING

WHAT DOES IT MEAN?

Attuning is being on the same wavelength, harmonizing, or being at one with other people, nature, objects, or situations and events. Attunement is a concept based on harmony and the interconnectedness of all things. As such, attunement requires that you consciously let go of a perspective limited to yourself, or your own agenda, in order to become one with a wider awareness.

Attunement might be used at the start of a task or activity with other people, connecting with each other to bring a sense of alignment toward the activity. It could be used when you are on your own, in order to tune into nature, your surroundings, or a task.

Here are two examples:

- *"We hold hands in a circle and focus on the activity we are embarking on as a way of linking at both outer and inner levels." Findhorn Foundation co-worker*

● *"I sit at the top of the hill sometimes, take time to calm down from the climb, and just look at the beauty spread out around me. After a while, I begin to feel more at one and in harmony with the surroundings." Sandra, Quest participant*

STARTING OUT

1. Allow your thoughts and your physical self to become still as you put aside other issues.

2. Focus your attention on the people you are with, the object with which you will work, the event in which you are participating. With that as your focus, imagine letting go of your self-concern and feel a sense of connection with the people or situation. Sometimes a group leader may say a few words to articulate the intention. Keep your attention on this focus for just a few moments. If your mind wanders, gently bring your attention back.

3. Review whether or not attuning in this way made any difference or not. What did you feel? What was different? Did the meeting/event flow more gracefully? Did you feel more connected, or notice a difference in any other way? How would you describe your experience?

PRACTICING

*1. **Attuning to a group** usually involves a short silence and a conscious sense of offering your own contribution to harmonize with other members of the group and the task or activity that you will undertake together. This might be likened to members of an orchestra bringing their instruments in tune with each other so that their combined music is in harmony rather than discord. Some people make a physical link, such as holding hands, to help create a sense of flow between them.*

*2. **Attuning to nature** helps you to be receptive to the diversity of life around you. Take time to look and listen. Even in a city street you can see the sky, clouds, birds, even plants growing up through cracks in the pavement. Those who take time to attune to nature sometimes begin to feel a connection with nature that helps them to work with plants, animals, and trees in a more sensitive and creative way.*

*3. **Attuning to objects or things** helps to cultivate a more respectful and mindful relationship with the object or thing on which you are focusing. This can be done with everyday objects, things that you normally do not think about at all. Taking time to attune to these things helps you to feel appreciation and respect for them.*

*4. **Attuning to events or situations** is a way of focusing on a particular event or situation in which you are taking part. Pause and be silent briefly to connect* *yourself (and all members of the group if there is one) with the vision of the event or situation ahead so you can flow outwards to work creatively with the event or situation.*

Attuning is a skill of spiritual reflection well-adapted to the idea of being loving. It has been found to create the space for living in a sacred way with those you are with, events, situations, nature, and even objects you might regard as inanimate, such as the computer that is used to write *The Quest.*

Being with other people, however, is one of the most potent learning experiences in being loving and living lovingly that you encounter. This learning may arise in your family, at work, through leisure and hobby interests, or any time in which you are in a group. You have the opportunity to see yourself as others see you; other people mirror back to you different aspects of yourself and you have to take account of them, their needs and wishes, and different perceptions. Many people experience one-to-one relationships or membership of a group as a big learning in love or the difficulties of love.

Here the word "group" is meant to include any forum where people come together. It can include family, workplace and club, group activity, and so on. You might also choose to use an example of a one-to-one relationship as your focus in the next few activities by reading through the activity to see what it's about and then substituting the example of your one-to-one relationship for a group.

Activity: **You With Others**

- *Have you been a member of any group?*
- *Which aspects of different groups worked well and which didn't?*
- *What was the biggest gift in being in the group?*
- *What was the biggest challenge?*
- *If you are following* The Quest *with others, what has that experience been like for you?*

When you have responded to the questions, spend some time reflecting on them. Try to identify any new information that you receive about yourself from membership of a group.

Turn back to Being Your Own Observer *(page 27) and re-read it. Next time you have an opportunity, try to observe yourself as if you were another member of the group. Add any insights this brings to the notes you have just compiled.*

There are many examples, from religious communities and secular groups, suggesting that, at their best, groups can provide an extraordinary opportunity to bring your capacity for being loving into living in a sacred way. At the Findhorn Foundation working with others in a group is the basis of most activity. It is no different to many similar situations that will be familiar to you. What is different, perhaps, is the way the life of a group is viewed.

One experienced group leader at the Foundation told us about her experience:

> "We always pay a lot of attention to the life of the group as well as the people in it. We attune to each other and the task before we start work or begin a workshop session. Honesty and loving are important, as are times to share together, to celebrate. We try to practise actively listening to each other, not just to the words, but from the heart."

Activity: Finding Out More About Living Lovingly

●*What do you think are the most important guidelines in a group that wants to practice being loving?*

●*Have you found ways in which you are able to bring yourself into more harmony and alignment with a group, a task, or other elements you are engaged with?*

●*How far does being loving affect how you feel and behave and does it make any difference?*

●*Can you begin to jot down your own guidelines for living lovingly?*

Make a note of your guidelines. As you read the next few paragraphs, check out your ideas against the experience that other people have had and the conclusions they have drawn from it.

LIVING LOVINGLY WITH OTHERS: SHIFTS AND CONFLICTS

The Findhorn Foundation staff member went on to talk about her experience in facilitating workshops for Foundation guests:

> "Over the years, I have found that whatever the topic of a workshop – whether it's dance, conflict resolution, or team building – the same thing is happening. Participants experience:

○ Trusting
○ Sharing with others in a deeper way
○ Feeling valued
○ Feeling listened to
○ Becoming more aware
○ Experiencing being vulnerable
○ Seeing themselves as having a contribution to make

○ Having a sense of something greater than themselves
○ Seeing that we all have strengths and vulnerabilities
○ Seeing themselves mirrored in and by others
○ Being open to love and trust within a group."

Finally, she observed that in response to these experiences, participants open up and are more able to live in a sacred way. Of course, none of this means that problems, such as disagreements, dislikes, and conflict, stop happening in such groups. It suggests though, that they have a different approach to dealing with them.

The Dingle Community Learning Programme, located in inner-city Liverpool, is another example of a group trying to be loving and live in a sacred way in their life together. The Dingle Programme provides an example of how individuals may change even when the social environment in which they live does not subscribe to the kind of changes they are making. It is different to the example of the Findhorn Foundation; generally people living in Dingle have not chosen Dingle as their place to live in the same way as residents at the Findhorn Foundation. The Dingle Programme is based on:

○ Ensuring a wholly democratic framework which respects the views
   and rights of others as well as the way they relate to each other
○ Belief in service to others
○ Trying to generate a change in attitude where, as one participant
   puts it, life can be "celebrated rather than endured".

The Dingle Programme believes these elements are essential to provide security for individuals to find space to explore their own needs and be listened to so that they can grow. Lynne Wilson, a staff member at the Open University who has been involved with the Dingle Programme since it was founded, has said:

"They are building up an experience of being loving with others. It is
showing that the presence of a unified and caring unit in the
community, where no one is simply in it for themselves, causes ripples
that move gently out. This gives others an opportunity to stop and
think again."

Another interesting dimension of the Dingle Programme is their intention that each person encountering experiences and formal courses in personal growth is not acting just for their own benefit, but on behalf of the development of the community as a whole. This may remind you of the fifth and final stage of the heroic journey (*Passion and Change*, pages 126-127) where the purpose of the heroic journey is revealed as bringing back the fruits of experience for the benefit of all.

Another example, based on experience within a group, is Quaker worship. One form of Quaker meeting is silent, unless someone is prompted to speak from the silence. What turns a Quaker meeting from an ordinary meeting of people into the extraordinary is that it is a collective and shared experience. Jan Arriens (*The Friend*, 25 August, 2000) describes:

> "It is as though we begin with the circle of our individuality, and then find ourselves embraced by the wider circle of those present. That circle in turn is not sealed off but spread seamlessly into society – which is why, coming out of Meeting, we do not have any sense of being set apart from the rest of society."

Research into strong, healthy, and loving groups shows another critical difference: they evolve more effective ways of dealing with interpersonal and group problems. The most critical factor is attitude and especially the attitude of people toward one another.

A radically different approach to living lovingly with others is Process Oriented Psychology, devised by Arnold Mindell (1995). A feature of Process Oriented Psychology is that when a dispute or conflict arises, all parties involved are seen as part of a whole. Therefore, each party is a "voice" that holds a part of the answer. In order for any individual, and indeed the whole group, to resolve the conflict every voice must be heard and its truth included. This is a very different perspective to a belief, based on separation and fear, that in order to resolve a conflict, one side must win or prevail. The next activity is an opportunity for you to experiment with shifting your attitude while in a disagreement or conflict. The activity gives you three ways to experiment with making a shift.

Activity: Living Lovingly With Others And Shifts In Attitude

Read through the activity and familiarize yourself with the shifts that are explained. When you are in a disagreement or conflict, try one of these shifts and notice what happens.

1. Hearing all the voices

Adopt the attitude that all views in the disagreement or conflict hold part of the truth and it is your job to help tease out the part each one holds. You might imagine yourself taking someone else's part, standing where they stand to experience how that feels. Try to take an attitude of allowing other points of view to be fully heard. Identify yourself with their points of view instead of just your own for a while and notice how that feels for you.

2. Loosening around the edges

While in the disagreement or conflict, if you are aware of feeling angry and distressed, ask yourself if there is any way that you can let go a little of your view or feelings. Can you loosen around an edge and feel less charged?

3. Whose business is it anyway?

Byron Katie, a teacher in the USA who calls her approach The Work of Byron Katie, *says that all suffering is caused by our attachment to a belief about somebody or some event. "I can find only three kinds of business in the universe," she says: "mine, yours, and God's. (For me, the word God means 'reality.' Reality is God, because it rules. Anything that's out of my control, your control, and everyone else's control — I call that God's business.)"*

- *We suggest letting go of your attachment through the following exercise:*
- *When you find yourself experiencing distress in a situation, ask yourself:*
- *Is this my business? Then focus on being present and seeking a positive resolution to my concern.*
- *Is this your business? Then resist the desire to become involved in someone else's business or imagine that we know best. Leave it to them.*
- *Is this God's business? Then the way forward is to hand the matter over to the God of your understanding.*

After you have tried these alternatives to shift your attitude in a disagreement or conflict, reflect on:

- *What you noticed, felt, thought*
- *How other people responded*
- *What you have learned.*

In the example and exercises in the previous activity you may have encountered paradox; times when the idea that the answer must be either/or and an issue is black/white doesn't seem to fit and there is a different kind of answer.

The next activity introduces the possibility that you can develop an ease with paradox that can be used as a skill of spiritual reflection for integrating spiritual values and your sense of soul into daily life.

Activity: Skills of Spiritual Reflection:
Practicing Integrating

This activity introduces a new skill of spiritual reflection associated with Integrating

LIVING WITH PARADOX

WHAT DOES IT MEAN?

According to an Orphic inscription, each of us is both "a child of the earth and the starry heavens". We are not one or the other; we are "both/and". Living with paradox is a conscious attempt to find One-ness within seemingly contradictory options.

In the paradigm that is passing, the whole has been seen as a sum of its separate parts. The contemporary message is that the whole is more than the sum of its parts. Instead of being isolated everything interacts, interrelates, and is connected. Yet you may still feel alone and separate from others and your surroundings. Finding a way of living with apparent contradictions like this is what living with paradox is all about.

In living with paradox, you shift away from the conventional assumption that opposing possibilities are mutually exclusive. Frequently, you assume there is only one option in something, as the possibilities are mutually incompatible. Living with paradox is inclusive, searching to embrace "both" and "and", instead of "either" and "or".

STARTING OUT

1. You already live with paradox in your daily life but you may not recognize it. See if you relate to any of the following experiences:

- *I thought that the answer was "x" and "y" was wrong but I find that actually it is "x" and "y" too*
- *I love my partner and I can't agree with him/her*
- *I am a man and I experience feminine qualities within me*
- *I am a woman and I experience masculine qualities within me*
- *I am an individual with my own preferences and I am part of a community where I accept the different priorities of the whole*
- *I am both who I was and who I am now*
- *I am a spiritual being having a human experience and a human being having a spiritual experience.*

2. Accept the nature of paradox, but concentrate on the area of overlapping interest, where you are "both/and". The following diagram is an ancient symbol, called the Vesica Pisces, which illustrates the nature of the paradox, and the area of "both/and".

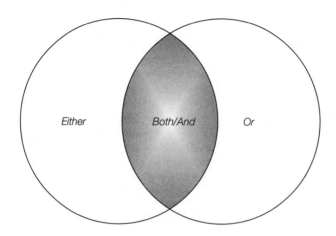

Fig 38: The Vesica Pisces And Paradox

PRACTICING

1. *Work with a specific example of a paradox in your life. Explore both sides of this paradox. You may find that you have a preference for one side rather than the other, and that one is stronger. Consciously try to prefer the other side. You may find that you can then find the meeting point in the middle much more easily.*

2. *Look on the different facets of paradox as different viewpoints that you can play with. The importance here is on playing, experimenting, trying things out, acting out different scenarios, enjoying the paradox.*

3. *Reflect on yourself as a spiritual being having a human experience, and as a human being having a spiritual experience. How does that change the way you think? Explore the way this idea gives you different perspectives on paradox.*

4. *Let go of your need to find a solution to paradox. Just accept it and that you can strive to live in a balanced state between "both/and".*

5. *Use the diagram above to explore and practise varying the relationship and relative size of "either" and "or" with the shaded "overlap". Notice how you feel, or what happens if the both/and overlap disappears.*

6. *Remember that humor and many jokes highlight paradox!*

Acceptance of both/and is one step. Psychotherapist Robin Skynner (1996), however, points out that healthy groups show another particular characteristic, also demonstrated by healthy schools and healthy families: "the fundamental principle is an affiliative attitude. There is a benign, supportive, caring attitude to the people as well as their environment." He goes on to say there is respect for the individual and communication is open and easy, with a good balance between structure and freedom.

The attitudes and qualities that Skynner describes would be recognized in religious traditions as a starting point for unconditional love. It is certainly seeing love very differently from the very conditional nature of many relationships. The next activity, therefore, asks you to try to go a little further in this direction yourself.

Activity: Experimenting With Loving

In this activity, you are asked to practice giving love unconditionally, with no expectation or likelihood of reward.

Every day for one week choose someone or something toward which you will experiment with being loving. You might do this in the moment while out in the street, when you see something disturbing on the television, or see a beautiful flower. The choice is yours. Reach into yourself and be loving toward the things or person chosen in a way that is appropriate in the circumstances.

Notice each day how you feel doing this and be aware of anything that happens that you feel is related to it.

At the end of the time, record what happened in some way, and allow yourself time to reflect on your experiences.

You may have found the last activity challenging. Don't worry if you think that you have been unable to let go of your expectations and hopes as you thought you could. Remember to appreciate your intention to experiment with loving and consider trying again in the future.

In addition to being loving toward others, it is important that you are loving toward yourself. In the Buddhist tradition there is a long-established *Metta*, or loving kindness, meditation. We suggest that you try it as a way to combine being loving both toward yourself and others. If you have read about meditation or practiced it for a while, you may find the next activity familiar. If so, just use it as an opportunity to experience this kind of meditation again.

Activity: Compassion And Loving Kindness Meditation

Read through the meditation completely, and then try it out.

Begin by breathing out tension, worry, and negativity and breathing in patience, kindness, and appreciation. After a while, as you feel yourself settling into the meditation, visualize yourself surrounded by a light that warms you. As you do this, you experience yourself as valued and valuable, dearly loved and being loving.

Now imagine this warmth of loving appreciation spreading out from yourself to embrace those people nearest and dearest to you.

Next, choose to direct your loving kindness toward people with whom you find it difficult to be loving. Forgive them if that is needed and wish them well on their journey. If you feel resistance to this, allow that to be there too, loving yourself for your ongoing willingness to try to expand your capacity to be loving.

Now let your loving kindness encompass the whole Earth and everything in it, the places and parts you know and those you do not. See the planet as a whole, both the beauty and the scars of injustice, aggression, and pain. Send loving kindness to all plants, animals, and places, naming qualities, such as love or peace, that you wish them and the planet.

Lastly, come back to yourself and take a few moments to wish these same qualities for yourself too. Give thanks for everything before bringing your meditation to a close.

Before leaving this quiet time you might reflect, then note down how you feel and the images and sensations that are close to you now.

LIVING LOVINGLY ON THE EARTH

From the beginning of *The Quest* we have emphasized that exploring a sense of soul embraces both spiritual and personal work. Living in a sacred way is the principle *The Quest* uses to integrate your values and understanding of spiritual principles into active expression.

Some contemporary commentators liken the state of humanity to that of a caterpillar as it reaches the end of the caterpillar stage. At this stage in its evolution a caterpillar becomes voracious and over-consuming. For many people, injustice, poverty, and environmental degradation demonstrate that humanity has become voracious and over-consuming. Events early in the century have brought war and terrorism to international attention, highlighting a crisis in relationships of power and a deep polarization in human affairs.

As a caterpillar becomes voracious and over-consuming, however, imaginal cells awake within it and provide a pattern for its emergence as a butterfly. In the natural world, living systems model a process of change which both responds to change and participates in its creation. Human beings are living systems and while you may commonly perceive change as happening to you, it also happens through you. Is it possible that humanity can awaken its "imaginal cells," providing a pattern for co-creating and participating in the future?

The Earth Charter, a declaration adopted by UNESCO in 2003, sets out principles for building a just, sustainable, and peaceful global society that show an agenda for change can be built collaboratively. The principles of the Earth Charter were established through extensive consultations conducted worldwide over a number of years. "Successive drafts of the Earth Charter were circulated around the world for comments and debate by nongovernmental organizations, community groups, professional societies, and international experts in many fields." Every effort was made from the beginning to make it inclusive and culturally diverse, involving people from many nations, religious beliefs and spiritual traditions, to articulate a universally valid and acceptable set of values and principles. The authors of the Earth Charter continue::

> "The drafting of the Earth Charter has involved the most open and participatory consultation process ever conducted in connection with an international document. Thousands of individuals and hundreds of organizations from all regions of the world, different cultures, and diverse sectors of society have participated. The Charter has been shaped by both experts and representatives of grassroots communities. It is a people's treaty that sets forth an important expression of the hopes and aspirations of the emerging global civil society."

You, along with many others, might choose to use the Earth Charter as an entry point into action for change. You might, alternatively, choose to define and express change in a way that is individual to you. Change rooted in the home or your existing way of life also embodies living in a sacred way. Buckminster Fuller articulated key questions: "If the world depended on me, what would I be? What would I do?"

The next activity is a major step in working out what living in a sacred way means to you in a practical sense and also serves as a review of the work you have done in this chapter.

Activity: Expressing Your Life In A Sacred Way

Read this activity in full before working through it. You might read the activity first and dwell on it for a while then answer the questions and come back another time to draw your conclusions.

1. Look carefully at the diagram (page 218) that identifies different aspects of life and steps toward living in a sacred way. You may wish to re-draw it on a larger sheet of paper.

2. Choose one of the aspects from the boxes around the edge of the circle or add your own idea in the blank box. We suggest you choose something that is important to you or currently a challenge. Note down which area you have chosen.

3. Now work from the center circle outward, responding to the points below and noting your responses for each concentric ring:

a. From both **your inner and outer perspectives**, briefly review yourself in relation to this area of your life. Note your response and any ways in which you are already trying to live in a sacred way.

b. Identify any **issue(s)** you have in this area of your life. Describe them.

c. What **symptoms** do you observe about yourself in relation to this focus? You might note how things are at present, e.g. signs of stress and illness, out of balance, not much fun, calm, peaceful, etc.

d. What is your **intention** – in what direction would you like things to change? e.g. take a more holistic approach, be more creative, less busy, know more ...

e. Review briefly the **alternatives** you can choose instead.

f. Make a specific **choice**, e.g. "I am willing to ... focus on ... and look at it in a new way" or "I am willing to continue as I am with greater awareness ... "

g. My first steps: e.g. I will take the first step of ... on ...

4. Make sure that you record the first steps you are going to take. You might find it useful to use the activity: Beginning It Now from **Passion and Change** (page 135) again here.

5. Take some time to reflect on the connections you make between your ideas on living in a sacred way and acting with awareness to pursue the steps above. Look again at the skill of Acting With Awareness (page 33).

Try to share this with someone else. If you are following The Quest on your own, share it with a friend. If you are in a group, use it as an activity to share in the group.

Tell them the first steps you will take and agree that they will ask you again in a month what action you have taken. This helps you to reinforce your willingness to change.

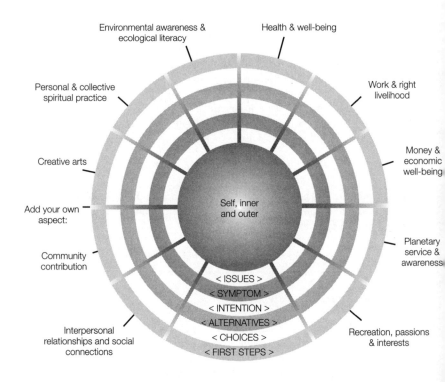

Fig 39: Dimensions Of Living In A Sacred Way
(Adapted from Pedlar and Boydell, 1985)

This activity can be used in many ways to explore the different dimensions of living in a sacred way. Similarly you have explored the idea of living in a sacred way from a number of perspectives – what it means to you, acting as if, being loving, living lovingly with others – and lastly, in a major review of areas in your life in which you might apply all this. But the key to living in a sacred way has to be your will to do it. So the final activity in this chapter offers you a skill of spiritual reflection that helps you develop the "inner muscles" to put living in a sacred way into practice.

Activity: Skills of Spiritual Reflection:
Developing Your "Inner Muscles"

This activity introduces a new skill of spiritual reflection associated with Opening

GOOD AND SKILFUL WILL

WHAT DOES IT MEAN?

Will is the power to choose, which implies the confidence to act and the commitment to go through with it. When you commit yourself to act you create a capacity for change in yourself, in others, and in your environment. Any act of Will calls for self-discipline, determination, and courage.

Transpersonal psychology understands your Will as a central force intimately connected to your sense of soul, and bringing feeling of connection to something beyond. In young children, evoking Will may be one of the ways in which they first connect with their sense of soul.

Will-power is needed to turn intention into action, but a strong Will alone is insufficient. You need to be able to discriminate and make wise informed choices. This calls for Good and Skilful Will. Good Will puts a premium on co-operation and harmony and acts for the greatest good of all. Skilful Will is identified as the capacity to develop an effective strategy and carry it out competently and conscientiously.

STARTING OUT

These stages of Good and Skilful Will are based on the work of Roberto Assagioli. He calls the Will "more than any other factor the key to human freedom and personal power" (Assagioli, 1974).

An act of Will can be broken down into a number of stages. For a major project, these stages will need to be carried out separately and in great detail. For something smaller, they may take place very quickly one after the other.

*1. **Purpose**. Defining what it is that is to be done and, if appropriate, writing it out and consulting with other people.*

*2. **Deliberation**. Considering all the various ways in which you might execute your act of Will based on Skilful Will, and carefully considering the impact of each way on others, the environment, and on yourself, choosing to put Good Will into action.*

*3. **Choice**. Making a planned and informed choice about which course of action to follow.*

*4. **Affirmation**. Gathering the elements of Skilful Will together, bringing your imagination, feelings, thoughts, highest dreams, and desires in unity bent toward this common purpose.*

*5. **Action**. Calling upon the power of your Will to carry out your action, taking constant account of progress, obstacles, and concerns as you go ahead.*

PRACTICING

1. Choose a task you have been putting off. Check that your mind and heart are in agreement with it, and it is aligned with your values. Make a sensible and realistic decision about when and how to get it done. Then do it!

2. Recall a project with which you have been involved, whether on your own, as part of a group, or as the leader. Try to choose something that was significant as far as you were concerned. Now recall it in detail. Note the stages that it went through, how well it worked, how things could have been done better. Appreciate the personal qualities that you contributed to it. Make a list of the aspects of the project that you consider demonstrated Good Will and those that demonstrated Skilful Will.

3. Offer your strength and support and advice to someone else when they need assistance with implementing an act of Will.

We suggest that you re-use this skill as you explore the different dimensions of living in a sacred way – it is your intention to live in a sacred way, allied to good and skilful will that changes the world.

"Our words and actions testify to our hidden thoughts; together they express our inner spirit. This is our life's testimony, our purpose here on earth: to manifest the very nature of our spirit, which is touched by the spirit of God."

Rumi (in Mabey, 2000)

ENDING – OR CONTINUING YOUR QUEST?

"Creativity itself is what is evolving in the cosmos,
and we are at the growing edge."

Beatrice Bruteau, (1997).

As you embarked on your journey with *The Quest* we put forward a number of strands for you to consider:

○ That the essence of exploring your sense of soul is awareness, being present, and connection to a Presence or Ultimate Reality that represents the ground, or fabric, of existence. This creates an inner space in which your sense of soul is enhanced by spiritual reflection.

○ That you can reflect upon your present and past through profound but gentle enquiry into yourself and your experience, in its personal and spiritual domains. This, in turn, brings greater clarity to your values and spiritual principles.

○ That collectively we are in a period of transition. A *zeitgeist* of this paradigm shift is that we are between stories. But you are not making this transition alone. By following *The Quest* you are able to contribute toward the compilation of a new story.

So you start drawing this phase of your journey to a close by literally returning to where you began and seeing it again through your eyes of today. At the beginning, your first activity was *Picturing The Present* (page 10). Now you picture the present again but from the perspective of reflecting on where you have traveled in your weeks and months with *The Quest*. Use this activity to get a "felt-sense" picture or impression. You will look at your journey in more detail in a while.

Activity: Picturing The Present Again

Imagine that you are going to meet an old friend and bring them up to date on your life.

- *Where are you as you complete* The Quest? *Look around and recognize what is important or meaningful now so you can remember it.*
- *What is your life like today?*
- *Very generally, what has changed since you first turned the pages of* The Quest?

As you imagine bringing your old friend up to date, take time to dwell, however briefly, in the current experience of your life. It may be helpful to stop using words and just be aware of this, without having to think about it or describe it. Focus on the main elements and what is uppermost in your attention.

    Then make a record of this in a way that suits you.

You may have noticed changes in the outward circumstances of your life, whether or not they were generated by following *The Quest*. But the important aspect is your inner domain and how you are able to bring that into harmony with the outer. What has your sense of soul come to mean to you in practice?

Activity: Your Sense Of Soul Today

This activity is best done with a partner, someone with whom you feel relaxed. It can also be done on your own; if so, value your response by recording it as imaginatively as you can.

    First, go outside and find a natural object; it may be a leaf, a stone, a piece of moss — whatever appeals to you and bring it back to where you will do the activity.

- *As you hold the object in your hands, first try to attune to the object. Imagine that you can take on the identity of the object and lend it your voice, speaking as if you are the object.*
- *As the object, speak about what it is and its outer being. Then speak of its sense of soul: how might it speak of that inner core that holds its potential and wholeness, its connection to the ground or fabric of existence that feels "radically alive" and the meaning this holds?*

Now put this object to one side. As you do so, take a few moments to quietly center yourself and resume your own identity. Then begin to speak of yourself, using the same questions as above but now applying them to yourself and your sense of soul.

When you have completed your story, pick your object up again and compare how you spoke as the object and when you spoke of yourself.

To complete the activity, take some time to be quiet in whatever way nurtures you and make any record you wish of your reflections.

Throughout *The Quest* a major part of your time and investment focused on reflecting on your story; as you read the next sentences, carry out a quick résumé of your journey. If it helps, you can turn back through the book to refresh your recollections.

You began your journey with **Heart of The Quest** in which you were *Having An Experience* and familiarizing yourself for the first time with exploring your sense of soul. In **Developing Your Skills** this was linked with a framework of skills of spiritual reflection and you practiced four core examples, one of each type of the skills of spiritual reflection. By **Telling Your Story** you concentrated on what has happened in your life and the particular beliefs, blocks, barriers, values, etc., that arose in you. Moving into **A Growing Sense of Soul** you made the connection between this, the language with which you can express spirituality, and your spiritual experience. You also considered the possibility of spiritual intelligence.

Through **Changing Faces of Faith** you revisited key formative influences in your life, both in your individual surroundings and in finding your way amid the cultural and intellectual movements of our times. As you explored **Encountering Direct Experience** you experimented with varied ways of knowing. You reflected on the particular experiences and forms that have been – and could become – your individual connection with Spirit.

Passion and Change introduced the idea of change as an enduring attribute of life, one that can be harnessed to give you a different way of engaging with both your passion and purpose and your pain. You re-framed change as your heroic journey, and thought about what excites and inspires your sense of purpose. But not all change is welcome and in **Dark Nights** you took a detailed and, perhaps, challenging walk through crisis, anger, despair, jealousy, and revenge before relieving the strain by working with love and fear and, finally, letting go into death and dying!

In **Wholeness and Connection** you began to turn your attention toward the outer world and how you might derive your own sense of wholeness and connection from recognizing that inner and outer are inalienable and indivisible aspects of yourself. This all culminated in **Living in a Sacred Way**, which Thich Nhat Hanh expressed as "Each thought, each action in the sunlight of awareness becomes sacred. In this light, no boundary exists between the sacred and the profane. I know that it can take me a bit longer to do the dishes, but I live fully in every moment, and I am happy." In *The Quest* this was translated into reflecting on the challenge of living lovingly, with yourself, with others, and on the earth.

The next activity pulls these threads together as you complete this journey –
even though each completion is no more than a provisional resting place
before you continue on your way.

Activity: Engaging With Your Story

*Remember that the various chapters gave you different ways to explore different
aspects of your spiritual and personal journey. Work through the recollections
below. This may take some time and the trigger questions are broken into groups
to encourage you to take a break between them.*

- *What have you learned about yourself in general?*
- *What have you learned about yourself in relation to your experience of
spirituality in your life?*
- *What have you learned about your present framework of faith?*
- *What, if anything, has changed in your world-view and your perception of other
world-views?*
- *What, for you, are the most natural ways of encountering direct experience and
does variety of approach help you?*
- *What other avenues of exploration might you wish to explore?*

- *How would you describe your 'passion and purpose' and your 'pain' now?*
- *Has anything shifted for you during the time that you have been following* The
Quest? *If so, what is it?*
- *What, if any, are the differences in your attitude to change now compared to
when you started* The Quest?

- *What is your current experience of wholeness and connection both with other
dimensions and through life and the Earth?*
- *What have you identified as ways in which you currently try to live in a sacred
way?*
- *What have you experienced about being loving?*
- *What next steps or specific actions did you identify for any outer changes you
have decided to make? How will you check back on your experience of putting
them into practice?*

SUMMING UP

*Complete the following sentences in any way that suits you. It doesn't have to be
writing – you may well have a different and creative way of your own but let the
sentences act as a focus.*

- *What I have learned during* The Quest *is ...*
- *An important insight for me during* The Quest *was ...*

- *The things from* The Quest *that I shall continue to use most often are ...*
- *New things I have discovered are ...*
- *The parts of* The Quest *I would like to return to are ... because...*
- *In exploring my sense of soul I have ...*
- *I want to continue ...*
- *I want to begin or develop ...*
- *I want to change ...*
- *My next steps are ...*

Lastly you turned to consider your contribution to the new story. Earlier, you explored the heroic journey, in which the final stage is reward and return, during which you share the experience and learning of your journey with others. In one such story, the hero is a Knight who was charged to go to a holy place, light a new torch from a sacred flame, and take this flame back to his hometown. After much traveling and endeavor, the Knight finds the flame and embarks on his return journey carrying the holy flame in his torch. On the way back he encounters an old woman by her house. She asks for a light from the flame to kindle her fire. Reluctantly he stops and grants her request, then continues on his way. A little later he is engulfed in a huge storm. Despite his best efforts to protect his torch, the rain and wind extinguish the flame. The Knight is distraught as he contemplates the failure of his quest. Suddenly he remembers that the flame still burns in the old woman's house. He retraces his steps to her house where she remembers the bold Knight and rekindles his torch from her fire. Now he is able to complete his journey with the flame back to his hometown.

The message of the quest here seems to be that the gifts of the quest, whatever they may be, must be shared and used if they are to stay alive to benefit both the adventurer who sought them and those the adventurer meets on the return journey.

The fruits of your individual journey will be many and varied, perhaps including insights, awareness, change, healing, and self-knowledge. The nature of our collective journey, however, is still fluid. Many researchers and commentators find evidence that people's experience and aspirations of spirituality are changing; we have referred to some of these in the text (e.g. Berry page 16, Heelas page 58, Forman page 184, Bloom page 185, Griffiths page 83, etc.). This trend seems to be true both for those whose path is within an existing religious tradition and among those not currently associated with them.

Key characteristics of these shared experiences and aspirations have been explored throughout *The Quest* and include:

○ People giving more weight to claims to truth that are rooted in their own experience rather than simply passed down unquestioningly through dogma or creed.

○ Perceiving language and thought as one among a number of valid modes of access to Spirit. Many people now value a holistic approach that also embraces emotion, intuition, and direct experience of varying kinds and conveys wonder, beauty, and mystery through images and symbols as well as words.

○ A profound and deeply felt re-connection with the environment and natural world is one of the major shifts of recent decades and it is frequently complemented by a strong sense of global unity.

○ Old authorities are challenged and under strain, whether these are based on hierarchy, gender, ethnicity, institutions, or bureaucracies.

○ A groundswell and yearning to feel whole within one's own life, to be able to talk about spirituality as a natural dimension of human experience.

This, then, may sum up the changing "hometown" toward which you are returning with the flame alight in your new torch. Consider the people you encounter en route, who may wish to kindle their fire from your torch as you pass by. Consider, also, as you look toward your destination, what fruits your return may bring in your "hometown". The next, and final, activity in *The Quest* offers one more gift – the skill of spiritual reflection in working with vision – that may help you perceive more deeply gifts of the flame, the new torch that you carry, and the contribution that you may make to compiling the new story with which we began.

Activity: Skills of Spiritual Reflection:
Practicing Opening

This activity introduces a new skill of spiritual reflection associated with Opening.

WORKING WITH VISION

WHAT DOES IT MEAN?

Vision helped invent the wheel and the printing press, helped explorers sail the oceans to new lands and land on the moon. Vision sparks creative power and turns something abstract into something concrete. But it does not have to be world changing.

Every idea turned into reality, even an everyday matter, is a demonstration of a vision turned into reality. It is a very powerful ability, and it needs care. We are, in a sense, co-creating with Spirit. Vision is Spirit's agent for change, and creativity is the agent's toolkit.

STARTING OUT

1. Vision may begin as a barely perceptible idea, an image, or a fluttering in the heart. Take time and space to be receptive to the vision. Wait a while, and see if anything becomes clearer. Allow time for the process of conception.

2. Ground the vision by translating the idea into thoughts, words, or images. Share it with others if appropriate. Begin to think what needs to be done to translate the vision into reality. Surrender to the vision, and consciously commit yourself to be a focus for vision, letting go of your own ego or personal agenda. Keep your antennae at the ready, stay open and receptive.

3. Make a commitment to the vision and clarify it further. Sharpen up the concepts; work on detail, and further steps and functions. Vision requires sincerity and passion. It also demands your integrity, patience, tenacity, and commitment.

4. Nurture the vision by finding the resources you need and communicating more publicly your sense of purpose and a clear plan and sense of direction. Stay attuned to the vision, and try to stay on course. Be open to valuable feedback and insight from others, or from elsewhere.

5. Review and adjust the vision according to how it is developing. Hold a balance between the clarity of the vision and adapting it to overcome obstacles. Take time also to celebrate success.

6. Keep the vision sustained in spite of drawbacks and challenges. Trust that it will serve the highest good.

7. Keep in your mind what you have learned from the experience and how you might continue to work with vision in your life.

PRACTICING

1. *Walking into the unknown.* Bringing a vision into reality often means stepping out into the unknown. You may find that a chasm opens ahead of you between the known and present state and an unknown future state. This is the void, where you summon all your trust in life to keep your footing, and keep sight of the vision.

2. *Working with the "Laws of Manifestation".* One way of finding and following a vision is to use a range of techniques such as Visualization (page 137), goal setting, or affirmation, all of which apply the power of positive thought toward a specific goal to fill a need or lack. Ask for direction and go ahead in the faith that your needs will be met, giving thanks that this is so. The mental images have a power that leads to a concentration of energy.

3. David Spangler (undated) suggests a second process. His four aspects of

this process are a more concisely defined way of what we describe above in Starting out.

Right identification – *means "knowing oneself as timeless, infinite Spirit", growing in consciousness and nourished by all life.*

Right imagination – *involves us in using "higher imagination" to attune, to identify, and understand the essence of the vision we seek to realize and to become one in consciousness with it.*

Right attunement – *is attuning with the essence of the vision in its pre-form state. For essence to be expressed, it must be "cloaked in the energy substance of either the mental, emotional, or physical realms, or all three of them." For a vision to be expressed, it needs to take form.*

Right action – *relies on our willingness and ability to do whatever is necessary on the physical level to bring the vision into form.*

Vision does not have to be individually conceived. It can be shared with others and it can be an exciting challenge to bring it to reality. Welcome the opportunity to participate in the compilation and development of a new story and a shared vision.

We, the writers of *The Quest*, will be continuing our journey too. May yours and ours be blessed, remain open to opportunity and challenge, and grow in wisdom. We encourage you to value your contribution and continue to quest in exploring your sense of soul.

MAKING THE MOST OF
THE QUEST

While many people follow *The Quest* on their own, many others find companionship and support helpful. Douglas V. Steere writes, "to 'listen' another's soul into life, into a condition of disclosure and discovery, may be almost the greatest service that any human being ever performs for another." Such discussion and sharing of your journey and insights can significantly deepen and enrich your own exploration and use of *The Quest*.

Although many bookshops have shelves dedicated to personal development and spirituality, it is still not necessarily part of personal or work settings for people to share their inner journeys, personal issues and challenges, or spiritual experiences and searching. At the same time many of us want to talk about these areas of our life and appreciate being heard by another or several others. Sometimes other people's stories are very similar to your own; sometimes they are very different. Either way the experience of sharing can help you feel that you are not alone, reassured that other people have comparable experiences and also appreciate that *your* journey is unique in its own way too.

FINDING SUPPORT

You may already know someone who is a kindred spirit – someone who is on the same wavelength and whom you can entrust with your deeper thoughts and feelings – and you may decide to follow *The Quest* together. In *Making The Most of The Quest*, however, we suggest some ways to develop companionship and support if you are not sure where to find it. You can also look at *The Quest* website (www.thequest.org.uk) to find further resources. *The Quest* website offers a directory of relevant information, including News & Updates, Resources, Events, and a Library of links that supplement and update the bibliography and further reading in *The Quest*.

A QUEST FRIEND

If you do not already have such a friend you might try to seek out such a person. Once you are looking, you may find that the person next door or sitting at the next desk may be interested to follow *The Quest* with you and you can offer companionship and support to each other. Alternatively, you may find support through people trained to accompany others on their spiritual journey, such as spiritual directors, those with a ministry of listening, people trained as interfaith ministers, or coaches, counselors, and mentors with an interest in the spiritual journey.

CONVERSATIONS AND CAFÉS

Sometimes you may welcome companionship and discussion but want to keep it informal and easy to organize; a meeting that is easy, convivial, and welcoming while providing an opportunity for meaningful conversation.

Meeting regularly with friends in a café to have conversations that go deeper than the normal social round can be one answer. This can take the form of just agreeing to meet a few friends in a convenient location, where the ambience and noise levels allow you to have a conversation. You can agree to each read a section of *The Quest* beforehand and bring some thoughts and responses with you to serve as a way in to deeper conversations.

Some people organize it a bit further and find a place where they can use a room, put a list of topics for meetings together and expect a mixture of regular participants and others who drop in sometimes. Activities, sections, or themes from *The Quest* can be used as a starting point for discussion.

QUEST GROUPS

You may prefer to start a Quest group to meet regularly and use *The Quest* to explore your own spiritual journey and enjoy the enrichment of companionship and discussion with others. Any information on existing Quest groups will be on *The Quest* website (www.thequest.org.uk).

STARTING A GROUP
1. RUNNING A TASTER SESSION

One way to get a group together is to invite some people for tea / coffee, show them your copy of *The Quest*, and share your own interest and enthusiasm.

You may find that people want to experience *The Quest* for themselves before making a commitment. One way of doing this is to do an activity together, so people start talking and sharing at a deeper level than before and generate interest in taking the exploration and discussion further.

A number of activities in *The Quest* give a practical experience of both an activity and sharing discussion of it with others. Choose one or two that you would enjoy (suggested activities are below), make sure you have read them carefully beforehand, and consider what you might say to introduce the activity to the group.

Activity: Skills For Spiritual Reflection: Opening to Creative Inspiration (page 30)
Ask people to think about what inspires them or brings them joy. Then ask them to find a partner and share their responses. Bring the group back together and give them time to hear from each other.

Activity: Skills For Spiritual Reflection: Your Personal Values (page 48)
Ask people to sit back, maybe close their eyes so they concentrate on the questions you are going to ask, then take them through the questions under Starting Out point 1. Allow time between each question for people to think and write. Then suggest that they share in pairs before sharing in the group. This might be used in conjunction with the activity below.

Activity: Qualities You Respect in Others (page 46)
A safe activity as a starter.

Activity: Who Am I? (page 43)
This activity allows people to introduce themselves to each other in a positive light. It may be helpful to share in twos or threes before speaking in the whole group.

Activity: Finding Your Own Language (page 61)
If you use this as a taster, write out the quotations on page 60 on a large sheet of paper (or similar quotations of your choice) beforehand. Read the quotations and give people a few moments to think about them before gathering in threes or fours to talk about the activity itself on page 61. This can be followed by the activity below.

Activity: What Has Been Your Experience? (page 58)
This is a good activity for a group who can be open to explore their own experience.

Activity: Developing Your SQ (page 66)
This is a useful activity to encourage people to start talking about what "exploring a sense of soul" means to them. You might also write Zohar and Marshall's 10 characteristics of spiritual intelligence (see page 66-67) on a large sheet of paper for the group to discuss after the activity.

Activity: *Your Response To Change* (page 125)
This may be a good activity to introduce into an existing support group

of some kind, e.g. single parent group, new business support group, as a way of deepening the issues discussed. You don't need to ask people to fill in a chart but jot down their thoughts and feelings in response to a change in their life.

Activity: _What is Sacred_? (page 190)
Read the quotation at the beginning of _Living in a Sacred Way_ by Thich Nhat Hanh (page 189) then use this as an introduction to the activity on page 190 If you wish to extend this, you could go on to read out the activities on pages 192 and 193 and invite responses to them.

2. RUNNING A GROUP

The idea of a group is that it is a community where people can share their spiritual journeys; where its members feel it is a safe place to be, where each person's story is valued, where leadership is exercised gently (perhaps peer leadership which is held in rotation by each of you), where questioning is valued and where change is welcome. Fenelon, a seventeenth-century French pastor, gave sound advice:

> "Speak little; listen much; think far more of understanding hearts and of adapting yourself to their needs than of saying clever things to them. Show that you have an open mind, and let everyone see by experience that there is safety and consolation in opening his mind to you."

The notes below offer some basic elements to give you the confidence to start a group; you can also find more ideas and skills through _The Quest_ website (www.thequest.org.uk), or from books in a local library or bookshop on running and facilitating a group. Imagine what would help you feel at ease in a group and ask the others in your group to share the responsibility – agree together what will make your group meetings something you look forward to, share the responsibility of keeping yourselves to these guidelines, encouraging each other to be able to speak in the group if you find yourself less happy to come to meetings.

Role of Group Convenor

The person who is the convenor of a group deals with practical arrangements. A welcoming venue and agreed timing that provides a safe and informal setting is needed. Simple refreshments will be appreciated as they provide time for informal introductions and building of relationships.

If you have not convened a group before the following checklist may help you:

○ Use of _The Quest_ – each person will need to have their own copy of

The Quest. The group cannot function as well if people try to share copies between them

○ <u>Size</u> – a group of between 3 and 8 people is preferable

○ <u>Location of group</u> – while people might be keen initially, they will only keep coming if their journey is practical for them

○ <u>Venue</u> – a room that is as light, airy, warm, and as comfortable as possible, with chairs arranged in a circle. Some groups appreciate flowers or a candle or background music to provide a welcoming atmosphere

○ <u>Refreshments</u> – look into how/whether to provide tea/coffee/biscuits and whether this is before or after the main part of the meeting. Refreshments can provide an opportunity for people to meet socially but not everyone has time to come early or start late

○ <u>Timing</u> – check everyone knows the date and time (and venue) of the meeting

○ <u>Cost</u> – be clear about costs involved, e.g. possible hire of room, refreshments and how expenses are shared

○ <u>Communication</u> – follow up on members who are absent and make sure they know the date, time, and venue for the next meeting and any tasks the group agreed to prepare

○ <u>Rotating the role of convenor</u> – the role of convenor can be regular for a series of sessions or it can be rotated. It can be combined with the role of group facilitator or it might be preferable to separate these tasks.

Role Of Group Facilitator

A facilitator is essentially an enabler. Unlike a teacher, tutor, or chairperson it is not the role of a facilitator to control or direct the proceedings. The role of a group facilitator is to enable the group to come together and collectively agree and maintain a process that will help both the individuals and the group as a whole to follow an agreed task or course in an enjoyable and effective way.

Group facilitators do not "know it all" but are on a journey of discovery and relationship along with everyone else in the group. Additionally, they try to set an atmosphere that will be warm, welcoming and 'safe' for honest sharing and discussion. As a facilitator you do not need to be an authority but it will help if you are familiar with some of *The Quest* or can read ahead before the group meets. You will then be more able to make suggestions as to how the group might start and proceed.

It is important to keep in mind that the purpose of the group is to follow *The Quest* in companionship with others. While it is a healthy part of the exercise to encourage participants to share from their personal experience and insight, be careful not to let it become a group therapy session. Keep focused and keep to your purpose.

If you already have experience of being a group facilitator these notes may act as a reminder. If you are new to this role they outline some basics that help a group organize itself.

Setting a Safe Atmosphere
The atmosphere in a group comes from a mix of factors – physical, social, and emotional. Remember that the purpose of *The Quest* is for each person to explore their own answers and responses. The benefit of doing this in a group is to hear different points of view from others and be heard in an open, non-judgmental way.

Relationship building in the early stages is important, perhaps through sharing in twos or threes before sharing in a larger group.

A practice of collective stillness or attunement may help introduce a sense of comfort around the spiritual element. Look at *Skills For Spiritual Reflection: Finding Inner Stillness* (page 25) and *Skills For Spiritual Reflection: Attuning* (page 205), and suggest something that seems to suit the people present.

Ice-breakers are useful at the start of a group. You might consider one of the following suggestions:

○ A simple name round and one short sentence to introduce oneself e.g. "I'm Tony and I live in the next village."
○ Introducing yourself in pairs, then each partner introducing the other to the group.
○ Moving around the room to music introducing yourself to another person each time the music stops.

The purpose of ice-breakers is to introduce people to each other, establish rapport between the individuals and dispel initial anxieties. So, make sure that the activity is one appropriate to the age and culture of the particular group.

Agreeing ground-rules
When you meet for the first time you will find it helpful to agree some guidelines for yourselves about how the group will operate. Each group will work out its own rhythm for working on *The Quest* alone and working together; our experience is that every Quest group uses the material differently and proceeds in its own way so be ready to trust what the group feels is right for them. We suggest you meet as a group not more than once a fortnight and not less than once a month. During the first meeting you might ask people to suggest some ground-rules you can all agree to. You could then suggest any possible gaps. Useful ground-rules include:

Confidentiality – as quite personal and sensitive issues might be shared an agreement to keep confidentiality within the group is important to creating safety.

Listening without interrupting also creates safety. Remember that in such personal areas it is important to treat each other with respect; "tread carefully because you tread on my dreams."

Sharing time fairly among the group members is important so enthusiastic or dominant members do not get more than their share of "air time" and more timid or tentative people get too little and are dissatisfied or feel put-down.

Using "I" statements is a way to own and be honest about feelings. We commonly use generalizations and stereotypes to express our own opinions as if they were facts. "I" statements enable the speaker to own their personal view in what they are saying, e.g.

"When you think about it you get confused" becomes "When I think about it I get confused"

"One often feels depressed" becomes "I often feel depressed"

"Most people think that is the easiest way" becomes "I think that is the easiest way".

In this way, real exchange and dialogue can take place. But bear in mind that the purpose is for authenticity not political correctness!

Commitment to the group also needs to be agreed. Group members feel frustrated when others do not turn up without a prior explanation, or have not done the agreed work or activities beforehand.

Group Development

A successful group usually takes off on its own after the first few sessions. You can help this process by encouraging other group members gradually to take over responsibility for planning the sessions and for taking up any suggestions that are practical. Don't be alarmed if the group goes through a difficult patch; it is a normal part of a cycle of developing relationship and establishing a capacity to be real with each other rather than just on your "best behavior" all the time. Difficulties may enable disagreements or personality difficulties to be aired and can be followed by a higher level of trust and co-operation.

Do encourage the members of your group to take turns in the role of group facilitator. This shares responsibility, provides different styles of approach, and helps everyone gain greater awareness of the energy and life of the group.

Having Variety . . . perhaps begin by going round your circle, coming together with each other, before getting down to the focus for the meeting. We suggest you set a time limit to this first circle and just listen to each other. Do not get sidetracked into a discussion or conversation that goes off track.

Sometimes you will spend the whole meeting together as a group working on an agreed topic and sometimes you might vary it by splitting into twos or threes to look at something, then all feed back into the whole group. Be prepared to experiment to find what you like. Try a variety of ways to keep the group alive and avoid any sense that it is stuck in just one way of doing things.

Having Conversations ... these will vary too. Sometimes they might explore and probe something; some might be about sharing difficulties or challenges; some might go in depth into differences of view to tease out different perspectives. But it is not helpful if people try to win an argument or prove one view against another. Be respectful in challenging one another; no one knows all the answers or all the truth. You are there to reflect on and clarify your own perspective but so is everyone else.

When sharing or listening, don't try to tell each other the solution to a dilemma. Often just by listening you enable another person to find their own answer. If someone asks "What should I do?" turn the question back for them to look for their own response. Encourage people to be clear with each other and to address inter-personal niggles as an opportunity to practice what they are working with. If the group can value the importance of trust, being transparent and clear, and respectful of each other early on, then the life of the group will be built on a more solid base.

Having Silence ... don't be afraid of silence and try to avoid rushing in to fill it. Silence can often be fruitful and can sometimes lead into an agreed period of inner stillness.

If in doubt ... trust the process, don't rush in to fix it, allow the situation to unfold itself while you wait to see what happens!

Dealing with Difficulties

However trusting or experienced the group, difficulties may arise and the group may look to the facilitator to give a lead on these. While you may take a lead, you are not solely responsible for the group; it is also the responsibility of everyone in the group. It may be helpful to observe or sum up to the group what seems to be happening and invite other people's suggestions on the next step for the group to take. Common difficulties include:

Dealing with emotional upsets such as acute anxiety, tears, or anger, can be quite challenging. All change generates emotion. Sadness may scare us and anger can be quite frightening. Very often the situation seems difficult because we are afraid that we, or others, might be overwhelmed. At all times, try to stay calm; you might make a neutral observation on what is happening in a non-judgmental way; offer the person concerned some support and maybe suggest a short break or cooling-off period.

Dealing with difficult individuals can range from the person who dominates and talks too much, to the person who is silent and makes no contribution at all, to a person who argues and puts other people down. Try to ensure that everyone gets an equal chance to take part. A quiet person may join in only by nodding and leaning forward and is often waiting for an invitation to contribute.

Remember that people's difficult behavior is rarely purposeless and can often be a defensive response to perceived fears or threats. See if you can perceive the emotional need behind what is being expressed and, once again, limit your interventions and try to trust the process. Be assured that most people want a session to work for them, each other, and for you!

<u>Starting and finishing</u> on time and with a short period of quiet helps to sustain the flow and togetherness of the group. Begin with a short attunement or meditation and consciously call forth qualities, such as clarity or understanding, which will help the meeting. Finish with an opportunity for any remarks or observations of unfinished business from the meeting and a goodbye check-in to make sure everyone feels complete as they leave.

A useful guideline for facilitators is to try to balance the needs of each individual, the group as a whole, and the agreed plan for the session. Your aim might be that:

- O **each person** leaves a session feeling that they have been heard and have satisfied at least some of the needs they came with
- O **the group** was able to set its own agenda and work well together
- O **at least some of the areas to be discussed or activities selected** received a fair amount of attention and you decided what, if anything, is needed to address those you did not cover
- O **everyone** left re-inspired in some way**.**

RESOURCES

The following list gives a few signposts to organizations and networks with a focus on spirituality. These resources concentrate on the UK; suggestions for additions outside the UK are welcome. A fuller (and more international) list of resources can be found on *The Quest* website: www.thequest.org.uk

Alternatives, St James' Church, 197 Piccadilly, London W1J 9LL, UK.
Tel: +44 (0) 207 287 6711
Email: alternatives@ukonline.co.uk
Website: www.alternatives.org.uk

Association of Interfaith Ministers, Halsecombe House, Parsons Hill, Porlock, Somerset TA24 8QP, UK. Tel: +44 (0) 1643 862621

Email: info@interfaithministers.org.uk
Website: www.interfaithministers.org.uk

CANA (Christians Awakening To A New Awareness), 102 Church Road, Steep, Petersfield GU32 2DD, UK. Tel: +44 (0) 1730 265591
Email: treasurer@canaweb.info
Website: www.canaweb.info

Esalen Institute, Highway 1, Big Sur, CA 93920-9616, USA. Tel: +1 831-667-3000
Email: info@esalen.org
Website: www.esalen.org

Findhorn Foundation, The Park, Findhorn, Forres, Moray IV36 3TZ, Scotland. Tel: +44 (0) 1309 690311
Email: enquiries@findhorn.org
Website: www.findhorn.org

Findhorn Foundation College, Cluny Hill College, St Leonards Road, Forres, Moray IV36 2RD. Tel: +44 (0) 1309 672288
Email: college@findhorncollege.org
Website: www.findhorncollege.org

Future Church New Zealand, Rosemary Neave, Massey Rd, RD2 Waipu 0254, Aotearoa, New Zealand. Tel: 09 4321234
Email: rosemary@futurechurch.org.nz
Website: www.futurechurch.org.nz

Hawkwood College, Painswick Old Road, Stroud, Gloucestershire GL6 7QW, UK. Tel: +44 (0) 1453 759034
Email: info@hawkwoodcollege.co.uk
Website: www.hawkwoodcollege.co.uk

Institute of Noetic Sciences (IONS), 101 San Antonio Road, Petaluma, CA 94952, USA. Tel: +1 707-775-3500
Email: membership@noetic.org
Website: www.ions.org

The Interfaith Seminary, 7-11 Kensington High Street, London W8 5NP, UK. Tel: +44 (0) 0207 368 3325.
Email: theinterfaithseminary@community.co.uk
Website: www.interfaithseminary.org.uk

Living Spirituality Network, The Well at Willen, Newport Rd, Willen, Milton Keynes MK15 9AA, UK. Tel: +44 (0) 1908 200675
Email: spirituality@ctbi.org.uk
Website: www.living-spirituality.org.uk

Naropa University, 2130 Arapahoe Ave, Boulder, Colorado, 80302, USA.
Tel: +1 303-444-0202
Email: admissions@naropa. edu
Website: www.naropa.edu

The New Seminary, PMB#344, Broadway, NY 10025-5657, USA. Tel: +1 212-222-3711 and +1 888-688-4884 (Toll-free within the USA)
Email: info@newseminary.org
Website: www.newseminary.org

New York Open Center, 83 Spring Street, New York NY 10012, USA. Tel: +1 212-219-2527
Email: info@opencenter.org
Website: www.opencenter.org

Onespirit Learning Alliance And Interfaith Seminary, 330 West 38th Street, Suite 1500, New York NY 10018, USA. Tel: +1 212.931.6840
Email: info@onespiritinterfaith.org
Website: www.onespiritinterfaith.org

Open Centres, Avils Farm, Lower Stanton St Quentin, Chippenham, Wilts SN14 6DA, UK. Tel: +44 (0)1249 720202

Psychosynthesis & Education Trust, 92-94 Tooley Street, London Bridge, London SE1 2TH, UK. Tel: +44 (0)20 7403 2100
Email: enquiries@petrust.org.uk
Website: www.psychosynthesis.edu

The Retreat Association, The Central Hall, 256, Bermondsey Street, London SE1 3UJ, UK. Tel: +44 (0) 845 456 1429
Email: info@retreats.org.uk
Website: www.retreats.org.uk

Schumacher College, The Old Postern, Dartington, Devon TQ9 6EA, UK.
Tel : +44 (0)1803 865934
Email: admin@schumachercollege.org.uk
Website: www.schumachercollege.org.uk

Social Venture Network, General Secretariat SVN Europe, Kalkovenweg 30, 2401 LK Alphen a/d Rijn, The Netherlands. Tel: +31 (0)172 - 423 845
Email: info@svneurope.com
Website: www.svneurope.com

Spirit @ Work Trust, (New Zealand), contact: Ann Smith, PO Box 6127, Dunedin North, New Zealand.
Email: athene@paradise.net.nz

The Spirituality, Leadership and Management Network (SLaM), (Australia), SLaM Network, PO Box 1171, Hartwell VIC 3124, Australia. Tel: +61 (0)3 9681 9111
Email: steve.mcdonald@slam.net.au
Website: www.slam.net.au

Postgraduate Certificate in Spiritual Development & Facilitation, School of Management, University of Surrey, Guildford GU2 7XH, UK. Tel: +44 (0) 1483 689760
Email: spirituality@surrey.ac.uk
Website: www.som.surrey.ac.uk

UK Directory of Resources, listing providers of spiritual learning programs with a universal outlook and allied resources such as publications and learning aids.
Email: resources@ufsforum.org
Website: www.ufsforum.org/
Enquiries can also be made to the Wrekin Trust (contact details below).

Wrekin Trust, Courtyard Lodge, Mellow Farm, Hawcross Lane, Redmarley d'Abitot, Gloucestershire GL19 3JQ, UK. Tel: +44 (0) 1452 840033
Email: info@wrekintrust.org
Website: www.sirgeorgetrevelyan.org.uk/WT1.html

WYSE (World Youth Service and Enterprise) International, Fox Cottage, Kensington Place, London W8 7PP, UK. Tel: +44 (0) 207 727 5198.
Email: internationaloffice@wyse-ngo.org
Website: www.wyse-ngo.org

MAGAZINES AND PERIODICALS

Caduceus, 38 Russell Terrace, Leamington Spa, Warwickshire CV31 1HE, UK. Tel: +44 (0) 1926 451897
Email: caduceus@ caduceus.info
Website: www. caduceus.info

Kindred Spirit, Foxhole, Dartington, Totnes, Devon TQ9 6EB, UK. Tel: +44 (0) 1803 866686
Email: mail@kindredspirit.co.uk
Website: www.kindredspirit.co.uk

Positive News, Positive News Publishing Ltd, Bicton Enterprise Centre, Clun, Shropshire, SY7 8NF, UK Tel: +44 (0) 1588 640022
Email: office@positivenews.org.uk
Website: www.positivenews.org.uk

Resurgence, Ford House, Hartland, Bideford, Devon EX39 6EE, UK. Tel: + 44 (0) 1237 441293
Email: info@resurgence.org
Website: www.resurgence.org

What Is Enlightenment? PO Box 2360, Lenox, MA 01240, USA. Tel: +1 413-637-6000 or +1 800 -376-3210 (Toll-free within the USA)
Email: wie@wie.org
Website: www.wie.org

A LIST OF VALUES AND QUALITIES

Accountability	Empathy	Intuition	Self-knowing
Adaptability	Enthusiasm	Joy	Sharing
Awareness	Equality	Justice	Simplicity
Balance	Equilibrium	Kindness	Sincerity
Beauty	Fairness	Leadership	Steadfastness
Belonging	Flexibility	Learning	Stillness
Calmness	Forbearance	Love	Strength
Caring	Forgiveness	Loyalty	Sympathy
Clarity	Forthrightness	Non-violence	Transparency
Commitment	Freedom	Obedience	Tenderness
Compassion	Fun	Openness	Tolerance
Concentration	Generosity	Peace	Trust
Co-operation	Gentleness	Perseverance	Truth
Courtesy	Gratitude	Power	Welcoming
Creativity	Harmony	Purpose	Willingness
Dedication	Honesty	Reliability	Unity
Delight	Hope	Resourcefulness	Reason
Determination	Humility	Respect	Tranquility
Dignity	Humor	Responsibility	Wisdom
Discernment	Independence	Satisfaction	Understanding
Diversity	Initiative	Self-acceptance	Detachment
Duty	Inspiration	Self-confidence	
Efficiency	Integrity	Self-discipline	

BIBLIOGRAPHY AND FURTHER READING

The bibliography is organized by chapter. Items marked ★are referred to in the text; other references suggest follow-up reading. References may appear under more than one chapter.

References and recommended reading relating to the Skills of Spiritual Reflection follow the general bibliography.

The Quest website – www.thequest.org.uk – has a Library with updated references as well as links to Internet resources.

GETTING STARTED

★Berry, Thomas (1988) *The Dream of the Earth*, Sierra Club Books, San Francisco, USA

Forman, Robert (2004) *Grassroots Spirituality: What It Is, Why It Is Here and Where It Is Going*, Imprint Academic, USA and UK

Matousek, Mark (1998) *Should You Design Your Own Religion?* Utne Reader, July-August 1998, an article on www.utne.com

★Moss, Richard (1987) *The Black Butterfly: an Invitation to Radical Aliveness*, Celestial Arts, Berkeley, California, USA

Sands, Helen Raphael (2000) *Labyrinth, pathway to meditation and healing*, Gaia Books, UK

★Spangler, David (1998) *The Call*, Riverhead Books, USA

Tomlinson, Dave (1995) *The Post Evangelical,* Triangle, UK

HEART OF THE QUEST

Brussat, Fredric and Mary Ann (1996) *Spiritual Literacy: Reading The Sacred In Everyday Life*, Turnstone, New York, USA

Cori, Jasmin Lee (2000) *The Tao of Contemplation*, Samuel Weiser Inc, ME, USA www.redwheelweiser.com

Gendlin, Eugene (2003) *Focusing*, Rider, UK

Griffiths, Bede (1994) *Universal Wisdom: A Journey Through The Sacred Wisdom Of The World*, Fount, HarperCollins, London, UK

Holden, Miranda (2002) *Boundless Love*, Rider, UK

Houston, Jean (1997) *A Passion for the Possible*, Harper, San Francisco, USA

Lacey, Paul (1999) *Nourishing The Spiritual Life*, Quaker Home Service, London, UK

Levine, Stephen (1997) *A Year Left To Live*, Thorsons, London UK

★Loring, Patricia (1997) *Listening Spirituality: Personal Spiritual Practice Amongst Friends*, Quaker Books of Friends General Conference and available from www.quakerbooks.org or e-mail at bookstore@fgcquaker.com and Quaker Book Shop, London, UK

★Parsons, Tony (1995) *The Open Secret*, Open Secret Publications, HDTV & Media, Cranborne, Dorset BH21 5PZ, UK

Steere, Douglas V. (1955) *Where Words Come From*, Quaker Home Service, London, UK

Vardey, Lucinda, (ed.) (1995) *God In All Worlds: An Anthology Of Contemporary Spiritual Writing,* Chatto & Windus, London, UK

DEVELOPING YOUR SKILLS

(See also *Index to Skills of Spiritual Reflection*, page 259)

★Blake, William – Jerusalem (1804) in *William Blake's Illuminated Books: Jerusalem (William Blake's Illuminated Books (Collected Edition))* William Blake (Illustrator), Morton D. Paley (Editor), Tate Publishing 1998, London, UK

Bloom, William (2001) *The Endorphin Effect: A Breakthrough Strategy for Holistic Health and Spiritual Well-being,* Judy Piatkus (Publishers) Ltd, UK

Das, Lama Surya (1999) *Awakening To The Sacred*, Bantam Books, USA and UK

★Evans and Russell, (1992) *The Creative Manager,* John Wiley & Sons, London, UK

★Ferrucci, Piero (1982) *What We May Be,* Aquarian/Thorsons, London, UK

Gruber, Louis N (2000) *Psalms for Breathing: Meditating the Psalms With Music, Movement and Silence,* 1stBooksLibrary, USA

★James, William (1961) *The Varieties Of Religious Experience*, Collier Macmillan, New York, USA

Lawrence, Brother (various) *The Practice Of The Presence Of God: The Best Rule Of The Holy Life*, and www.ccel.org/ccel/lawrence/practice.toc.html

Leonard, George and Murphy, Michael (1995) *The Life We Are Given*, Jeremy Tarcher/Penguin Puttnam, New York, USA

Mello S. J., Anthony de (1984) *Sadhana: A Way To God – Christian Exercises in Eastern Form*, Image Books, part of the Random House Group, USA

Neeld, Elizabeth Harper (1999) *A Sacred Primer*, Renaissance Books, USA

Roberts, Elizabeth and Amidon, Elias (eds) (1999) *Prayers For A Thousand Years:*

Blessings and Expressions for Hope for the New Millennium, HarperCollins Publishers, USA

*Rogers, Carl (1977) *Becoming a Person*, Constable & Co, UK

*Rogers, Natalie (1993) *The Creative Connection*, Scientific & Behavior Books Inc, USA

*Scott, Mike (1992) *Open* From the CD album *Still Burning* (Chrysalis Records, 1997). Words and Music by Mike Scott, ©1996 Sony Music Publishing Limited

Simpson, Ray (2003) *The Joy Of Spiritual Fitness*, Zondervan, UK & USA

Sinetar, Marsha (1992) *A Way Without Words: A Guide For Spiritually Emerging Adults*, Paulist Press, USA

Teasdale, Wayne (1999) *The Mystic Heart; Discovering a Universal Spirituality in the World's Religions*, New World Library, CA, USA

Tolle, Eckhart (2001) *The Power Of Now*, Hodder & Stoughton, London, UK

Walsh, Roger (1999) *Essential Spirituality – Exercises From The World's Religions To Cultivate Kindness, Love, Joy, Peace, Wisdom And Generosity*, J Wiley & Sons Inc, NJ, USA

Whyte, David (1990) *Where Many Rivers Meet*, Many Rivers Press, Langley, USA

TELLING YOUR STORY

*Barber, Paul and Bates, Anna (2000) *Transpersonal Explorations for Personal and Community Change: Experiential Reflections for Group Facilitators, Therapists and other Travelling Souls*, Renewal, 7 Ridgeway Road, Redhill, Surrey RH1 6PQ, UK

Barrett, Richard (1995) *A Guide To Liberating Your Soul*, Fulfilling Books, USA and an article on www.richardbarrett.net/download/liberating_your_soul.pdf

Berger, Peter L. and Brigitte (1976, revised edition) *Sociology: A Biographical Approach*, Penguin Books, UK

Bloom, William (2002) *Feeling Safe*, Judy Piatkus (Publishers) Ltd, London, UK

Boorstein Seymour (ed.) (1996) *Transpersonal Psychotherapy*, State University of New York Press, New York, USA

Brown, Molly Young (1997, revised) *Growing Whole: Self-Realization On An Endangered Planet*, Psychosynthesis Press, CA, USA

Caddy, Eileen and Platts, David Earl (2004) *Findhorn Book Of Learning To Love*, Findhorn Press, Forres, UK (formerly published as *Learning To Love*, now revised)

Campbell, Joseph (1993) *The Hero with a Thousand Faces*, Fontana, U.K.

*Cori, Jasmin Lee (2000) *The Tao of Contemplation*, Samuel Weiser Inc, ME, USA   www.redwheelweiser.com

Covey, Stephen (1999) *7 Habits Of Highly Effective People*, Simon & Schuster, USA and UK

Dass, Ram (1988) *Grist for the Mill*, Celestial Arts, UK

Ferrucci, Piero (1982) *What We May Be*, Aquarian/Thorsons, London, UK

★Gandhi, Mohandas, taken from an interview with a reporter, cited at www.mkgandhi.org/

Goleman, Daniel (1998) *Working With Emotional Intelligence*, Bantam Books, New York, USA

Goleman, Daniel (2003) *Destructive Emotions*, Mind and Life Institute, published by arrangement with Bantam Books, USA

★Halberstam, Joshua (1993) *Everyday Ethics: Inspired Solutions To Real-Life Dilemmas*, Penguin, New York, USA

★Heschel, Abraham (1997) *God in Search of Man*, Noonday, USA

★Hugel, Baron Friederich von (1995) *Letters To A Niece*, Zondervan, MI, USA

Hugel, Baron Friederich von, (1964) *Spiritual Counsel And Letters / Edited with an introductory essay by Douglas V. Steere*, Darton, Longman & Todd, London, UK

Kohn, Alfie (1990) *The Brighter Side of Human Nature*, Basic Books, USA

★Kornfield, Jack (1994) *A Path with Heart*, Rider, London, UK

Leonard, Alison (1995) *Telling Our Stories*, Darton, Longman & Todd, UK

★Levine, Stephen (1997) *A Year To Live*, Thorsons, HarperCollins, London, UK

McDermott, Ian and O'Connor, Joseph (2001) *Thorsons Way Of NLP*, HarperCollins, UK

★Marks, Linda (1989) *Living with Vision*, Knowledge Systems Inc., Indianapolis, USA

Maslow, Abraham (1998, 3rd edn) *Towards a Psychology of Being*, John Wiley & Sons Inc., USA

Millman, Dan (2004) *Sacred Journey Of The Peaceful Warrior: Second Edition*, H J Kramer, USA

Myss, Caroline (1996) *Anatomy Of The Spirit*, Random House Inc, New York, USA

Parfitt, Will (1990) *The Elements of Psychosynthesis*, Element Books, UK

Peck, M. Scott (1978) *The Road Less Travelled, A New Psychology Of Love, Traditional Values and Spiritual Growth*, Simon and Schuster, USA

★Rilke, Rainer Maria, trans M. D. H. Norton (1903, re-issue edition 2004) *Diaries of a Young Poet*, W.W. Norton & Co Inc, New York USA

Rothberg, D & Kelly. S (eds) (1998) *Ken Wilber in Dialogue: Conversations With Leading Transpersonal Thinkers*, Quest Books, USA

A GROWING SENSE OF SOUL

★Assagioli, Roberto (1991) *Transpersonal Development*, Crucible Books, London, UK

Belitz, Charlene and Lundstrom, Meg (1997) *The Power Of Flow*, Harmony Books, USA

★Black Elk, an Oglala Lakota elder, cited at www.spiritwalk.org/blackelk.htm

*Britain Yearly Meeting of the Religious Society of Friends (Quakers) (1995) *Quaker Faith And Practice*, Introduction to Chapter 26. Friends House, London, UK

*Brown, Molly Young (1997, revised) *Growing Whole: Self-Realization On An Endangered Planet*, Psychosynthesis Press, CA, USA

Csikszentmihalyi, Mihaly (1990) *Flow: The Psychology Of Optimal Experience*, HarperCollins, USA

*Gardner, Howard (1993) *Frames Of Mind: The Theory of Multiple Intelligences*, Basic Books, USA. Also articles at www.pz.harvard.edu/Pls/HG.htm and www.swopnet.com/ed/TAG/7_intelligences.html

*Goleman, Daniel (1996) *Emotional Intelligence*, Bantam Books, New York & London

*Heelas, Paul, Woodhead, Linda and Szerszynski, Bronislaw (2004) *The Spiritual Revolution*, Blackwell, UK. See also *The Kendal Project*, Department of Religious Studies, Lancaster University, Lancaster LA1 4YG, UK and cited at www.lancs.ac.uk/depts/ieppp/kendal/

*Howatch, Susan (1999) *The High Flyer*, Little, Brown & Co, London, UK

*James, William (Centennial Edition, 2002) *The Varieties Of Religious Experience*, Routledge, USA

Kelly, Thomas (1942) *A Testament of Devotion*, HarperCollins, New York, USA

Kornfield, Jack (2000) *After The Ecstasy, The Laundry: How The Heart Grows Wise On The Spiritual Path*, Bantam Books, USA and UK

*Lacey, Paul (1999) *Nourishing The Spiritual Life*, Quaker Home Service, London, UK

*Leonard, Alison (1995) *Telling Our Stories*, Darton, Longman & Todd, UK

*Levin, Michal (2000) *Spiritual Intelligence: Awakening The Power of Your Spirituality and Intuition*, Hodder Mobius, London UK

*Moss, Richard (1987) *The Black Butterfly: an Invitation to Radical Aliveness*, Celestial Arts, Berkeley, California, USA

Neeld, Elizabeth Harper (1999) *A Sacred Primer*, Renaissance Books, USA

O'Donohue, John (1997), *Anam Cara; Spiritual Wisdom from the Celtic World*, Bantam Press, London, UK

*O'Donohue, John (2004) Interview with Joan Bakewell for BBC Radio 4, extract printed in *The Tablet*, 10 April 2004, London, UK and www.thetablet.co.uk

Sinetar, Marsha (1986) *Ordinary People As Monks And Mystics: Lifestyles For Self-Discovery*, Paulist Press, USA

*Schweitzer, Albert (1993) *Reverence for Life: The Words of Albert Schweitzer, ed Dr Harold E. Robles*, HarperCollins Publishers Inc, USA

*Skynner, Robin & Cleese, John (1996) *Life and How to Survive It*, William Heinemann, part of the Random House Group, UK

*Thompson, Richard (2000) Articles in *The Friend*, 5 May 2000 and 7 July 2000, The Friend, 173 Euston Rd, London NW1 2BJ, UK

★Tolle, Eckhart (2001) *Practicing The Power Of Now: Essential Teachings, Meditations, and Exercises from The Power of Now*, New World Library, USA

Tolle, Eckhart (2003), *Stillness Speaks*, Hodder and Stoughton, UK

Vaughan, Frances (1985) *The Inward Arc*, Shambhala, USA and iUniverse.com, edition part of the Authors' Guild Back in Print Series available as print on demand.

★Whitmore, Diana (1990) *The Joy of Learning,* Crucible, UK, available from the Psychosynthesis & Education Trust, Tooley Street, London SE1 2TH, UK

★Woolf, Virgina (1927) *To The Lighthouse*, Hogarth Press Ltd, London, UK

★Woolman, John (1762) *The Journal and Major Essays* (ed. Phillips Moulton) (1971), Friends United Press, USA

★Zohar, Danah & Marshall, Ian (2000) *SQ: Spiritual Intelligence, the Ultimate Intelligence*, Bloomsbury, London, UK

CHANGING FACES OF FAITH

Anderson, Sherry R & Hopkins, Patricia (1992) *The Feminine Face of God; the unfolding of the sacred in women*, Bantam Books, UK

★Arberry, Arthur. J, trans (1998) *The Koran (Oxford World's Classics)*, Oxford Paperbacks, UK

Armstrong, Karen (1999) *A History of God,* Vintage, UK

★The Bahá'í, (unknown) *Gleanings from the Writings of Bahá'u'lláh*, http://bahai-library.com/writings/bahaullah/gwb/066.html

★Bahro, Rudolph, quoted in Tomlinson, Dave (1995) *The Post Evangelical,* Triangle, UK

Beckerlegge, Gwilym, ed (2000) *The World Religions Reader*, Routledge, an imprint of Taylor & Francis Books Ltd, UK

★Bloom, William ed., (2000) *The Holistic Revolution*, Penguin Press, UK

★Bloom, William (2004) *Soulution: The Holistic Manifesto*, Hay House, UK

★Bodhi, Bhikkhu (trans and ed) (2002) *The Connected Discourses of the Buddha: A Translation of the Samyutta Nikaya*, Wisdom Publications MA, USA

★Borg, Marcus. J. (1997) *The God We Never Knew,* Harper San Francisco, USA

Borysenko, Joan (2000) *A Woman's Journey To God: Finding The Feminine Path*, Riverhead Books, USA

Bowker, John (2004) *God: A Brief History*, Dorling Kindersley, UK

Bowker, John (2004) *World Religions*, Dorling Kindersley, UK

Briggs, John & Peat, F. David (1990) *The Turbulent Mirror, an illustrated guide to chaos theory and the science of wholeness*, Perennial Library, Harper Row, New York, USA

★Campbell, Joseph, ed Diane Osbon (1995, reprint) *A Joseph Campbell Companion,* Perennial, HarperCollins Group, USA

Capra, Fritjof (2003) *The Hidden Connection: A Science For Sustainable Living*, Flamingo, UK

Childre, Doc Lew et al (1999) *The HeartMath Solution for Engaging the Power of the Heart's Intelligence*, Harper SanFrancisco, USA

★Chopra, Deepak (2000) *How to Know God*, Rider, UK

★Clarke, Abdassamad, trans (2000) *The Complete Forty Hadith of Imam an-Nawawi*, Ta-Ha Publishers, UK and
www.islamworld.net/nawawi.html#hadith9

★Dharma, Krishna, ed (1999) *The Mahabharata Anushaasana Parva*, Torchlight Publishing, CA, USA and
http://bombay.oriental.cam.ac.uk/john/mahabharata/statement.html

Dyer, Wayne (1999) *Wisdom Of The Ages: Eternal Truths For Everyday Life*, HarperCollins, UK and PerfectBooks (eBook)

★Easwaran, Eknath, trans and ed (1987) *The Upanishads*, The Blue Mountain Center of Meditation, USA

★Eck, Diana (1994) *Encountering God: A Spiritual Journey from Bozeman to Banaras*, Beacon Press, New York, USA

Elgin, Duane (2001) *Promise Ahead: A Vision Of Hope And Action For Humanity's Future*, Quill/Harper Collins, USA

★Epstein, Isidore trans and ed (1985) *Babylonian Talmud*, Soncino Press Ltd, USA. Also at www.sacred-texts.com/jud/talmud.htm and www.come-and-hear.com/shabbath/shabbath_31.html

★Ferrucci, Piero (1982) *What We May Be*, Aquarian/Thorsons, London, UK

Firmage, Joe (2001) Science and Consciousness Conference, Albuquerque, New Mexico, USA

Freke, Timothy (2000) *Encyclopaedia of Spirituality*, Godsfield Press Ltd, UK

★Fry, Christopher (1951) *A Sleep of Prisoners*, written for the Religious Drama Society, Oxford University Press, UK

Gallagher, Winifred (1999) *Working On God*, The Modern Library, New York, USA

★Griffiths, Bede (1982) *The Marriage of East and West*, Fount, HarperCollins, London, UK

★Griffiths, Bede (1989) *A New Vision of Reality*, Fount, HarperCollins, London, UK

Griffiths, Bede (1994) *Universal Wisdom: a journey through the sacred wisdom of the world*, Fount, HarperCollins, London, UK

★Gwyn, Doug (1997) in *Words in Time,* Bellafonte, Kimo Press, USA

Harries, Richard (2002) *God Outside The Box,* SPCK, UK

★Heelas, Paul (1996) *The New Age Movement: Religion, Culture & Society in the Age of Post-modernity*, Blackwell, UK

★Heron, John (1998) *Sacred Science*, PCCS, UK

Hicks, John (1999) *The Fifth Dimension: an exploration of the spiritual realm*, Oneworld Publications, Oxford, UK

★Hillman, James (1996) *The Soul's Code: In Search of Character and Calling*, Bantam Books, London, UK

Holitzka, Klaus (2002) *Islamic Mandalas,* Sterling Publishing, UK

Holloway, Richard (2002) *Doubts and Loves: What Is Left Of Christianity,* Canongate Press, UK

★Jacobi, Hermann trans (2003) *Kritanga Sutra Jaina Sutras, Vol. II. The Uttaradhyayana Sutra; The Sutrakritanga Sutra,* Satguru, New Delhi, 2003, India

★Li Ying-chang, Eva Wong (1994) *Lao-Tzu's Treatise on the Response of the Tao to Human Actions: Tai-Shang Kan-Ying P'Ien* (The Sacred Literature Series), HarperSanFrancisco, USA and www.sacred-texts.com/tao/ts/ts05.htm

★Maclaine, Shirley (2000) *The Camino,* Simon and Schuster, New York, USA

McTaggart, Lynne (2003) *The Field,* HarperCollins, UK

★Muller, F. Max and West, E.W. trans (1996) *Dadistan-I-dinik The Sacred Books of the East/ Pahlavi Texts Vols: 18,* Low Price Publications, RoutledgeCurzon 2001 USA and UK and www.tanenbaum.org/resources/golden_rule.asp

Novak, Philip (1994) *The World's Wisdom,* HarperSanFrancisco, USA

O'Murchu, Diarmuid (1987) *Coping With Change in the Modern World,* Mercier Press Ltd, Dublin, Ireland

★O'Murchu, Diarmuid (1997) *Quantum Theology,* Crossroad Publishing Company, New York, USA

★Picasso, in *The Soul's Code: In Search of Character and Calling* (1996) by James Hillman, Bantam Books, London, UK

Prime, Ranchor, translator (2003) *The Illustrated Bhagavad Gita,* Godsfield Press, UK

Redfield, James (2003) *God And The Evolving Universe,* Putnam Publishing Group, UK

★Roberts, Elizabeth and Amidon, Elias, eds (1991) *Earth Prayers from Around the World,* HarperCollins Publishers, USA

★Russell, Peter (1998) *Waking up in Time: Finding Inner Peace in Times of Accelerating Change,* Origin Press, California, USA

★Russell, Peter (2003) *From Science to God: Exploring the Mystery of Consciousness,* New World Library, USA

★St John, Gospel of: from the King James Version Bible (Authorized), New Testament

★St Luke, Gospel of: from the King James Version Bible (Authorized), New Testament

★Sacks, Jonathan (2002) *The Dignity Of Difference,* Continuum International Publishing Group, Academi, London, UK

★Sahtouris, Elisabet (2003) *After Darwin. Dr. Elisabet Sahtouris talks to Big Picture about reuniting spirituality with science in order to form a new world view.* 30 August 2003, Wasan Island, Canada. A Barbara Luna Production. www.ratical.org/LifeWeb/Articles/AfterDarwin.html

★Schwartz, Gary and Russek, Linda (1999) *The Living Energy Universe,* Hampton Roads Publishing Co, USA

★Silesius, Angelus, source unknown

Smith, Huston (1991) *The World's Religions – Our Great Wisdom Traditions*, HarperSanFrancisco, USA

Spangler, David (1996) *A Pilgrim in Aquarius*, Findhorn Press, Scotland

Spong, John Selby (2003) *A New Christianity For A New World,* HarperCollins, UK

★Steiner, Rudolf (2003) *Self Transformation,* Rudolf Steiner Press, UK

★Swimme, Brian and Berry, Thomas (1994) *The Universe Story: a celebration of the unfolding of the Cosmos*, HarperSanFrancisco, USA

★Tagore, Rabindranath (unknown) www.spiritwalk.org/tagore.htm#quotations

Teasdale, Wayne (1999) *The Mystic Heart: discovering a universal spirituality in the world's religions,* New World Library, CA, USA

Tze, Lao, trans Ralph Alan Dale (2002) *Tao Te Ching,* Watkins Publishing Ltd, UK (see also *Tao Te Ching* under references in *Encountering Direct Experience*)

★Walker, Alice (1991) *The Color Purple*, Cambridge University Press, UK

Watts, Alan (2002) *Zen: The Supreme Experience,* Vega Books, UK

★Wilber, Ken (1998) *The Marriage of Sense and Soul*, Newleaf, Gill & Macmillan Ltd, Ireland

Wilber, Ken (2001) *A Theory of Everything,* Gill & Macmillan Ltd, Ireland and Shambhala Publications, USA

Zeolla, Gary F. (1999) *Overview of Process Theology*, www.dtl.org/index.html.

ENCOUNTERING DIRECT EXPERIENCE

Anderson, Sarah, ed (1997) *The Virago Book of Spirituality*, Virago Press, London

★Arberry, Arthur. J, trans (1998) *The Koran (Oxford World's Classics)*, Oxford Paperbacks, UK

★Assagioli, Roberto (1991) *Transpersonal Development*, Crucible Books, London, UK

Borysenko, Joan (1997) *7 Paths to God: the Ways of the Mystic*, Hay House, CA. USA

★Caddy, Eileen (1986) *Opening Doors Within*, Findhorn Press, UK

★Chapman, Dom John (unknown)
http://homepage.virgin.net/david.torkington/Page9%20FAQ.htm

★Cori, Jasmin Lee (2000) *The Tao of Contemplation*, Samuel Weiser Inc, ME, USA www.redwheelweiser.com

★Csikszentmihalyi, Mihaly (1990) *Flow: The Psychology Of Optimal Experience*, HarperCollins, USA

Das, Lama Surya (2000) *Awakening to the Sacred*, Bantam Books, UK

★Dolley, Janice – in conversation

★Ferrucci, Piero (1982) *What We May Be*, Aquarian/Thorsons, London, UK

★Fowler, James (1981) *The Psychology of Human Development and the Quest for Meaning*, Harper Row, San Francisco, USA

★Heron, John (1998) *Sacred Science*, PCCS, UK

*Howatch, Susan (1999) *The High Flyer*, Little, Brown and Company, UK

Hughes, Gerard (2003) *God In All Things,* Hodder & Stoughton, UK

*Jung, Carl Gustav (original 1921, 1990) *Psychological Types, trans R Foundation C Hull*, Routledge, Taylor & Francis Books, UK

*Keats, John (1973) *The Complete Poems (Penguin Classics)*, Penguin Books, UK

Krishnamurti, J (1995) *The Book Of Life,* HarperSanFrancisco, USA

*Loring, Patricia (1997) *Listening Spirituality: Personal Spiritual Practice Amongst Friends*, Quaker Books of Friends General Conference and available from www.quakerbooks.org or e-mail at bookstore@fgcquaker.com and Quaker Book Shop, London, UK

Mello S. J., Anthony de (1984) *Sadhana: A Way To God – Christian Exercises in Eastern Form*, Image Books, part of the Random House Group, USA

*Moss, Richard (1987) *The Black Butterfly: an Invitation to Radical Aliveness*, Celestial Arts, Berkeley, California, USA

*Progoff, Ira (1992) *At a Journal Workshop*, Jeremy Tarcher/Penguin Puttnam, New York, USA

*Psalms, The: from the King James Version Bible (Authorized), Old Testament

*Redfield, James (1993) *The Celestine Prophecy*, Satori Press, Hoover, Ala, USA

Sahajananda, John Martin (2003) *You Are The Light,* O Books, UK

*Spangler, David (undated) *Attunement*, a paper at the Findhorn Foundation, UK

Tolle, Eckhart (1999) *The Power Of Now*, New World Library, USA

*Tze, Lao trans Stephen Hodge (2002) *The Illustrated Tao Te Ching (chapter 25)*, Barron's Educational Series, UK

*Vaughan, Frances (1985) *The Inward Arc*, Shambhala, USA and iUniverse.com, edition part of the Authors' Guild Back in Print Series available as print on demand.

*Whitmore, Diana (1990) *The Joy of Learning,* Crucible, UK, available from the Psychosynthesis & Education Trust, Tooley Street, London SE1 2TH, UK

Williams, Rowan (2003) *Silence and Honey Cakes: The Wisdom Of The Desert*, Lion Publishing, UK

*Wordsworth, William ed. John Morley (1983) *Complete Poetical Works of William Wordsworth*, Arden Library, UK

*Zohar, Danah & Marshall, Ian (2000) *SQ: Spiritual Intelligence, the Ultimate Intelligence*, Bloomsbury, UK

PASSION AND CHANGE

Barber, Paul & Bates, Anna (2000) *Transpersonal Explorations for Personal and Community Change: Experiential Reflections for Group Facilitators, Therapists and other Travelling Souls*, Renewal, 7 Ridgeway Road, Redhill, Surrey, RH1 6PQ, UK

Beck, Don and Cowans, Christopher (1995) *Spiral Dynamics: Mastering Values, Leadership and Change*, Blackwell Publishers, UK

Borysenko, Joan (1997) *7 Paths to God: the ways of the mystic*, Hay House, USA

★Buttner, Judi – in conversation

★Drake, Susan (1993) *Planning Integrated Curriculum: The Call to Adventure*, Association for Supervision & Curriculum Development, USA

★Edwards, Gill (1991) *Living Magically*, Judy Piatkus (Publishers) Ltd, London, UK

Gleick, James & Porter, Eliot (1996) *Nature's Chaos*, Abacus Books, Little, Brown and Company, UK

★Goethe, popularly ascribed to Goethe from a translation by John Anster of *Faust (1835)*, full quotation appears in W. H. Murray in *The Scottish Himalaya Expedition*, 1951 (information supplied on the website of the Goethe Society of North America)

★Jones, Rufus (1937) *Friend of Life: the biography of Rufus M Jones* by Elizabeth Gray Vining (1981), Philadelphia Yearly Meeting, USA

★Jung, Carl Gustav (original 1921, 1990) *Psychological Types, trans R Foundation C Hull*, Routledge, Taylor & Francis Books, UK

Kolb, David (1994) At an international conference *A Global Conversation about Learning*, Washington D.C., USA

★Kornfield, Jack (1994) *A Path with Heart*, Rider, UK

Leite, Elizabeth (1980) *Simply Beautiful*, Naturegraph Publishers Inc, CA 96039, USA

Mello S.J., Anthony de (1986) *Wellsprings: A Book Of Spiritual Exercises*, Image Books, New York USA

★Merton, Thomas (unknown) cited at www.creationethics.org/index.cfm?fuseaction=webpage&page_id=134

Moody, Harry R. and Carroll, David (1997) *The Five Stages Of The Soul: Charting The Spiritual Passages That Shape Our Lives*, Doubleday, USA

Moore, Thomas (1992) *Care of the Soul*, HarperCollins Publishers Inc, USA

Parry, Danaan (1991) *Warriors of the Heart*, Sunstone Publications, NY 13326, USA

Sinetar, Marsha (1992) *Developing A 21st Century Mind*, Ballantine Books, USA

★Spangler, David (2004) *Inner Citizenship, Part 1: The Soul of America*, an article on www.lorian.org

Vaughan, Frances (1985) *The Inward Arc*, Shambhala, USA and iUniverse.com, edition part of the Authors' Guild Back in Print Series available as print on demand.

★Whitmore, Diana (1990) *The Joy of Learning*, Crucible, UK, available from the Psychosynthesis & Education Trust, Tooley Street, London SE1 2TH, UK

★Williamson, Marianne (1992) *A Return to Love: Reflections on the Principles of A Course in Miracles*, HarperCollins, New York, USA

Zohar, Danah & Marshall, Ian (2000) *SQ: Spiritual Intelligence, the Ultimate Intelligence*, Bloomsbury, London

DARK NIGHTS

★Anamaire, Phyllida (2001) *Death – The Final Healing,* unpublished transcripts from a workshop

★Bly, Robert with William Booth (1998, reissue) *A Little Book on the Human Shadow,* HarperSanFrancisco, USA cited on www.robertbly.com/b_prose.html

Bloom, William (2002) *Feeling Safe,* Judy Piatkus (Publishers) Ltd Books, UK

★Bridges, William (1980) *Transitions,* Perseus, USA

★Brussat, Fredric and Mary Ann (1996) *Spiritual Literacy: Reading The Sacred In Everyday Life,* Turnstone, New York, USA

★Cohen, Andrew (2000) *Embracing Heaven and Earth,* Moksha Press, Mass, USA

★Dass, Ram (1999) *On Hearing What Is* in Eddie and Debbie Shapiro, Eds, *Voices From the Heart,* Jeremy Tarcher /Penguin Puttnam, New York, USA

★Dawes, Joycelin – in conversation

★Frankl, Victor (1959) *Man's Search for Meaning,* Beacon, UK

★Gandhi, Mohandas (unknown) cited at www.ieer.org/latest/oct2quot.html

★Gibran, Khalil (1926) *The Prophet,* Heinemann, London, UK

Griffin, Kathleen (2003) *The Forgiveness Formula,* Simon & Schuster, UK

★Grof, Stanislas and Grof, Christina eds (1989) *Spiritual Emergency: When Personal Transformation Becomes a Crisis (New Consciousness Reader),* J P Tarcher/Penguin Puttnam, New York, USA, and the Spiritual Emergence Network at the California Institute of Integral Studies at www.ciis.edu/comserv/sen.html

Halifax, Joan (1993) *The Fruitful Darkness,* HarperCollins, London, UK

★Hanh, Thich Nhat (1991) *Peace is Every Step,* Bantam, USA

★Howatch, Susan (1999) *The High Flyer,* Little, Brown and Company, London, UK

Kabatt-Zin, Jon (1996) *Full Catastrophe Living,* Judy Piatkus (Publishers) Ltd Books, UK

★Kheema, Ayya (1987) *Being Nobody, Going Nowhere,* Wisdom, Boston, USA

★Kubler-Ross, Elisabeth (1998) *The Wheel of Life,* Bantam, UK

Levine, Stephen (1997) *A Year to Live,* Thorsons, HarperCollins London UK

Lewin, Kurt (1981) *Field Theory in Social Sciences,* Harper & Row, London, UK

Lynn, Joanne and Harrold, Joan (2001) *Handbook For Mortals: Guidance for People Facing Serious Illness,* Oxford University Press (Inc) , USA

★Mascaro, Juan trans (1965) *The Upanishads,* Penguin, Harmondsworth, UK

Moore, Thomas (2004) *Dark Nights of the Soul,* Penguin Group (USA) Inc and Piatkus Press, UK

★Myss, Caroline (1996) *Anatomy of the Spirit,* Random House Inc, New York, USA

★Ono, Yoko (1999) *Revelations* in Eddie and Debbie Shapiro, Eds, *Voices From the Heart,* Jeremy Tarcher/Penguin Puttnam, New York, USA

★Parsons, Tony (2000) *As It Is: the open secret to living an awakened life,* Cranborne, BH21 5PZ, UK

*Rohr, Richard (1999) *Everything Belongs: the gift of contemplative prayer*, Crossroads Publishing Company, New York, USA
*Spangler, David (2004) *Inner Citizenship Part 1: The Soul of America,* an article on www.lorian.org
*St John of the Cross (various) *The Dark Night of the Soul*
Taylor, Allegra (1989) *Acquainted with The Night: A Year on the Frontiers of Death*, Fontana Books, UK
*Zohar, Danah (1990) *The Quantum Self,* Bloomsbury, London, UK

WHOLENESS AND CONNECTION

*BBC poll, cited at www.williambloom.com/f-BBCGod.html
*Barrett, Richard (1995) *A Guide to Liberating your Soul*, Fulfilling Books, Virginia USA
*Beck, Don and Cowan, Christopher (1995) *Spiral Dynamics: Mastering Values, Leadership, and Change*, Blackwell Publishers, UK
*Beck, Don (2002) *Spiral Dynamics in the Integral Age*, an article on www.spiraldynamics.net
*Bloom, William (2004) *Soulution: The Holistic Manifesto*, Hay House, UK
Capra, Fritjof (2003) *The Hidden Connection*, Flamingo, UK
*Chopra, Deepak (2000) *How to Know God*, Harmony Books, UK
Combs, Allan (2002) *The Radiance of Being: Understanding The Grand Integral Vision; Living The Integral Life*, Continuum Publishing Group, USA
Elgin, Duane (1999) *Our Living Universe*, Institute of Noetic Science, Review No 54, and www.ions.org
*Featherstone, Cornelia (2004) *The Healing Dynamic of Community*, a presentation at a conference *The Spirit of Healing*, Findhorn Foundation, April 2004
*Forman, Robert (2004) *Grassroots Spirituality*, Imprint Academic USA & UK
*Fox, Matthew (2000, revised) *Original Blessing: A Primer in Creation Spirituality*, Jeremy Tarcher/Penguin Puttnam, New York, USA
*Gawain, Shakti (2000, 2nd edition) *The Path of Transformation: How Healing Ourselves Can Change The World*, New World Library, USA
Gendlin, Eugene (1981) *Focusing*, Bantam Books, UK
Handy, Charles (1995) *The Empty Raincoat*, Arrow, UK
Hill, Stuart B. (2002) *Redesign for Soil, Habitat and Biodiversity Conservation: Lessons from Ecological Agriculture and Social Ecology*, School of Social Ecology & Lifelong Learning, University of Western Sydney, Australia
*Kung, Hans and Schmidt, Helmut (Eds), (1998) *A Global Ethic and Global Responsibilities*, SCM Press, UK
*Lacey, Paul (1999) *Nourishing The Spiritual Life*, Quaker Home Service, London, UK
Laszlo, Ervin (2002) *You Can Change The World*, Positive News Publishing, UK
Lawrence, Brother (various) *The Practice Of The Presence Of God: The Best Rule Of*

The Holy Life, and www.ccel.org/l/lawrence/practice/htm/i.htm

★Locke, Angela (2001) *Sacred Earth*, Pleiades Press and Beaconside Community Development Centre, UK

McMahon, Edwin and Campbell, Peter (1985) *Bio-Spirituality: Focusing As A Way To Grow*, Loyola University Press, USA

★Mitchell, Edgar (2000) Report on two lectures, *A New Scientific Look at Consciousness* and *The Quantum Hologram: Nature's Mind* given at the College of Psychic Studies on 17 May 2000 and reported in The College Journal *Light* Volume 120, No.3, London, UK

★O'Donohue, John (1997) *Anam Cara; Spiritual Wisdom from the Celtic World*, Bantam Press, London, UK

★Parfitt Will (1997) *The Elements of Psychosynthesis*, Element Books, UK

Pert, Candace B (1999) *Molecules Of Emotion: The Science Behind Mind-Body Medicine*, Simon & Schuster, USA

★Peters, David (2004) *Vitalism, Holism and Healing*, a presentation at a conference *The Spirit of Healing*, Findhorn Foundation, April 2004, UK

★Ray, Paul H. and Anderson, Sherry Ruth (2000) *The Cultural Creatives*, Three Rivers Press, USA

Sahtouris, Elisabet (2000) *EarthDance: Living Systems in Evolution*, Praeger, USA, and www.ratical.org/LifeWeb/

Spangler, David (2004) *Incarnational Spirituality*, an article on www.lorian.org

Spangler, David (2004) *Sun to Star – Reimagining the Center*, an article on www.lorian.org

★Suzuki, David (1997) *The Sacred Balance: Rediscovering Our Place in Nature*, Greystone Books, BC, Canada

Tarnas, R (1996) *The Passion of The Western Mind*, Pimlico, UK

Trevelyan, Sir George (1980) *Magic Casements: the Use of Poetry in Expanding Consciousness*, Coventure Press, UK

Trevelyan, Sir George (1981) *Operation Redemption*, Turnstone, UK

Vaughan, Frances (1985) *The Inward Arc*, Shambhala, USA and iUniverse.com, edition part of the Authors' Guild Back in Print Series available as print on demand.

Walker, Alex, ed et al (1994) *The Kingdom Within: a Guide to the Spiritual Work of the Findhorn Community*, Findhorn Press, UK

Wilber, Ken (1996) *A Brief History of Everything*, Gill and Macmillan Ltd, Ireland

★Wilber, Ken (2001) *A Theory of Everything*, Gill and Macmillan Ltd, Ireland and Shambhala Publications, USA

★Zolar Entertainment (2004) information on www.questforlife.com

LIVING IN A SACRED WAY

★Arriens, Jan (2000) *The Shared Silence*, in The Friend, 25 August 2000, The Friend, 173 Euston Rd, London NW1 2BJ, UK

★Assagioli, Roberto (1974, reprint 2002) *The Act of Will: A Guide to Self-Actualization & Self-Realization*, available from the Psychosynthesis & Education Trust, Tooley Street, London SE1 2TH, UK

★Blake, William (1827) *Auguries Of Innocence* quoted by Francis Thompson, cited at www.bartleby.com/73/196.html

Brussat, Fredric and Mary Ann (1996) *Spiritual Literacy: Reading The Sacred In Everyday Life*, Turnstone, New York, USA

Chittister, Joan (1995) *There is a Season*, Orbis Books, New York, USA

Davidson, Gordon and McLaughlin, Corinne, (2001) an article on www.visionarylead.org The Center for Visionary Leadership, 3408 Wisconsin Ave. NW Suite 200, Washington DC 200016, USA

★Earth Charter (2000) *The Earth Charter Initiative Handbook*, information available at www.earthcharter.org/ or from info@earthcharter.org

★Fox, Matthew (1983) *Meditations With Meister Eckhart*, Bear & Co, USA

Featherstone, Alan Watson: www.treesforlife.org.uk and www.restore-earth.org, Trees for Life, The Park, Findhorn Bay, Forres IV36 3TZ, Scotland

Ferrer, Jorge (2000) *Revisioning Transpersonal Theory: A Participatory Vision of Human Spirituality*, State University of New York Press, USA

★Goldfarb Peter in Shapiro, Eddie and Shapiro, Debbie (1999) *Voices from the Heart*, Jeremy Tarcher/Penguin Puttnam, New York, USA

★Hahn Thich Nhat (1991) *Peace is Every Step*, Bantam, USA

★Jane – in conversation

★Judith (Berry) – in conversation

Holland, Gail Bernice (1998) *A Call for Connection*, New World Library, CA, USA

Jenkins, Palden (2003) *Healing The Hurts Of Nations*, Gothic Image Publications, UK

★Katie, Byron and Mitchell, Stephen (2002) *Loving What Is: Four Questions That Can Change Your Life*, Harmony Books, USA and quoted from www.thework.com

Kay, Kay, ed (2001) *Growing People: People's Personal Experiences At The Findhorn Community*, Pilgrim Guides, 5A1 Ka Nam Village, Yung Shue Wan, Lamma Island, Hong Kong

Kiuchi, Tachi, Shireman, Bill and Shireman, William K (2002) *What We Learned in the Rainforest: Business Lessons from Nature*, Berrett-Koehler, San Francisco, USA

★Main, John (1984) *Moments of Christ: The Path of Meditation*, Darton, Longman & Todd, UK

McAleese, Mary (1997) *Reconciled Being: Love in Chaos*, The John Main Seminar 1997, Medio Media/ Arthur James, Herts UK

McMahon, Edwin (1993) *Beyond the Myth of Dominance – an alternative to a violent society*, Sheed and Ward, USA

McMahon, Edwin and Campbell, Peter (1985) *Bio-Spirituality: Focusing As A Way To Grow*, Loyola University Press, USA

*Mindell, Arnold (1995) *Sitting in the Fire*, Lao Tse Press, USA
*Pedlar, M. & Boydell, T. (1985) *Managing Yourself*, Fontana/Collins, London, UK
*Rumi, (2000) *Rumi: A Spiritual Treasury* compiled by Juliet Mabey, Oneworld Publications, Oxford, UK
Shapiro, Eddie and Shapiro, Debbie, Editors (1999) *Voices From the Heart*, Jeremy Tarcher/Penguin Puttnam, New York, USA
*Skynner, Robin and Cleese, John (1996) *Life and How to Survive It*, Heinemann, part of the Random House Group, UK
*Spangler, David (2004) *Incarnational Spirituality*, an article on www.lorian.org
Spangler, David (2004) *Sun to Star – Reimagining the Center*, an article on www.lorian.org
*Teasdale, Wayne (1999) *The Mystic Heart; Discovering a Universal Spirituality in the World's Religions*, New World Library, CA, USA
*Thompson, Francis (2003, reissue/print on demand) *The Works of Francis Thompson, Vol 3*, R A Kessinger Publishing Co, USA and www.bartleby.com/73/196.html
*Tutu, Desmond (1994) in Robert Siegel, *The NPR Interviews 1994*, Houghton Mifflin Company, USA
Walsch , Neale Donald (2002) *The New Revelations: Conversations With God*, Atria Books, NY, USA
Williamson, Marianne (2000) *Imagine: What America Could Be In The 21st Century*, Global Renaissance Alliance
*Wilson, Lynn – in conversation

ENDING – OR CONTINUING YOUR QUEST?

*Bruteau, B. (1997) *God's Ecstasy: The Creation of a Self-Creating World,* The Crossroad Publishing Company, New York, USA
*Fénelon, François (1980) *Spiritual Letters to Women*, cited in Benner (1998) *Care of Souls*, Baker Books, USA
Tomlinson, Dave (1995) *The Post Evangelical,* Triangle, UK

MAKING THE MOST OF *THE QUEST*

*Steere, Douglas V. (1955) *Where Words Come From*, Quaker Home Service, London, UK

SKILLS OF SPIRITUAL REFLECTION: INDEX, BIBLIOGRAPHY AND FURTHER READING

The *Skills of Spiritual Reflection* were described in **Heart of The Quest** (pages 21-22) and **Developing Your Skills** (pages 24-37). By using each of the skills of spiritual reflection regularly, you establish a regular rhythm and habit of reflection that helps you reach greater self-awareness and engage with a nourishing spiritual life at a deeper level.

The diagram below is a reminder of *The Quest* framework and how it combines the four skills into a coherent framework of spiritual reflection. Each of the *Skills of Spiritual Reflection* is indexed according to types of skills, together with a bibliography and guide to further reading for each one. The further reading resources are not exhaustive but include a variety of approaches.

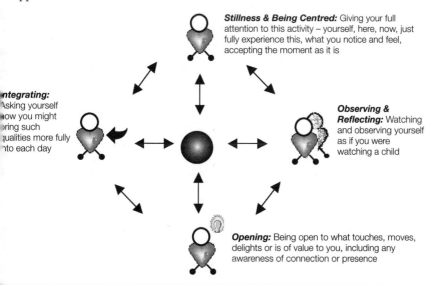

Stillness & Being Centred: Giving your full attention to this activity – yourself, here, now, just fully experience this, what you notice and feel, accepting the moment as it is

Integrating: Asking yourself how you might bring such qualities more fully into each day

Observing & Reflecting: Watching and observing yourself as if you were watching a child

Opening: Being open to what touches, moves, delights or is of value to you, including any awareness of connection or presence

SKILLS OF SPIRITUAL REFLECTION: *STILLNESS AND BEING CENTERED*

FINDING INNER STILLNESS (PAGES 25-26)

<u>Aim</u>: Gently quietening the mind, minimizing the clamor of thought and bodily needs, finding an inner stillness and point of equanimity.

Gendlin, Eugene (2003) *Focusing*, Rider, UK
Harris, Paul (ed) (1998) *The Fire of Silence and Stillness*, Darton, Longman & Todd, London
Skolimowski, Henryk (1994) *Eco Yoga: Practice And Meditations For Walking In Beauty On The Earth*, Gaia Books Limited, UK
Tolle, Eckhart (2003) *Stillness Speaks*, Hodder and Stoughton, UK

MEDITATION AND CONTEMPLATION (PAGES 115-116)

<u>Aim</u>: Reaching a point of silence and stillness where awareness unfolds and you experience inner peace.

Braybrooke, Marcus (2001) *Learn To Pray: A Practical Guide To Faith And Inspiration*, Chronicle Books, UK
Bloom, William (1987) *Meditation in a Changing World*, Gothic Image, Glastonbury, UK
Cooke, Grace (1965) *Meditation*, White Eagle Publishing Trust, UK
Ferrucci, Piero (1982) *What We May Be*, Aquarian/Thorsons, London, UK
Jacka, Judy (1990) *Meditation: The Most Natural Therapy*, Lothian Books, UK
Keating, Thomas (1996) *Open Mind Open Heart: The Contemplative Dimension Of The Gospel*, The Continuum Publishing Company, NY, USA
Le Shan, Lawrence (1974) *How to Meditate*, Turnstone Press, Wellingborough, UK
Parfitt, Will (1990) *The Elements of Psychosynthesis*, Element Books, UK
Twyman, James (2000) *Praying Peace*, Findhorn Press, UK
Williamson, Marianne (2001) *Illuminata: Thoughts, Prayers and Rituals For Everyday Life*, Rider, USA/UK

ATTUNING (PAGES 205-207)

<u>Aim</u>: Bringing yourself into harmony and alignment – being at one – with people, events, objects or nature that are your current focus of attention.

Bloom, William (1993) *First Steps: An Introduction To Spiritual Practice*, Findhorn Press, UK
Spangler, David (undated) *Attunement*, Findhorn Foundation, UK

VISUALIZATION (pages 137-139)

<u>Aim</u>: Combining stillness and being centred with the power of imagination, working with symbols and metaphor to explore experience, possibilities and access the unconscious.

Gawain, Shakti (1978) *Creative Visualization*, Bantam Books, USA
Glouberman, Dina (1992) *Life Choices And Life Changes Through Imagework: The Art Of Developing Personal Vision*, Aquarian Press, London, UK

SKILLS OF SPIRITUAL REFLECTION: *OBSERVING AND REFLECTING*
BEING YOUR OWN OBSERVER (PAGES 27-29)

<u>Aim</u>: Developing your capacity to observe, or witness, yourself from an independent position without judgment as if you were a wise person standing at your own shoulder.

Bond, Jean (1993) *Behind the Masks*, Gateway Books, Bath, UK
Dolley, Janice et al (1995) *People & Potential* (K502), Open University, Milton Keynes, UK
Ferrucci, Piero (1982) *What We May Be*, Aquarian/Thorsons, London, UK
Walsh, Roger (1999) *Essential Spirituality – Exercises From The World's Religions To Cultivate Kindness, Love, Joy, Peace, Wisdom And Generosity*, J Wiley & Sons Inc, NJ, USA
Yeomans, Tom (1999) *Presence, Power and the Planet*, Occasional Paper no. 5, Concordia Institute, USA

JOURNALING (PAGES 116-118)

<u>Aim</u>: To reflect and record from your intuitive side, balancing out the rational, linear and logical approach more frequently used in reflective writing.

Baldwin, Christina (1991) *Life's Companion: Journal Writing as a Spiritual Quest*, Bantam, New York, USA
Cerwinske, Laura (1999) *Writing as a Healing Art*, Berkeley Publishing Group, USA
Gamin, Barbara and Fox, Susan (1999) *Visual Journaling: Going Deeper Than Words*, Quest Books, USA
Progoff, Ira (1992) *At a Journal Workshop*, Jeremy Tarcher, Penguin Puttnam, USA

CRITICAL INCIDENT ANALYSIS (PAGES 101-102)

<u>Aim</u>: A structured, analytical approach to reflection that allows you to stand back from your reactions and emotions and look at what was going on.

Dolley, Janice et al (2000) *Clinical Supervision* (K509), Open University, Milton Keynes, UK
Johns. C, (1992) *Holistic Model of Nursing Practice* in *The Bunford Nursing Development Units*, Journal of Advanced Nursing 16, 1090-98, UK
Senge, Peter (1991) *The Fifth Discipline*, Century, London, UK
Tipping, Colin (2000) *Radical Forgiveness*, Newleaf, Dublin, Ireland

WORKING WITH VALUES (PAGES 48-49)

<u>Aim</u>: To become clearer about the values that inspire and guide you, bringing focus and intention to your actions.

Angel Cards – obtainable from Phoenix Community Store, The Park, Findhorn, Moray IV36 3TZ, telephone +44 (0)1309 690110
Barrett, Richard (1995) *A Guide To Liberating Your Soul*, Fulfilling Books, USA and www.richardbarrett.net/download/liberating_your_soul.pdf
Kung, Hans & Schmidt, Helmut, (1998) *A Global Ethic and Global Responsibilities*, SCM Press, UK
Marks, Linda (1989) *Living with Vision*, Knowledge Systems Inc, Indianopolis, USA

SKILLS OF SPIRITUAL REFLECTION: OPENING
OPENING TO CREATIVE INSPIRATION (PAGES 30-32)

<u>Aim</u>: Developing your creative spark and capacity to live and express yourself spontaneously, staying in touch with what touches, delights and moves you, and brings value and meaning to your life.

Cameron, Julia (1993) *The Artist's Way*, Pan Books, London, UK
Campbell, Don (2001) *The Mozart Effect*, Hodder & Stoughton, London, UK
Evans and Russell, (1992) *The Creative Manager*, John Wiley & Sons, London, UK
Kenton, Leslie (1998) *Journey to Freedom*, Harper Collins, London, UK
Rogers, Carl (1977) *Becoming a Person*, Constable & Co, UK
Rogers, Natalie (1993) *The Creative Connection*, Scientific & Behavior Books Inc, USA
Vaughan, Frances (1985) *The Inward Arc*, Shambhala, Boston, USA

LISTENING TO THE WHISPERS (PAGES 131-133)

<u>Aim</u>: To become more aware of, and sensitive to, guidance whether that is a 'still small voice' or interpretation of meaning in events and apparent coincidences.

Caddy, Eileen (1992) *God Spoke To Me*, Findhorn Press, UK

Edwards, Gill (1991) *Living Magically*, Piatkus (Publishers) Ltd, UK
Edwards, Gill (1993) *Stepping into the Magic*, Piatkus (Publishers) Ltd, UK
Maclean, Dorothy (1980) *To Hear the Angels Sing*, Lindisfarne Press, USA
Main, Roderick (1998) *Jung on Synchronicity and the Paranormal*, Princeton University Press, USA
Roman, Sanaya (1988) *Spiritual Growth: Being your Higher Self*, H.J. Kramer CA, USA
Small-Wright, Machaelle (1987) *Behaving As If The God In All Life Mattered*, Perelandra Ltd, USA
White, Ruth (1988) *A Question of Guidance*, C. W. Daniel & Company, Essex, UK

USING INTUITION (PAGES 118-120)

<u>Aim</u>: Becoming more aware of your ways of knowing that are non-rational and, perhaps, unconscious, recognizing your own intuitive system and testing it out.

Dolley, Janice et al (1995) *People & Potential* (K502), The Open University, Milton Keynes, UK
Ferrucci, Piero (1982) *What We May Be*, Aquarian/Thorsons, London, UK
Glouberman, Dina (1992) *Life Choices And Life Changes Through Imagework: The Art Of Developing Personal Vision*, Aquarian Press, London, UK
Henry, J. (1990) *Training Creativity and Intuition*, Meta Publications, Miami, USA
Jung, C. (1966) *The Practice of Psychotherapy*, Routledge and Kegan Paul, London, UK
Vaughan, F. (1979) *Developing Intuition*, Anchor Press / Doubleday, London, UK
Whitmore, Diana (1990) *The Joy of Learning,* Crucible, UK, available from the Psychosynthesis & Education Trust, Tooley Street, London SE1 2TH, UK

WORKING WITH VISION (PAGES 226-228)

<u>Aim</u>: Developing your capacity to turn your creative or abstract ideas into reality and co-creating with Spirit.

Marks, Linda (1989) *Living with Vision*, Knowledge Systems Inc., Indianapolis, USA
Spangler, David (undated) *Manifestation*, Findhorn Foundation, UK (out of print)
Spangler, David (1996) *Everyday Miracles*, Bantam, USA

GOOD AND SKILFUL WILL (PAGES 218-220)

Aim: Using your power to choose, confidence to act and commitment to action to bring about change for the highest good of all beings.

Assagioli, Roberto (1974, reprint 2002) *The Act of Will: A Guide to Self-Actualization & Self-Realization*, available from the Psychosynthesis & Education Trust, Tooley Street, London SE1 2TH, UK
Brown, Molly Young (1997, revised) *Growing Whole: Self-Realization On An Endangered Planet*, Psychosynthesis Press, CA, USA
Green, T & Woodrow, P & Peavey, F (1994) *Insight And Action: How To Discover A Life Of Integrity And Commitment To Change*, New Society, Philadelphia, USA
Shapiro, Eddie and Shapiro, Debbie, Editors (1999) *Voices From the Heart*, Jeremy Tarcher/Penguin Puttnam, New York, USA

SKILLS OF SPIRITUAL REFLECTION: *INTEGRATING*
ACTING WITH AWARENESS (PAGES 33-35)

Aim: Using your senses and keeping your attention on the present moment so you participate fully in living in each moment, appreciating its gifts and in a flow with Spirit.

Borysenko, Joan (1987) *Minding the Body, Mending the Mind*, Bantam Books, USA
Brussat, Fredric and Mary Ann (1996) *Spiritual Literacy: Reading The Sacred In Everyday Life*, Turnstone, New York, USA
Hanh, Thich Nhat (1991) *Peace Is Every Step*, Bantam, USA
Hanh, Thich Nhat (1996) *The Miracle Of Mindfulness*, Beacon Press, USA
Tolle, Eckhart (2001) *The Power Of Now*, Hodder & Stoughton, London, UK
Walsh, Roger (1999) *Essential Spirituality – Exercises From The World's Religions To Cultivate Kindness, Love, Joy, Peace, Wisdom And Generosity*, J Wiley & Sons Inc, NJ, USA

GOING WITH THE FLOW (PAGES 120-121)

Aim: Being able to be absorbed in what you are doing as if you are "merging with the flow" with an increased sense of direction and purpose.

Csikszentmihalyi, Mihaly (1990) *Flow: The Psychology Of Optimal Experience*, HarperCollins, USA
Edwards, Gill (1991) *Living Magically*, Judy Piatkus (Publishers) Ltd, London, UK
Redfield, James (1993) *The Celestine Prophecy*, Satori Press, Hoover, Ala. USA
Redfield, J & Adrienne C (1995) *The Celestine Prophecy: An Experimental Guide*, Bantam Books, USA

LIVING WITH PARADOX (PAGES 212-213)

Aim: Shifting away from a paradigm that assumes opposing possibilities are mutually exclusive and, instead, seeing the possibility of inclusivity that embraces "both/and."

Clarke, Lindsay (1994) *Alice's Masque*, Jonathan Cape, UK
Yeomans, Tom (1999) *Presence, Power and the Planet*, Occasional paper no. 5, Concordia Institute, USA

DISCERNMENT (PAGES 139-140)

Aim: Being willing and able to test those things you perceive as 'guidance' from Spirit, checking their validity against the possibility that they bolster your personal preferences or are distortions that reinforce your habits and patterns.

Baldwin, Christina (1991) *Life's Companion: Journal Writing as a Spiritual Quest*, Bantam New York, USA
Green, T & Woodrow, P & Peavey, F (1994) *Insight And Action: How To Discover A Life Of Integrity And Commitment To Change*, New Society, Philadelphia, USA

ACKNOWLEDGEMENTS
AND PERMISSIONS

The creation and writing of *The Quest... Exploring A Sense Of Soul* was made possible by the support and assistance of many people. *The Quest* co-authors – Joycelin Dawes, Janice Dolley, and Ike Isaksen – wish to appreciate and celebrate the contribution of:

- ○ Vivienne Seabright, Penelope Hobman, Paul Maiteny, and Gillian Paschkes Bell, fellow members of the **writing team**, and Judith Berry, as our **Administrator**, for the unstinting contribution of their experience and skill.
- ○ Judith Bone, India Brown, Judi Buttner, Josie Gregory, Malcolm Hollick, David Lorimer, Sue Miles, Diana Whitmore, and Lynne Wilson for being **critical readers** of earlier drafts of our writing.
- ○ Phyllida Anamaire, Paul Barber, Judi Buttner, Pauline Compton, Janice Eddy, Miranda Holden, Lauri Makela, Sue Miles, Anita Rogers, Corinna Schmitz, and Courtenay Young as **advisers** who gave generously of their time and expertise to assist us in various ways, and Lesley Hill who gave us feedback from an open learning course in personal and career development .
- ○ The participants of **pilot study groups** of *The Quest* between November 2000 and March 2001 for their warm reception of the material and valuable feedback. These included people in groups from the Findhorn Foundation and wider Foundation community, the Wrekin Trust, the Dingle Community Learning Programme, and groups in Inverness, St Helens, London, and Bellingham, USA.
- ○ Miranda Holden and Pauline Compton who trained a pilot group of **Quest Companions**, and those who trained as Quest Companions in 2000 and offered their support voluntarily to the pilot students from November 2000 to March 2001.
- ○ Clive Kitson, then at the Findhorn Foundation, and Malcolm

Hollick, then at the Findhorn Foundation College, for their support, understanding, and enthusiasm for the project .

O India Brown, Pauline Compton, Joyce Ferne, Mari Hollander, Clive Kitson, Paul Maiteny, Brian McMullen, Javier Rodriguez, and Vivienne Seabright, who shared with us a weekend of telling our stories at the Coach House, Inverness; from this came many creative ideas that are embedded in *The Quest*.

We wish to acknowledge all those writers, thinkers, creators, and pilgrims on the spiritual path whose own records of their journeys and experience have contributed to *The Quest*.

PERMISSIONS

A comprehensive effort has been made to obtain the permission of copyright holders of extracts used in this text for which specific permission is required. If any acknowledgements have been overlooked or requests for permission to use extracts not been made, the error is unintentional. Numerous enquiries and requests have been made to which no reply has been received to date. If notified, we will be pleased to rectify the omission in future editions.

We appreciate permissions granted to quote from the following:

Phyllida Anamaire, for permission to quote from an unpublished transcript of a workshop *Death – The Final Healing*.

Jan Arriens, from an article in *The Friend*, 2000. Used by permission of the Editor of *The Friend*.

Roberto Assagioli, from *Transpersonal Development* granted by the Administration Board, Insitituto di Psicosintesi, Firenze, Italy.

William Bloom, from his Introduction to *The Holistic Revolution*, published by Penguin Press, UK, 2000. Used by permission of the author.

William Bloom, to quote from an early draft of *Soulution: The Holistic Manifesto*. Published 2004 by Hay House, UK. Used by permission of the author.

Deepak Chopra, Extract from *How to Know God* by Deepak Chopra published by Rider ©2000 by Deepak Chopra. Used by permission of The Random House Group Ltd, UK and permission of Harmony Books, a division of Random House, Inc.

Jasmin Lee Cori, excerpted from *The Tao Of Contemplation* by Jasmin Lee Cori with permission of Red Wheel/Weiser of Boston, MA and York Beach, ME, USA.

Ram Dass, extract from an interview with Eddie and Debbie Shapiro, eds, in *Voices From the Heart*, Jeremy Tarcher/Penguin Puttnam, New York, USA. Used by permission of Ram Dass.

Susan Drake, extract from *Planning Integrated Curriculum: The Call to Adventure*. Used by permission of the Association for Supervision & Curriculum Development, USA.

Evans, Roger & Russell, Peter, extract from *The Creative Manager* © 1992. Used by permission of Wiley-Liss Inc, a subsidiary of John Wiley & Sons, Inc, and by Peter Russell.

Cornelia Featherstone, for permission to quote from a presentation at a conference *The Spirit Of Healing* at the Findhorn Foundation, April 2004.

Findhorn Foundation, and the many co-workers who shared their views and experience and contributed to *The Quest* in a variety of ways.

Christopher Fry, from *A Sleep of Prisoners*, written for the Religious Drama Society, 1951, OUP ©. By permission of Oxford University Press. www.oup.com

Peter Goldfarb, an extract from an interview with Eddie and Debbie Shapiro, eds, in *Voices From The Heart*, Jeremy Tarcher, Penguin Puttnam, New York, USA. Used by permission of Peter Goldfarb.

Bede Griffiths, from *The Marriage of East and West* 1982 and *A New Vision of Reality* 1989, by permission of Templegate Publishers, Springfield, USA.

Joshua Halberstam, extract from *Everyday Ethics* by Joshua Halberstam, ©1993 by Joshua Halberstam. Used by permission of Viking Penguin, a division of Penguin Group (USA) Inc.

Thich Nhat Hanh, from *Peace Is Every Step*, published by Rider. Used by permisison of the Random House Group Limited, UK and Bantam Books, a division of Random House, Inc, USA.

Paul Heelas, for permission to use a graph and data from *The Kendal Project* led by Paul Heelas, Linda Woodhead and Bronislaw Szerszynski, published (2004) as *The Spiritual Revolution*, Blackwell, UK.

John Heron, from *Sacred Science*, (PCCS, UK, 1998), extracts and adaptations used with the permission of the author.

Susan Howatch, from *The High Flyer*, reprinted by permission of Time Warner Group, UK.

Ike Isaksen, for permission to use his design of a labyrinth.

Byron Katie, extract used by permission of Byron Katie.

Jack Kornfield, extract from *A Path with Heart* by Jack Kornfield published by Rider. Used by permission of The Random House Group Ltd, UK.

Paul Lacey, for permission to use extracts from *Nourishing The Spiritual Life*, Quaker Home Service, London, UK. © Paul Lacey. Used by permission of the author.

Alison Leonard, from *Telling Our Stories*, published and © 1995 by Darton, Longman and Todd Ltd and used by permission of the publishers.

Angela Locke, from *Sacred Earth*, published by Pleiades Press. Used by permission of the author © Angela Locke www.angelalocke.com

Patricia Loring, for permission to use extracts from *Listening Spirituality*

Volume 1: Personal Spiritual Practices Among Friends. Used by permission of the author.

John Main, taken from *Moment of Christ* published and © 1984 by Darton, Longman and Todd Ltd and used by permission of the publishers.

Edgar Mitchell, *A New Scientific Look at Consciousness* and *The Quantum Hologram: Nature's Mind*, reported in *Light* vol. 120, No.3, the journal of The College of Psychic Studies. Used by permission of the editorial board of *Light*.

Richard Moss, reprinted with permission from *The Black Butterfly: An Invitation to Radical Aliveness*, by Richard Moss. Copyright © 1986 by Richard Moss, Tenspeed Press, Berkeley, CA, USA. www.tenspeed.com.

Caroline Myss, extract from A*natomy of the Spirit* by Caroline Myss, Ph.D, Copyright 1996 by Caroline Myss, published by Bantam Books. Used by permission of The Random House Group Ltd, UK and Harmony Books, a division of Random House, Inc. USA.

John O'Donohue, permission to quote from an article based on an interview with Joan Bakewell for BBC Radio 4, printed in *The Tablet*, 10 April 2004, London, UK. Used by permission of *The Tablet*. www.thetablet.co.uk

Yoko Ono, to quote her poem *Revelations* © 1999. Used by permission of the author. All rights reserved.

Will Parfitt, from *The Elements of Psychosynthesis*, used by permission of the author.

Tony Parsons, from *The Open Secret*, used by permission of the author.

David Peters, for permission to quote from a presentation at a conference *The Spirit Of Healing* at the Findhorn Foundation, April 2004.

Rainer Maria Rilke, excerpts from *Diaries of A Young Poet*, edited by Ruth Sieber-Rilke and Carl Sieber, translated by Edward Snow & Michael Winkler. © 1942 by Insel Verlag, 1997 by Edward Snow & Michael Winkler. Used by permission of W.W. Norton & Company, Inc.

Peter Russell, from (1998) *Waking up in Time: Finding Inner Peace in Times of Accelerating Change*, Origin Press, California, USA and (2003) *From Science to God: Exploring the Mystery of Consciousness*, New World Library, USA. © Peter Russell. Used by permission of the author.

Albert Schweitzer, from *Reverence for Life: the words of Albert Schweitzer,* ed. Harold E.Robles. HarperCollins Publishers Inc. Used by permission of Dr Harold E.Robles.

Mike Scott, from the CD album *Still Burning* (Chrysalis Records, 1997), Words and Music by Mike Scott.© 1996 Sony Music Publishing Limited. All Rights Reserved.

Robin Skynner and John Cleese, extracts from *Life and How to Survive It*, (Heinemann) Used by permission of the Random House Group Ltd, UK.

David Spangler, from *The Call*, and articles published at www.lorian.org. ©

Used by permission of the author.

Richard Thompson, from an article in *The Friend*, 2000. Used by permission of the Editor of *The Friend*.

Frances Vaughan, from *The Inward Arc*, ©Frances Vaughan. Used by permission of the author. iUniverse.com, edition part of the Authors' Guild Back in Print Series available as print on demand.

Diana Whitmore, from *The Joy of Learning* © Diana Whitmore, 1986. Used by permission of the author. This book is available from the Psychosynthesis and Education Trust, 92-94 Tooley St, London SE1 2TH, UK.

Ken Wilber, from *A Theory of Everything* by Ken Wilber, ©2000. Reprinted by arrangement with Shambhala Publications, Inc., Boston, www.Shambhala.com and Gill and Macmillan Ltd, Ireland.

Lynne Wilson, and the Dingle Community Learning Programme, for their participation and interest in *The Quest*.

Danah Zohar & Ian Marshall, from *SQ: Spiritual Intelligence*. Used by permission of the authors. © Danah Zohar & Ian Marshall 2000.

PARTNERS AND SUPPORTERS

The Quest was developed through a partnership between *The Quest* co-authors and the Findhorn Foundation[1] who generously made available a loan to enable *The Quest* to be written. *The Quest* co-authors also gratefully acknowledge grants from the David Thomas Charitable Trust,[2] The Home Foundation,[3] and The Wrekin Trust.[4] However, all editorial policy, content, and decisions are the sole responsibility of *The Quest* co-authors.

THE FINDHORN FOUNDATION

The Findhorn Foundation (www.findhorn.org) is the educational heart of one of the world's best-known spiritual communities, founded by Peter and Eileen Caddy and Dorothy Maclean in 1962. It is a major international center of spiritual education and personal transformation and a registered educational trust offering many ways for people to visit, live, and work. It welcomes all people irrespective of race, color, ethnic origin, age, religion, or sexual orientation, and recognizes the essential truths of all religions and spiritual teachings. The Findhorn Foundation is an NGO (Non-Governmental Organization) associated with the Department of Public Information of the United Nations, a founder member of the Global Ecovillage Network, and part of the growing Findhorn Ecovillage, a positive and practical attempt to live sustainably on the Earth.

[1] The Findhorn Foundation, The Park, Findhorn, Forres IV36 3TZ, Scotland. Enquiries: +44 (0) 1309 690311. Website: www.findhorn.org

[2] The David Thomas Charitable Trust is a charity supporting writers, self-publishing, and a variety of projects. Details: PO Box 6055, Nairn, Scotland, IV12 4YB

[3] The Home Foundation is a charity with the object of demonstrating that ecology and economy are not in conflict with each other and that socially responsible projects can make a return on investment. Details: PO Box 178, 3940 AD Doorn, The Netherlands. Email: welcome@homefoundation.nl

[4] The Wrekin Trust is an educational charity concerned with the spiritual nature of humanity and the universe. Details: Courtyard Lodge, Mellow Farm, Hawcross Lane, Redmarley d'Abitot, Glos GL19 3JQ, UK. Tel/Fax: +44 (0) 1452 840033. Email: info@wrekintrust.org

ENDORSEMENTS FOR *THE QUEST*

1. **William Bloom, author of** *The Endorphin Effect* **and** *Soulution - The Holistic Manifesto*

The Quest is a serious, effective and intelligently structured approach to spiritual development for mature enquirers. I admire and am inspired by it.

2. **Tom Cook is an artist, a director of The Alternatives programme at St James's Church, Piccadilly, London and an Honorary Trustee of the Findhorn Arts Foundation, Scotland**

The Quest belongs alongside the dictionary or thesaurus as ready reference to the possibilities of spiritual connection in the same way that a dictionary and thesaurus help to find a word or develop an idea. It is guide that provides practical tools enabling us to explore the positive possibilities that the holistic approach to life offers in an increasingly fragmented and materialistic world.

I believe *The Quest* is equally effective for individuals, community groups and families for the exploration of personal development, social awareness and spiritual consciousness. As well as having sound professional credentials for the materials that are used, the exercises contained in *The Quest* are easily accessible and can be a much fun to do as they are revealing and profound in their deepest meaning.

3. **Joyce Ferne, Director, Coach House Retreat Centre, nr Inverness, Scotland**

I now know I have a soul – *The Quest...Exploring A Sense Of Soul* is a stimulating and effective way to grow on all levels of being for those exploring some of the core questions of life: it encourages a widening and deepening understanding of s/Self, the sacred in the everyday life of the world and our interconnection on all levels of being - in fact what spirituality/Soul is all about. It works well for group sharing as well as for the individual.

4. **Dr. Josie Gregory, Senior Lecturer in Management and Director of Studies for the PG. Cert in Spiritual Development and Facilitation. School of Management, University of Surrey, Guildford, Surrey. UK.**

The Quest...Exploring A Sense Of Soul is an apt title and description of the content of this book. The book is a very comprehensive guide to spiritual development and personal change that is relevant for the 21st Century. The book explores the richness of the spiritual processes from many faith traditions and nature mysticism in a manner that makes them accessible to individuals and groups exploring their own spiritual orientations and practices.

The book is one of the best examples I have seen in the personal development self-help movement, with a holistic and pragmatic approach and lots of simple, yet profound exercises to engage the enthusiast. I intend to recommend it as essential reading on the Spiritual Development and Facilitation programme I run at the University of Surrey, UK.

5. Dr Ann Smith, Chair of Spirit at Work Charitable Trust, New Zealand Research and Training Consultant in NZ and UK. 22nd August 2004

"*The Quest* is a wonderful self-reflective study course. I like the way it offers a clear structure for learning and for change. Primarily, *The Quest* offers a method for uncovering the deep thoughts, values and motivations that help shape who we are. *The Quest* works for personal and for group learning.

For those looking for clarity about their soul purpose, *The Quest* approach provides methods, practice techniques and readings to help individuals to reveal their true self. Taking the course to a deeper level one can also gain insight about living in a way that honours one's true purpose in life.

Most of all, I like the respectful way that the material has been put together. It values diverse contributions, without imposing any one particular approach to finding spirit, soul; or whatever one may call the motivational force that may guide the way in which we live our life.

The Quest came at the right time for me; it offered a deeply reflective and personal experience. I found I could dip in and out of it to look at issues that were important at the time, rather than observe a set order of learning. I have used it intermittently for the last two years in my personal life and for working with colleagues.

I can't speak highly enough of the material, if you are ready for a spiritual journey, for asking deep questions about who you are, what values drive you, if you are searching for meaning and purpose to become central to your work and personal life, *The Quest* is for you.

6. Diana Whitmore, President the Psychosynthesis & Education Trust and Director, Children Our Ultimate Investment UK

The Quest promises to be a transformative journey for the reader who is prepared to commit themselves to an exploration of their own well being and sense of meaning and purpose. *The Quest* not only supports the reframing of the personal challenges we face, but enables us to find our own style of spirituality - one which is uniquely our own - and universally fulfilling. For the sincere student of life, *The Quest* will provide a systematic, safe wholesome experience. I wholeheartedly recommend *The Quest*.

The *Quest* co-authors appreciate our partnership with the Findhorn Foundation, whose holistic approach to spirituality was reflected in *The Quest: Rediscovering A Sense Of Soul,* an open learning course on which this book is based (self-published 2001 to 2004)

FINDHORN FOUNDATION & COMMUNITY
Celebrating the Divinity in all Life

The Findhorn Foundation and Community, in north east Scotland, is a unique blend of spiritual community, ecovillage and educational centre-a rich context for exploring new ways of living.

Our educational programmes offer practical steps for personal and global transformation, bringing each person closer to knowing their own essential divinity and context in the world. Each year 3,000 people from than 70 countries are attracted to residential courses in the unique setting of a working spiritual community with organic gardens, innovative ecohousing and a common vision for humanity and the earth.

Over 30,000 people have participated in Experience Week, the Foundation's core programme which begins almost every Saturday of the year. It is a dynamic week offering a taste of community life and is often life-changing, involving you in a transformative process of self-discovery in the company of an international group of fellow explorers. Further programmes give you a chance to live and work in community, deepening the experience.

Specialist courses cover such areas as spiritual practice, nature and ecology, creative arts, relationships and healing, and the community also hosts large international conferences in the fields of ecology, education and spirituality.

Our Global Network offers a chance to engage with like-minded people all over the world and experience community online.

For further information
Write: Findhorn Foundation, The Park, Findhorn IV36 3TZ, Scotland
Visit: www.findhorn.org   Email: enquiries@findhorn.org
Phone: +44 (0) 1309 690311